The Transformation of Political Communication

Also by Ralph Negrine:

The Communication of Politics (1996) London: Sage
Parliament and the Media. A Study of Britain, Germany and France (1998)
London: Royal Institute of International Affairs/Cassell
Television and the Press Since 1945 (1999) Manchester: Manchester
University Press
The Professionalisation of Political Communication (2007) Bristol: Intellect,
(with Mancini, P., Holtz-Bacha, C. and Papathanassopoulos, S.)
The Political Communication Reader (2007) London: Routledge, (with
Stanyer, J.)

The Transformation of Political Communication

Continuities and Changes in Media and Politics

Ralph M. Negrine
University of Sheffield

palgrave
macmillan

First published 2008 by
PALGRAVE MACMILLAN
Houndmills, Basingstoke, Hampshire RG21 6XS and
175 Fifth Avenue, New York, N.Y. 10010
Companies and representatives throughout the world

PALGRAVE MACMILLAN is the global academic imprint of the Palgrave Macmillan division of St. Martin's Press, LLC and of Palgrave Macmillan Ltd. Macmillan® is a registered trademark in the United States, United Kingdom and other countries. Palgrave is a registered trademark in the European Union and other countries.

ISBN-13: 978–0–230–00030–8 hardback
ISBN-10: 0–230–00030–4 hardback
ISBN-13: 978–0–230–00031–5 paperback
ISBN-10: 0–230–00031–2 paperback

This book is printed on paper suitable for recycling and made from fully managed and sustained forest sources. Logging, pulping and manufacturing processes are expected to conform to the environmental regulations of the country of origin.

A catalogue record for this book is available from the British Library.

A catalog record for this book is available from the Library of Congress.

10 9 8 7 6 5 4 3 2 1
17 16 15 14 13 12 11 10 09 08

Printed and bound in China

To Angie and to Ruth, David,
Peter, Alice and Jonathan

Contents

List of Tables   x

Acknowledgements   xi

Chronology of a Selection of Significant Events in Media and Politics   xii

**1 The Transformation and Professionalization of
   Political Communication**   1

Introduction   1

Understanding historical change   4

The structure of this book   14

**2 Media and Politics: How, and Why, Political Parties
   Communicate Politics**   18

Introduction   18

Adaptation or transformation? The changing nature
   of political communication   21

Evolutionary and historical perspectives on changing
   campaign communications   23

Harnessing technology: newspapers, radio and film   28

Summary and conclusion: adaptation, transformation
   and professionalization   42

**3 The Transformation of Political Parties:
   Organizational Change and Communication
   Technologies**   44

Introduction   44

Political parties in the late 19th century: a background
   sketch   46

Political parties post-1945: organizing for success   52

New Labour: the 1997 election and all that   57

From the mass-membership party to the 'cartel' party:
   political communication in the 21st century   59

Summary and conclusion   67

4 The Transformation of Political Parties and the Use of Professional Advisers in the Communication of Politics   **69**
Introduction   69
Who are the professionals?   70
Transforming political communication: Political parties and communication professionals   75
New Labour: laying the foundations for a new campaigning template?   83
Parties and professionals: the nature of the relationship   87
Professionals and political parties: political communication transformed?   91

5 Political Actors: Transforming Practices   **93**
Introduction   93
Transforming the candidate: what does it mean to be a professional?   95
From amateur to professional: transforming prospective parliamentary candidates   106
From candidate to MP   109
Summary and conclusion   114

6 Transforming Government Communication   **117**
Introduction   117
Managing communication   121
New Labour and government communication: controlling and managing the process   125
The Mountfield Report and the Phillis Review   127
A transformation in government communication?   134
Post-Blair, what?   140

7 The Transformation of a Political Communication: the Global Context   **143**
Introduction   143
Understanding change: modernization   147
The transformation of political communication: Americanization and professionalization   152
Understanding transformations in a global context   157
Summary and conclusion   168

8 The Internet: Transforming Political Communication?   **170**
Introduction   170
The political impact of new media   172
Politics on the net   177
Politics as usual ... or new possibilities?   185
Summary and conclusion   192

9 Conclusion: The Transformation and Professionalization of Communication and its Impact on Politics   **195**

Notes   205
Bibliography   208
Index   220

List of Tables

2.1 Typology of the evolution of campaign communications 24
2.2 Political campaigns in historical perspective 25
2.3 The evolution of political parties and their role in changing forms of campaign communications 26
3.1 Total membership of British political parties, 1980–2006 61
3.2 The models of party and their characteristics 64
3.3 Three stages in the development of election campaigning 66

Acknowledgements

This book developed over a number of years and in a number of different conversations with colleagues. Many of these conversations and discussions took place at the regular meetings of Team 2 of the European Science Foundation (ESF) programme *Changing Media, Changing Europe*. I would like to thank Peter Golding and Ib Bondebjerg for running the ESF programme and colleagues in Team 2 for the many hours we spent together discussing political communication issues. Special thanks to Stelios Papathanassopoulos, Paolo Mancini and Christina Holtz-Bacha, and to Gianpietro Mazzoleni, Winfried Schulz and Philipe Maarek.

I would also like to thank the Economic and Social Research Council (ESRC) for funding the project *MPs and the Media* which helped me to think about the changes discussed in Chapter 5 of this book. My thanks also to Darren Lilleker who helped me on that project.

I am also deeply grateful to Emily Salz and Sheree Keep at Palgrave Macmillan for offering me the opportunity to develop this project. They were helpful and understanding and dealt with the numerous queries and quibbles with great patience.

Finally, my thanks to Rose Lewis and all at Aardvark Editorial for their help with the manuscript.

The author and publishers would like to thank Sage Publications Inc. Journals for the permission to reproduce Table 2.2, taken from 'Changing Campaign Communications: A Party-Centred Theory of Professionalized Campaigning' by Rachel Gibson and Andrea Römmele, in *Harvard International Journal of Press/Politics*. Copyright 2001 by Sage Publications Inc. Journals. Reproduced with permission of Sage Publications Inc. Journals in the format Textbook via Copyright Clearance Center.

Chronology of a Selection of Significant Events in Media and Politics

1850–90   Newspapers in Britain and the US become established as important media of communication

1896   *Daily Mail* launched in the UK as the first popular daily paper

1904   *Daily Mirror* launched in the UK

1910s   Limited use of film for political propaganda in the UK

1919   Radio Corporation of America (RCA) founded

1922   British Broadcasting Company (later Corporation) formed

1924   First radio political speeches in the UK

1927   British Broadcasting Corporation (BBC) formed

1930s   Use of propaganda films by political parties

1933   US President F. D. Roosevelt begins a series of evening radio speeches, known as 'fireside chats', which run until 1944

1933   Whitaker and Baxter join forces to establish the first US political consulting company, Campaigns Inc.

1936   Television launched by the BBC

1939   F. D. Roosevelt becomes first US President to appear on television

1946   BBC television service resumes after the end of the Second World War

1950   First US political ads by William Benton, Senator from Connecticut

1951   First Party Election Broadcast on television in the UK

1952   Richard Nixon delivers the 'checkers speech', to defend himself against accusations of accepting illegal campaign funding. The speech is often seen as one of the earliest personalized political uses of television

1955   Commercial television is launched in the UK

1955   President Eisenhower allows television cameras into the White House for the first time

1957   The '14-Day Rule' which restricted political coverage in the UK is abandoned

1958   First major television interview with a British Prime Minister (PM Harold Macmillan with Robin Day)

1958   ITN (Independent Television News) extensively covers the 1958 Rochdale by-election, so breaking away from previous limited coverage

1960   Joe Napolitan is described as the first political consultant

1968   Inauguration of the White House Office of Communication

1978   Gordon Reece, advertising executive, made Publicity Director of the UK Conservative Party

1978   Saatchi and Saatchi appointed to work for the UK Conservative Party

1978   Harvey Thomas appointed to organize UK Conservative Party rallies

1979   Commercialization of internet begins

1979   Margaret Thatcher becomes Prime Minister

1979   Bernard Ingham appointed as Margaret Thatcher's Chief Press Secretary (until 1990). He was also Head of the Government Information Service until 1990

1980s   Emergence of significant personal computer market

1980   Cable News Network (CNN), founded by Ted Turner, starts its 24-hour news service

1980s   European countries embark on processes of deregulation of broadcast media so bringing about greater competition into the fragmenting terrestrial and satellite television markets

1985   Peter Mandelson appointed as Director of Campaigns and Communication for the Labour Party. Mandelson headed the Campaigns and Communications Directorate which was reorganized into the Shadow Communications Agency

1985   Philip Gould, advertising executive, pollster and later political adviser, commissioned by Peter Mandelson to produce a report on what the Labour Party needed to do to win

1989   Sky News launches a 24-hour news service in Britain as part of the Sky satellite television service

1990s (late)   Bloggers begin to create significant audiences for their material

1991   James Carville, US political consultant for the Democrats, creates the 'war room' – all major campaign players in the

	same room – for the Clinton campaign. New Labour was later to use this model for the 1997 general election campaign
1992	Bill Clinton elected as US President. Remains in office until 2000
1993	The documentary film *The War Room* (dir. P. A. Pennebaker and C. Hegedus) is released. It shows Bill Clinton's presidential campaign centre, i.e. the 'war room', in action
1997	Election of New Labour, under Tony Blair, in the UK
1997	Alastair Campbell appointed as Director of Communications and Strategy by Tony Blair (PM 1997–2007)
1997	The Mountfield Report published after New Labour comes to power in UK. Recommends reforming the government communications service
2003	Alastair Campbell resigns his role as Director of Communications and Strategy for Tony Blair
2004	Howard Dean uses the internet to raise substantial sums of money for his presidential campaign
2005	David Cameron becomes leader of the British Conservative Party
2005	Tony Blair resigns as British Prime Minister
2005	Lynton Crosbie, Australian political consultant, employed by British Conservative Party in bid to win 2005 general election
2006	In September, David Cameron, leader of Conservative Party, launches the first blog by a leader of a political party, 'webcameron'

The Transformation and Professionalization of Political Communication

1

Introduction

In reviewing the literature in the field of political communication produced in the past half-century, one is inevitably struck by the speed, intensity and depth of change in the structures of communication and in the ways in which political communication is carried out. In the case of the former, we have seen the internet force the older media of communication – television, the printed press, radio – to adapt their styles and contents to a new environment. In the case of the latter, we have seen the emergence of 'spin' and the birth of the 'spin doctor', the growth of the 'public relations state' and the growing interest amongst political parties in 'political marketing'.

In these and other ways it is abundantly clear that things are not what they were and that new arrangements, structures, practices and ways of thinking abound. That, in other words, the nature of political communication – understood here as incorporating the means and practices whereby the communication of politics takes place – has been *transformed* and that there has been 'a marked change in its nature, form or appearance' (Compact Oxford English Dictionary online definition). The aim of this book is to explore the meaning of that transformation.

At the same time as exploring the nature and content of that transformation, this book will also highlight one of the dimensions of that transformation, that is, the professionalization of political communication. If transformation implies 'a marked change in nature, form or appearance', then the greater degree of professionalization that is now brought to bear on the conduct of political communication is one such transformation. The conduct of political communication in the late 20th century and certainly in the 21st century is an increasingly professional affair: the political parties are now more professional than ever, as are the candidates for office, party members and the many consultants brought in to advise on campaigning and strategy. Whether such a level of professionalization is part of a developmental process whereby things gradually change 'for the better' is clearly an issue that has to be discussed and more so since it may sit awkwardly alongside the notion of transformation as a *marked change* in the nature, form or appearance of things. Nevertheless, the two notions of transformation and professionalization are suggestive of change at a level that produces a set of arrangements or practices that can be interpreted as being very different from the past. One example of this – and many others will be offered in the book – relates to how political actors have changed their communication practices vis-à-vis the media in order to gain advantage from their appearances, statements and activities. This is discussed more fully in Chapter 5.

In suggesting that such change can be labelled 'professionalization', it is clear that a particular meaning is attached to it. In keeping with the work of Christina Holtz-Bacha, professionalization is seen as:

> a process of adaptation to, and as such a necessary consequence of, changes in the political system on the one side and the media system on the other and in the relationship of the two systems. These changes follow from the modernization of society, which is a development that is still going on and will take place in similar political systems sooner or later. Professionalisation in this sense is a general and not culture-bound concept. Its actual appearance and the degree of professionalisation in a given country are however dependent on a country's specific social and political structures and processes. (Negrine et al., 2007: 63)

More generally, professionalization suggests an ongoing process where structures and practices are continually revised and updated in order to make them more 'rational' and more 'appropriate' for the conduct of politics at any particular moment of time. We thus need to understand developments in political communication as part and parcel of a long and continuing process of adaptation and change whereby, for example, the skills of those outside politics are increasingly applied to the conduct of politics. But more than this, those who possess such skills – 'the professionals' – and the practices they advocate, in turn come to influence those in politics. Politics then begins to change from the inside, as it were, as the lessons of the world of commerce become internalized: political parties become more professional in their activities, as do the politicians who are now much more aware of the needs of proper communication skills, dress and manner.

Professionalization can be seen as a process of continual self-improvement and change towards what is deemed to be a 'better' way of doing things, be it winning an election or ensuring successful governance, that is made possible by technological and communications innovations, as well as a more general process of skills specialization. The idea of professionalization also encompasses the willingness to change, and the motivations underpinning that willingness.

The process of professionalization, however, takes place within societies that are themselves undergoing a process of modernization, that is, a process of differentiation and secularization, that:

> leads to growing numbers of subsystems of all kinds that develop to satisfy the specialized demands of particular groups and social actors. The rise of these subsystems undermines the traditional aggregative structures of socialization, authority, community, and consensus, producing social fragmentation and exclusion. (Swanson and Mancini, 1996: 253)

The idea of professionalization takes from the idea of modernization the knowledge that functional differentiation is part of the process of change but it does not see this as necessarily related to specific factors in contemporary political communication only. In this way, the idea of professionalization, as used here, cuts across the idea of modernization and other equally contested concepts such as Americanization and homogenization, since it deals with a more general process of change taking place in contemporary societies. (A fuller discussion of both professionalization and modernization can be found in Chapter 7.)

For this book to argue successfully that there has been a transformation and professionalization of political communication, it must demonstrate that there has been a *marked change* in, say, practices over the past century or so. It must offer a historical review of political communication that is sufficiently full and robust to confirm the nature and extent of the transformations that have taken place. The intention, it should quickly be added, is not to provide a historical account of changes in political communication per se but to draw on historical change as a way of providing a background that helps us understand contemporary events. Rather than take it for granted that there has been a wholesale transformation of political communication, this book will argue that the roots – and routes – of change are more complex and long-term than is often suggested, that there are both continuities and discontinuities in the changing nature and conduct of political communication and that both the continuities and discontinuities need to be explored.

In approaching the subject from this perspective, this book moves away from interpretations of change that are centred on particular technologies, be it the press or television. Instead, it suggests that there are different and equally valid ways of exploring changes in the content and nature of political communication that foreground significant continuities in the ways in which those who engage in politics adapt their practices to changing conditions in society, including changing media. Those continuities illustrate the extent to which political actors, for instance, are alert to changes in their environments and react to them or even sometimes introduce changes that then impact on the nature and content of political communication more widely. An example of the former would be the widening of the electorate in the early 20th century (see Chapter 2), of the latter, the greater centralization of government communication under New Labour from 1997 onwards (see Chapter 7). Although the focus will be primarily on the interaction between the world of politics – conceived here as governments and politicians and those who work within their orbits – and the worlds of the media – both 'old' and 'new' – the examples chosen to illustrate the arguments are widely drawn. Inevitably, though, many are taken from political communication at election times because those moments can be taken to reflect the coming together of trends and tendencies in the political culture more widely. Nevertheless, the lessons to be drawn from these, and other examples, feed into the broad historical sweep that is presented in this book as a way of drawing attention to the contemporary within a larger landscape of historical change.

Understanding historical change

As we begin to explore those complex changes, however, it is crucial that we also pay some attention to the way in which we come to analyse *how historical change is itself understood*. To put the matter fairly crudely, how do we make connections between practices in the past and today? Are we justified in seeing a continuous line of development between then and now, or is it more appropriate to see breaks and thus fairly loose connections between them? Furthermore, what sort of evidence would we need if we were to argue for continuity or discontinuity? Whilst these questions may appear esoteric, there are many examples in the book which call on the careful reader to make sense of events or practices across periods of time. Without that broad historical grounding, how is it possible to argue for or against transformation or in support of *marked changes* in political communication over time?

The questions of method and of historical understanding are, therefore, never far from the surface of much that appears in this book. At times, these questions intrude fully in the text, as in Chapter 2, when the discussion considers the extent to which each new medium of communication altered the nature and content of political communication. Does the 'new' completely replace the 'old' or is the process of adaptation subtle and intensive? These sorts of questions are familiar to the historian and the lessons from historiography are worth bearing in mind. As Black and MacRaild point out:

> For historians and students of history today, the point about the passage of time … is that we must strike a balance between judging the past by our own standards and entirely standing the past in its own frozen compartment of history. The problem, then, is one of extremes. If, on the one hand, we adopt a present-minded stance in our approach, we risk overplaying continuities, or indeed manufacturing continuities, between us and our past which do not actually exist. If, on the other hand, we adopt a historicist position, or posit the hermetically sealed epochal approach to history … we risk removing any thread which might connect our past and our present. This notion of time, of change and continuity, or similarity and difference, is the hardest balance to achieve; yet it is central to our understanding of the nature of history and the dynamics of social development. (2000: 19)

As well as these problems which are indicative of the range of problems that one must confront when studying change *within* a specific political context, for example Britain, there are others that are relevant when studying change *across* political contexts. In the case of the latter, it is a matter of exploring change across time, as well as across nations, and across media. A good example of these sorts of considerations is explored in Chapter 7 when the subject of 'Americanization' of media practices is tackled precisely because it shows how interactions between different systems alter practices across time and space. Such crossings of boundaries in the 20th century are part of what Werner and Zimmerman call for in their propositions for 'histoire croisée', that is, an approach to historical studies that includes explorations of 'comparative approaches, transfers, and, more generally, sociocultural interactions' (Werner and Zimmerman, 2006: 32).

This is particularly important from the 20th century onwards as technologies of communication not only changed forms and speeds of communication within one political and social system, but enabled speedier communication – and the transfer of forms – across physical boundaries as well as political and social systems. Unlike the printed press, radio and film moved across boundaries very easily and shaped and reshaped the forms of communication that took place within one political and social system: British film-goers could watch American films, as could Egyptian film-goers; British radio listeners in the 1920s could listen to commercial services from Luxembourg as well as the BBC's own output; and television viewers in 1950s Britain would become familiar with the content of American television through imports, alongside growing familiarity with commercial and non-commercial broadcasting. The internet completely breaks down any limitations of a physical or time-based kind.

As important as this 'collapsing of time and space' for the study of transformations in political communication, is the study of inter-media influences and continuities (or discontinuities). We may be familiar with the study of the impact of television on political communication but what of the impact of radio or film on political communication and of the links between one and the other? Did radio establish a framework for political communication that was then used for television? Are there differences between how one medium can be used compared with another, and how do we include them in our explorations? As Douglas Craig has observed, there are some important similarities and differences that one can take into account in looking at media over the past century or so:

> Although all national candidates after 1920 used newsreels to reach cinema audiences, few bothered with the time and expense involved in full-scale film production. ... Radio and television, on the other hand, evolved new forms of political advertisements, provided candidates with quick production and distribution facilities, and ... their operators were generally receptive to the needs of those candidates with the financial resources to employ them. (Craig, 2000: 174)

The three examples briefly presented here illustrate why understanding change is so important. The first relates to the changing organizational structures of political parties; the second to the changing nature of technologies of communication, and the third to the place of 'spin' in modern politics.

Example 1: Changes in the structures of political parties

In contemporary Western democracies, political parties have become lean organizations primarily directed at gaining political power. They have become, in the eyes of many, professionally run organizations pursuing electoral success, that is, professional electoral parties. The reasons why they have become transformed in this way will be explored in greater detail in later chapters, but it may be useful to identify some of the reasons here because they form an important part of the overall argument of this book.

Modern political parties are, in essence, organizations with particular types of characteristics. They are made up of a collection of individuals who have come together to push forward a particular agenda for the way a country is to be organized and run. Crucially, modern political parties are not loose federations nor are they 'flat' in their organizational structures. They are, increasingly, hierarchical organizations led by a small cadre of permanent employees who serve the political party as a whole and the leader more specifically.

With minor variations, this description would be valid for any of the major parties across Western democratic systems. There are obvious and significant differences between, say, the American and European models of political parties but the essential features remain unchanged, namely, a collection of individuals centred around a leader (or, more simply, an individual in the case of the US) seeking to persuade citizens to vote him or her into office.

But there are two features of the modern political parties that deserve to be mentioned and that are increasingly significant for our analysis of the processes and conduct of political communication. The first relates to funding; the second, to the membership of political parties. In many ways, these features are intertwined.

Funding

In the absence of unlimited state funding for political parties, funds must be collected from individual members, supporters and sponsors. The greater and more expensive the needs of the political party organization – for example in respect of employees, premises, political activities, canvassing, electoral expenses – the greater the amount of funds needed. In the summer of 2006, for example, the Labour Party faced a cash crisis as it was revealed that it had an overall deficit of £27 million and an operating deficit of £14.5 million in 2005. Jobs, it emerged, were likely to be lost in order to close the gap (Woodward, 2006).

The millions of pounds required to run a party and its activities do not usually come out of ordinary members' party subscriptions. Not only are there are too few members for this to be a source of substantial funding, but individual donations from ordinary members of the party are likely to fall short of what may be needed. This can make parties dependent on special 'loans' or large donations from wealthy individuals.[1] But if they do not want to become dependent on a few large donors – whether wealthy individuals or trade unions – parties need to draw on funds from their members.

Members

Members, however, do not usually want to be taken for granted. In an increasingly centralized political party structure, members are in danger of being seen as little more than fodder, taken for granted but given little in return. The danger for political parties is that members become insignificant *in the policy- and decision-making process of the party*. This has affected the Labour Party in recent years as it has seen its membership numbers tumble to around a quarter of a million (see Chapter 3). But the Labour Party is by no means unique and other parties have also suffered. In his report on the funding of political parties in Britain, Sir Hayden Phillips pointed out that:

> Our mass political parties, which sustained our democracy for most of the twentieth century, now seem to be in decline. Fifty years ago one in 11 of the electorate belonged to a political party. Today, that ratio is down to one in 88. (2007: 1)

The danger for parties is that they become centralized, insular and cut off from their core members. They cease to be mass membership parties and cease to be connected in any significant way with the public at large: just over 61% of the British electorate voted in the 2005 election.

The consequences of these two factors are significant for how parties act both in political contests and in the way they govern. Insularity will shield them from their members but it will undermine their support overall; it will also undermine their prospects of being able to run a *national* party organization on a day-to-day basis. On the other hand, a lack of a hierarchical and centralized organizational structure can create havoc and is ill-suited to the modern media age which tends to dislike chaos as it seeks those in responsible positions.

Political parties must therefore continually adapt to changing circumstances, be they in relation to funding, members, organizational needs, different media needs and so on. If they fail to adapt, they are unlikely to maintain a real and viable presence as a source of political ideas or as a potential government. And so, as circumstances change, for example an expanded electorate, a new party forming, a party splintering, political views changing and so on, political parties also need to change to keep in step with supporters and electors. The emergence of New Labour in the 1990s is a good illustration of how a political party changes its position in order to engage with an electorate that has also moved away from more socialist and radical politics (Shaw, 1994) and the Conservative Party under David Cameron similarly moved away from its traditional Conservative pursuit of lower taxes and toughness on crime (Hitchens, 2007). Both examples also illustrate the need to regularly redefine what a party stands for.

To suggest that political parties often behave in a rational way in their pursuit of organizational and electoral survival is not to point to any radical departure from the past. Like all other organizations, political parties need to adapt to changing circumstances. They cannot remain unchanged: that is the lesson of New Labour, just as much as it is the lesson that the Conservatives had to learn after three consecutive election defeats. Importantly, this process of adaptation to external circumstances – however brought about – is not new. Parties, this book will contend, have always adapted to changing circumstances in one way or another. However, the distinctive elements that in some ways distinguish recent adaptations from past ones incorporate the extent to which parties have become more professional in their organizational make-up and the extent to which they seek to alter their political make-up in order to win elections. That is, parties have increasingly shaped themselves as organizations that mirror modern management and organizational theories: lean, centralized, efficient and in control of all aspects of their remit. More than this, they have sought to win votes by engaging in the process of 'marketing' politics (Scammell, 1999) rather than pursuing more traditional, ideologically inflected positions.

Whilst this description can be used in the context of New Labour in the 1980s and 1990s and could be increasingly applied to the Conservative Party under David Cameron post-2005, it does have precedents. In the 1950s, as we shall see in Chapter 3, Lord Poole also ran the Conservative Party in ways that sought to maximize the advantages of a good organization able to make use of research and intelligence to defeat the Labour Party. A good organization, in other words, is one that is able to adapt to circumstances in order to maintain advantage: as did the Conservative Party in the 1950s and New Labour in the 1980s and 1990s.

The reference to Lord Poole and the Conservative Party in the 1950s shows that the logic of organizational adaptation is not new, although the forms it takes may be susceptible to particular and time-bound approaches to how organizations should be structured. Management and organizational theories do, after all, follow particular fads and fashions. But the logic of organizational adaptation remains constant, at least if the organization wishes to survive and prosper. And this is one of the lessons that one can draw from the work of John Gorst for the Conservative Party in the 1870s: the party had to attract new voters from an expanded electorate if it wished to survive and thrive. As E. J. Feuchtwanger notes in his study of the Conservative Party in the 1870s:

> The appearance of [National Union and the Central Office] is symptomatic of a parliamentary, aristocratic party, having somewhat reluctantly, to adapt itself to new electoral conditions and reaching out to organize new support. (1968: 131)

Such a process of adaptation took place in a particular context and with a particular set of circumstances at play and although it was short-lived, it highlighted the fact that political parties could not simply rely on 'traditional' and 'loyal' voters if they were to win elections. As the electorate expanded and/or became less strongly aligned with traditional parties, newer ways had to be found to persuade and mobilize them. Similarly, as the rationale and meaning of different political parties in the 21st century gradually shift away from what they once were – does Labour mean the same as New Labour? Does new Conservatism mean the same as old Conservatism? – new ways must be found to persuade voters to come out to vote and to vote for your party.

These references to past structures and individuals illustrate the bigger question of how we come to *understand change* over time. Given these examples, could it be argued that the modern political party is no more than an *evolution* of the party of the 19th century in both its structure and approach to persuading and mobilizing a changing electorate, or would it be more appropriate to see the current state of the parties as different in spirit and kind? Is there something qualitatively and quantitatively different between the party of the 21st century and that of the mid-20th century, say? In respect of understanding of both political parties and of historical change, is this an example of continuity or an example of discontinuity and radical transformation?

Example 2: Technologies of communication: new or just different?

If the discussion of political parties illustrates some fundamental issues about understanding change, the development of technologies of communication emphasizes the significance of these issues. Indeed, in an age of digital communication and 'electronic glut' (Seymour-Ure, 1996), it would be churlish to argue that such systems and such abundance are no more than mere adaptations to what had preceded them. Today's political party – and political actors more generally – are adept at using a range of communication systems to get their messages across and to try and mobilize support. And, in the age of the internet, it is no surprise that it would begin to move to centre stage in political communication: it has in so many respects superseded the medium of mass communication via television, radio and print: the 2008 American presidential election might be seen as a YouTube election given the degree to which the main contenders appear on the web (see www.youtube.com and www.prezvid.com).

Yet, as with the example above, there are reasons to think that the ways in which newer technologies of communication are now being used illustrate nothing more than a strategy, sometimes implicit sometimes explicit, to employ whatever technologies are available to better communicate to an expanding or disparate public. When the press developed, political parties sought ways to control and use it; when the gramophone came into existence, political parties exploited it by recording the speeches of their leaders for distribution (Cockett, 1994); when radio, film and television came into their own, the same desire applied: politicians, and leaders in particular, have sought to use the media to make themselves visible – aurally and visually – to the electorate. Regulatory constraints, particularly in European democracies, may have made it more difficult for the political parties to develop their strategies as they might have wished, for example, by buying airtime on television services as was the case in the US, but there were other ways in which they could promote their leaders. The aims and objectives of the political parties remained constant irrespective of the medium in question.

If this argument has any validity, then the internet is no more than the latest in a long line of technologies being used by political parties and others to spread content. It may differ from other technologies in the way that it can and should be used, but political actors nonetheless seek to exploit it just as they have done the technologies which preceded it. And this they have done in a variety of settings and ways, such as www.sarkozy.fr/home/, www.barackobama.com and www.youtube.com/labourvision.

But if one places these different technologies in a long line, one could be accused of minimizing those differences that make each technology unique or even minimizing the significance of the differences and the ways in which the conduct of political communication has been transformed. Pippa Norris (Norris, 2004), for example, sees the post-1990s as exemplifying an era of 'post-modern' political communication with the internet playing a large part in bringing about transformations in the conduct of political communication. The 'post-modern' era is therefore distinguishable from the 'modern' one in which the medium of television was dominant. For Norris the occurrence of change – in respect of media, organization and behaviour – marks one period off from another.

In contrast, if one treats new contemporary technologies as no more than developments in a long line of developments, the differences between 'periods' become more blurred and the idea of difference itself is open to question and analysis. One can illustrate these differences in perspective quite easily by exploring the question of whether television had a more significant transformative effect on the conduct of political communication than the internet. If one argues that the impact of television was far more significant, then one is bound to question the idea of a transition from a television dominated 'modern' period to an internet dominated 'post-modern' one. More so, since television is still the dominant medium of communication in most democracies. This is not to deny that there have been changes in the conduct and nature of political communication brought about by the internet. The question is whether those changes are significant enough to warrant classifying them as transformative (see the discussion in Chapter 4).

Inevitably such questions are open to interpretation and different assessments but they illustrate why it is important to explore how the notion of change is itself an object of study and discussion.

Example 3: 'Spin' and 'spin doctors'

The third example that illustrates the importance of coming to grips with how change is itself understood comes from contemporary British discussions about spin and the role of Alastair Campbell in coordinating and running the media relations operation of Tony Blair's government from 1997 to about 2005. There can be little doubt that

Campbell was very effective in that role and that he managed to deal with the media in a way that highlighted the level of coordination needed for modern government.

Yet when it comes to examining Campbell's role in a historical perspective, one also becomes aware of the fact that others may have played similar parts in earlier periods: Bernard Ingham (who worked for Margaret Thatcher in the 1980s) and Joe Haines (who worked for the Harold Wilson government in the 1970s) were, in their time, equally controversial figures. Should we, therefore, see continuity between these three figures or is there a way of judging the Campbell era as significantly different from the other two? At a deeper level, should we see the work of Campbell as part of a process of adaptation to the new era of 24/7 news where an absence of coordination is taken to signify chaos, disorganization and weakness? As more historical work emerges – for example Richard Cockett (1989) on Neville Chamberlain's control of the lobby (political journalists) in the 1930s, or Martin Moore's (2005) analysis of news management in the immediate post-war period in Britain – these questions of continuity and change must be revisited.

The point here, as with the two other examples above, is that it is important to see the broader contexts in which changes take place and the ways in which the incidence of change does not necessarily signify transformation. Change, after all, can be minimal, incremental and superficial; it can also be large-scale and significant. How it is interpreted can therefore be an issue in itself.

If the above examples suggest the possibility of continuity across decades in respect of the ways in which those in politics have conducted political affairs, are there any events or practices, technologies or people that may have brought about the possibility of transformative change? Asking that question risks degenerating into a game of 'any answers', yet the question is important because it can alert us to possibilities and, at the same time, the realization that we need to justify our preferences. Were the Nixon–Kennedy debates significant in alerting political actors to the importance of image and personality? Did Roosevelt's 'fireside chats' introduce a different way of talking to the public? Did Margaret Thatcher develop a whole new strategy to electioneering and image building? Is the internet creating a new network of political communication that is more horizontal than hierarchical? Did the medium of television completely redefine and re-present politics, political actors and political communication? And so on.

Many of these questions are discussed more fully in later chapters of this book, yet they each touch on the issue that has been central in discussions about the changing nature of political communication. As Jay Blumler and Denis Kavanagh asked in their article 'The Third Age of Political Communication' 'how [does] the present situation differ from what preceded it?' (1999: 209). Yet in posing such a deceptively simple question, Blumler and Kavanagh have alerted us not only to the task of identifying change but also to the problematic nature of historical explanation itself. What will hopefully emerge from this book is that simple accounts or descriptions of the changing nature of political communication, particularly in the context of election campaigns, throw up more problems than they resolve. We need a more nuanced and historically informed understanding of change in the study of political communication than is commonly available.

But to call for a more nuanced and historically informed understanding of change is not to deny that change has taken place. It is simply to attempt to situate change in a broader context in which one can better make sense of developments. It also implies that we need to be cautious in the words we use to describe those aspects of political communication that are often employed to signify change and difference. This would certainly be true of words such as 'Americanization' and 'professionalization': the former has been used to suggest that the nature of political communication has become more Americanized, whilst the latter has been used extensively to suggest that things – structures, practices, ways of doing things and so on – are different and more professional than in the past. But without a proper assessment of the meaning of either Americanization or professionalization and the process of professionalization, how can such judgements be made?

The structure of this book

The next eight chapters in this book deal with the ideas of transformation and professionalization in some of the key component elements of political communication, namely, political parties and their members, campaign communications, the technologies of communication, and governmental communication. Cutting across these, there are several other elements that also feature such as the changing nature of the electorate, the global dimension of the changes that are taking place, the increasing use of consultants and other communication professionals, the consequences of all these elements for the future conduct and content of political communication, and the implications of all these changes for the role of the public or citizen in the conduct of politics. Perhaps inevitably, many of the examples are drawn from recent British political and communication history. One reason for this is that, at times, the nature and details of the arguments require considerable layers of historical and political background. Replicating this in relation to other political systems would have created an unmanageable and possibly unreadable book. As it is, I draw on specific literatures in order to argue the case about the nature of transformation and professionalization in political communication.

The organization of the eight chapters reveals a degree of prioritization of importance.

The main theme of **Chapter 2** is that political parties continually adapt to their environment, including to new means of communication, and that just as newer media help 'condition' the nature of politics, politics too can 'condition' the dominant media of the day. Although this chapter reviews accounts of the changing nature of campaign communications   prime examples of political communication – its main focus is on the ways in which political parties have adapted to changing technologies of communication. Using examples relating to the use of radio, film and television it pursues the argument of adaptation reserving some specific comments for how the medium of television may have had a more transformative power.

Chapter 3 deals with political parties and how these have adapted to changing circumstances in their pursuit of electoral victory. Political parties represent coalitions of interest and are very much at the centre of a democratic political system. They organize interests and offer citizens alternatives. Without the possibility of choice and alternatives, there is a poverty of political debate. But political parties – like almost everything else – change over time. While there may be linkages between the present and the past, those linkages cannot necessarily be treated as continuous ones. The political parties in the 19th century were very different from what they are today, both ideologically and organizationally. Similarly, the role of the public or citizen has changed over that period. Appreciating the importance of that change means that it becomes necessary to adopt a framework for understanding change which allows one to grasp similarities, and continuities as well as discontinuities. In this respect, although political parties have changed enormously from what they were in the late 19th century, the pursuit of electoral victory is one of those eternal truths that link them together. As with the saying that 'in defeat one plans for victory', political parties are always pursuing some particular objective.

Chapter 4 develops more fully ideas initially presented in preceding chapters by exploring in some detail how a variety of professional advisers have come to play an increasingly important and often central role in the lives of political parties, especially in respect of electoral contests. If anything, professional advisers have become increasingly central in the conduct of politics and in political communication. As with other chapters in this book, the historical context of this discussion is important since there is evidence to show that paid consultants were in use in US elections in the 1920s although their use in Britain and elsewhere came later. By drawing attention to historical details, this chapter once again raises the question of whether there has been a transformation in the way consultants are used or whether there are lines of continuity.

While previous chapters explored the questions of adaptation, transformation and professionalization of political communication at the level of the political party, the changes that have taken place at that level cannot be seen in isolation from changes that have taken place, or are taking place, at a more local level or at the level of the individual politician. **Chapter 5** turns the focus onto the way individual political actors, mainly prospective candidates for Parliamentary seats and Members of Parliament, have changed their practices alongside changes in technologies of communication and different understandings of what does and does not work in the media.

The primary theme of **Chapter 6** is that changes in the communication of government information in the British context have accelerated in recent decades as governments have had to confront more ubiquitous media. These changes can be likened to transformations as new refined practices and ways of looking at communications issues have become embedded. Once these changes have taken place, this chapter argues, it becomes difficult to undo them. The secondary theme of this chapter is the extent to which changes brought about since New Labour came to power in 1997 represent a transformation per se rather than a greater professionalization of practices that have been in use in previous decades. As with other chapters in this book, this chapter explores not only the present configuration of forces but also the broader historical and political context so as to give a better understanding of the significance of change.

The aim of **Chapter 7** is to explore some common accounts of transitions and transformations in political communication and to look at these in the context of a number of country-specific studies of transformations in political communication. The first substantive part of the chapter looks at different accounts of change and, in particular, at accounts that privilege the idea of 'modernization', whilst the second part looks at transformations of political communication in three quite different countries: Germany, Greece and Italy. In reviewing accounts of change and 'modernization' this chapter connects with ideas presented in Chapter 2 where different accounts of changes in campaign communications are presented. In this way, it is useful to look at Chapter 7 in the context of ideas also discussed in Chapter 2.

Chapter 8 focuses specifically on the internet but looks at it in the context of discussions about the transformation of political communication. In this way, there is a clear attempt to make connections between 'old' and 'new' media and between ideas that envisage radical and transformative change and ideas that highlight elements of continuity.

Chapter 9 concludes with a review of the key themes presented in this book and tries to answer the main question that is posed throughout, that is, has there been a transformation and professionalization of political communication? In seeking to answer this question it is inevitably forced to confront another one that features less often in such discussions, namely, what role, if any, has the public – as voters, electorate, audiences, citizens or consumers (Lewis et al., 2005; Livingstone, 2005) – played in respect of the changes documented in the chapters of this book?

In the following chapters, a case will be made to the effect that there has been a transformation as well as a professionalization of political communication. Neither of these ideas is presented as hypotheses that can be tested in a quantitative way for a simple reason: when endeavouring to do historical work tracing changes in political communication, one is struck by continual change so that what is considered to be professional in one period may be very old-fashioned in another. Attempts to test such hypotheses must, therefore, take into account those sorts of changes. To give one final example: when fax machines were first used for sending political literature to constituents sometime in the 1970s it was hailed as a momentous leap forward from what had gone on before. By the late 20th century, fax machines were being moved out of offices and into cupboards as email took over. It does matter, therefore, at what points one makes judgements about what it means to be professional and when transformations took place.

As this book seeks to show, there have been many transformations and many changes at numerous levels throughout the past 100 years or more. It is up to the reader to decide how significant each of these sets of changes has been.

Media and Politics: How, and Why, Political Parties Communicate Politics

2

Introduction

The broad theme of this chapter is that political parties continually adapt to their environment, including to new means of communication, and that just as newer media help 'condition' (Seymour-Ure, 1977: 114) the nature of politics, politics too can 'condition' the dominant media of the day. In pursuing this argument, this chapter will illustrate the process of adaptation by exploring how political parties have, in the recent past, dealt with technologies of communication, such as radio and television.

One early admission of the need to adapt to changing circumstances can be seen in Stanley Baldwin's comments in 1929, when he observed that:

> the whole organisation, the political organisation of a party, has to adapt itself to the modern condition of electioneering, and to the enormous electorate that has come into existence after the [1918] war; and I doubt if any party has yet adapted itself fully to meet the new conditions. (Quoted in Hollins, 1981: 62)

In drawing attention to the changed circumstances in which political parties found themselves at the end of the First World War, Stanley Baldwin showed that he – and presumably others – were alert to the dangers of atrophying, of remaining as before and of being out of step with modern conditions. The key task of the political party, as expressed by Baldwin, was to 'adapt'. But what, in these circumstances, does 'adapt' mean? On the one hand, it can mean to acknowledge changing political and social circumstances and ensuring that the political party is able to respond to these by, for example, modifying political positions; on the other hand, it can also mean to engage with, and become immersed in, what Baldwin called 'the modern condition of electioneering'. In both these readings of 'adapt', there is an implicit readiness to deal with changing circumstances and to deal with these in such a way as to ensure that the political party continues to survive and thrive.

The view expressed by Baldwin resonates with comments made by Hazel Blears, MP and Chairwoman of the Labour Party, in 2006. In an article in *The Times* she argued that the Labour Party needed 'to analyse the success of membership organizations such as the RAC or RSPB, and learn how to recruit and retain members. ... We need to harness technology such as podcasting, texting and blogging, learning from campaigns such as *Make Poverty History*' (2006a).

In a radio interview later that same day, she observed that:

> as a modern campaigning organisation ... we need to use a whole range of ways to attract more people and keep them engaged. ... We, in the Labour Party, do not have a monopoly on wisdom. That's why I am keen to look at other organisations: how do you bring people in, how do you particularly harness that idealism of young people who want to change the world? (Blears, 2006b)

Although separated by some 80 years, what these comments reveal is not only an appreciation (and realization) of the imperative of change but also a readiness to deal with it. When Stanley Baldwin was first elected in 1906, campaigning essentially consisted of local meetings and newspaper reports in a newspaper industry that had only been revolutionized some ten years before with the launch of the first newspaper aimed at a mass readership, the *Daily Mail*. By the 1930s – and still at the heart of political life – Baldwin had already been involved in radio broadcasts and his speeches had been filmed for distribution (http://www.screenonline.org.uk/film/id/1196906/index.html). By contrast, Hazel Blears entered Parliament in 1997 when all the means of communication we know today were already in place, and yet her comments still reflect the critical importance of continually reappraising how politics has to be communicated to a continually changing electorate.

For these two politicians, the transformation and professionalization of political communication may thus mean little more than a process of adapting politics, and how it should be communicated, to the newest medium of significance, but it probably has consequences also for how they would see changes that political party organizations themselves have to undergo in order to communicate more effectively.

And just as Baldwin could not ignore the new media of radio and film, so too Blears could not ignore the potential of the internet – and both could not ignore the fact that some forms of political organization are better than others. In this respect, they would probably agree with the comments made by Colin Seymour-Ure in his study of the media and politics:

> Politics has no existence apart from the communications media prevalent in society. When the hustings, the country house and the political club were important places for communication, politics suited them. With mass politics and modern technology, forms of political communication have necessarily changed. TV is the prevalent medium and inevitably tends to impose its own manners on its subjects. This is not to 'distort' politics, for there have never been politics that were not conditioned by the dominant media of the day. (1977: 114)

As will be argued in Chapters 5 and 6, one of the ways in which political actors and governments from around the late 1980s onwards adapted to television (and also the press) was to seek to control it by coordinating their communication strategies. But the media sought to unravel attempts to control them by revealing the background and intention to control. In this process – in effect, the introduction and subsequent unmasking and denigration of the 'spin' machine (McNair, 2004) – the form and content of politics and of political communication changed. Not only did politics adapt to media, but media also adapted to politics. The same argument can also be applied to the newest technology of all, the internet. Rather than seeing it as completely transforming the nature of politics, political parties might simply adapt to it and incorporate it into their overall strategies, seeing it as no more than part and parcel of, what Baldwin had called, 'the modern condition of electioneering'. As Hill and Hughes conclude from their study of 'cyberpolitics':

> the Net is not going to radically change us; we are molding it to our own ways of thinking and action. It is neither a monstrosity nor a savior; it is a new venue for the same old human compunction: politics. (1998: 186)

Adaptation or transformation? The changing nature of political communication

The idea that the 'dominant media of the day' 'condition' politics (Seymour-Ure, 1977: 114) suggests that in the relationship between media and politics it is the media that force change. But the media are as much a product of politics as they are an influence on it, so that the nature of the power they bring to bear on the world of politics is anything but straightforward. This is particularly true of the medium of television which had been fairly heavily regulated in most Western European democracies until the 1980s. Yet, and irrespective of the regulatory structures imposed on the broadcast media, the audio-visual character of television inevitably forced politicians to come to terms with it: to learn how to appear on screen, how to handle television reporters, how to present their case, how to control the interview situation and so on.

In its formative years, or while heavily regulated (as in most West European countries), the medium of television did begin to condition and transform the nature of political communication by, at the very least, making politicians aware of the need to come to terms with it. In that process of transformation – or is adaptation a more apt word? – both those working in the media and those working in politics became more professional, that is, more adept and more skilful, at using the medium. In other words, rather than seeing the relationship between media and politics as comprising just one single transformative moment, for example television takes over from other media or the internet takes over from television, the 'conditioning' power of any new medium, at least as it connects to the world of politics, may be made up of several phases in which one can also find evidence of processes of adaptation and professionalization. Furthermore, as 'newer' means of communication do not tend to replace other 'older' media, the processes of adaptation also include the media adapting to one another.

In arguing that the relationship between media and politics is a complex one and that it might include different phases, this chapter is proposing a more nuanced understanding of change in the nature and content of political communication. (See also Chapter 7 for a lengthier discussion of this point.) At the same time, it will suggest that while politics may be 'conditioned' by media, those who engage in politics, either as individuals or as part of organizations, grasp opportunities for change if those opportunities are able to offer them some advantage over their competitors. As the section on television below will show, a number of key British political players within the political parties were fully cognizant of the potential of television in the early 1950s and even before it had developed its own arrangements and approaches to the coverage of politics. The same would be true in the case of the emergence of radio and film: there were always those who sought to exploit the new media well before they became fully established. While radio had more of a transformative effect than the medium of film (see the section on film and radio below), their use by political actors demonstrates the willingness and readiness of politicians to exploit all available means of communication. Instead of seeing politicians/political parties as being forced to adapt to the media – the strongest sense of the meaning of 'conditioned' – it may be that politicians/political parties, aware as they are of their transient existence, take on board all means that are likely to improve their fortunes.

There is one other consideration that should be noted. Political parties are organizations that change over time. Their shape – and their relations with their members, the wider public and the state – change over time. As Chapter 3 argues, political parties have adapted to their surrounding circumstances, of which the media are only a part, in a number of ways and these changes also condition their relations with their members and their use of the media. The mass-membership party is a very different one from the 'cartel' party which, it is argued, is distanced from its members, dependent on the state for its existence and no more than a machine for waging electoral contests (see Katz and Mair, 2002; Krouwel, 2003). In this respect, different organizational forms of political parties may be better at dealing with different media structures and practices: the centralized, leader-directed party is better suited to media practices that privilege a communication strategy that leaves little room for dissent and deviation; conversely, the 24/7 adversarial media culture may force parties to become centralized and highly organized. The interplay between media and political parties/politicians is thus complex and, more importantly, constantly shifting.

Yet in studying the transformation and professionalization of political communication, too often the primary focus has tended to be on campaign communications and of a broadbrush nature. Consequently, as we shall see presently, subtle changes can be overlooked, and evolutionary change and adaptation to new circumstances or new media can take on the role of transformative agents bringing about epochal change. This is not to deny that the media can bring about fundamental change in the nature and content of political communication, merely that one needs to be careful about making judgements concerning the transformative nature of that change. To give an example: television has had an enormous impact on the way politics and political communication are conducted and one needs only to compare output in the 1950s with output in the 1990s to see this. But what of radio's impact in the 1920s and 1930s, and how did changes vis-à-vis radio impact on practices that developed vis-à-vis television? Furthermore, are some media (which?) more transformative than others, while others (again which?) politicians/political parties merely adapt to? The point here is not that change does not take place but that one can become very easily seduced by apocalyptic visions of transformative change.

What this chapter seeks to do is to explore not only how change has been dealt with in some of the literature – the next section – but also to illustrate how political parties have continually adapted to newer media over the past 100 years. In offering a historical overview, I hope to show how political parties responded to developing technologies – film, radio, television and the web – and how their responses can be placed within a framework that underplays the simplistic sense of transformation as epochal change and emphasizes elements of adaptive strategies to meet implicit objectives of electoral success. Part 4 of this chapter will seek to establish some general themes relating to the way politics meets the challenge of new technologies.

Evolutionary and historical perspectives on changing campaign communications

One of the more popular accounts of the changing nature of campaign communications is Pippa Norris's 'typology of the evolution of campaign communications' (see, for example, Norris, 2000, 2004) (Table 2.1). Two features of this, as of other accounts, are worthy of note. The first is the designation of the different forms of campaigns using labels that may have normative qualities to them. Hence, the label 'premodern' as against the contemporary 'postmodern' or, in the case of Gibson and Römmele (2001) (Table 2.2), 'premodern' as against the contemporary 'professional campaign'. While there can be little doubt that campaigns in the 21st century are run differently from campaigns in the 1920s, it is not clear why earlier campaigns should be designated as 'premodern'. Such a judgement implies amateurishness, a lack of familiarity, almost backwardness in the ways campaigns were organized. Yet I would argue that at those moments in time, campaigns might have been considered *by contemporaries* as modern. To put this point differently, the labels are contemporary lenses through which we see the past and, one must presume, that in twenty or thirty years time, today's 'post-modern campaign' or 'professional campaign' will be somewhat less 'post-modern' and less 'professional' than we perceive it to be today.

Table 2.1 Typology of the evolution of campaign communications

	Premodern	**Modern**[1]	**Post-modern**
Predominant era	Mid-19th century to 1950s	Early 1960s–late 1980s	1990s+
Campaign organization	Local and decentralized party volunteers	Nationally coordinated with greater professionalization	Nationally coordinated but decentralized operations
Media	Partisan press, local posters and pamphlets, radio broadcasts	Television broadcasts through main evening news, targeted direct mail	TV narrowcasting, direct and mediated websites, email, online discussion groups, intranets

Source: Adapted from Norris, 2004, Table 1

The second point to make about these accounts is that they are essentially built around the existence, and use, of different media: the 'premodern' campaign is basically a campaign built around the press; the 'modern' is the campaign built around television and the 'post-modern'/professional campaign is the campaign in the digital age where media have proliferated and 'electronic glut' (Seymour-Ure, 1996) is the order of the day. Yet in no election campaign has an older campaign mode been abandoned. Even when television was the dominant medium in the 1980s, say, – and arguably it still is in the early 21st century – the press continued to be a very significant player. By breaking up historical time – even for heuristic purposes or for reasons of simplicity – there is a danger of separating elements which could really be seen as part of a continuous process of adaptation and change.

While such frameworks can be useful in illustrating how elements of campaigning have changed, one of their weaknesses is that they mask the presence of knowing and acting political actors adapting to

Table 2.2 Political campaigns in historical perspective

	Premodern Campaigns	Modern Campaigns	Professional Campaigns[2]
Tools	Print media, rallies, meetings, foot soldiers	Broadcast television news, news, news advertisements, polls	Internet, direct mail
Mode/style	Labour-intensive, interpersonal, amateur	Capital-intensive, mediated, indirect	Capital-intensive, marketed, targeted, continuous
Orientation to voter	Mobilizing voters = loyal partisans	Converting and mobilizing, voters = loyal partisans and floating	Interactive, voters = consumers
Internal power distribution	Local-centric	National-centric	Local/national-centric, bifurcation

Source: From Gibson and Römmele, 2001: 34. Reproduced with permission of Sage Publications Inc. Journals

changing media environments. Interestingly, none of these accounts of change incorporate a way of looking at the transformation of political parties themselves alongside changing media environments. This is, as it were, the other side of the evolution of campaign communications and it may be an equally valid way of looking at changes in campaign communications, namely, that the changes are as much a response of the political parties to changed circumstances, including media, as to the media changing the nature and style of campaigning. This can be illustrated as in Table 2.3 where the role/nature of the political party becomes a key factor in accounting for change rather than a subsidiary or invisible one.

As political parties change and as new media join old media in the campaigning practices of political parties, new relationships develop between the media, political parties and the public. These new relationships then feed into the communication strategies of political parties, as well as media practices: the 'cartel' party has a different relationship to its members than does the mass-membership party, for example, and would consequently communicate with its members in different ways. *Importantly, as newer media come on stream and develop and as media practices change, the place of political parties in the world of politics can change quite significantly.*

Table 2.3 The evolution of political parties and their role in changing forms of campaign communications

	Premodern	**Modern**	**Post-modern**
Predominant era	Mid-19th century to 1950s	Early 1960s–late 1980s	1990s+
Nature of political parties	Mass membership	Catch-all party	Cartel party
Campaign organization	Local and decentralized party volunteers	Nationally coordinated with greater professionalization	Nationally coordinated but decentralized operations
Media	Partisan press, local posters and pamphlets, radio broadcasts	Television broadcasts through main evening news, targeted direct mail	TV narrowcasting, direct and mediated websites, email, online discussion groups, intranets

Source: Adapted from Katz and Mair, 2002; Norris, 2002

We can see this in the development of different media over the past century or so. In the 19th century in both Britain and the US, political parties or factions were able to exercise some measure of direct control over the press either through ownership, subsidies or strong ideological links. But as newspapers became too expensive to run, too costly to organize and developed a more commercial approach to news content, the relationship between political parties and newspapers changed (see, for example, Seymour-Ure, 1996) leaving political parties without direct control over any means of mass communication. The absence of direct controls over the press meant that other forms of control and connections – ideological, indirect and behind-the scenes – would need to be deployed to disseminate the message, but it left political parties generally exposed to a press that was more independent – perhaps even 'unhinged' (Seymour-Ure, 1998) – and less subservient than in the past.

Subsequent developments in technologies of communication – the gramophone, radio, film and even television – took place outside the control of political forces or, at the very least, kept them at a distance. Film, for example, developed as a commercial and entertainment medium, as did the gramophone. In most West European countries, radio and then television developed within the framework of public service which ensured, to a significant extent, some measure of balance between the political parties. (See pp. 39–41.)

The internet, as with the gramophone and film, is developing as an essentially commercially driven system. In the 1930s, when political parties made their own films for propaganda, those films had to be shown in commercial cinemas (Hollins, 1981: 62) although there were also indications that cinema proprietors 'did not like having their (mostly working-class) audiences upset by contentious political material' (Thorpe, 1991). The only ways in which political parties could fully control the dissemination of their filmed messages was through their own film vans which toured the country. Once political parties lost direct control over the press, they would no longer be 'in control' of any mass medium; they would have to find ways of disseminating their messages through means of communication over which they had no direct control.[3] Their ability to control how the message was communicated to a mass public became negligible.

In the early days of radio and television, political parties were able to exert some pressure on broadcasters but that soon waned.[4] By the 1960s, television and radio – both mostly controlled by the BBC – were able to move away from under the shadow of political parties and began to develop their own ways of dealing with them. This included presenting a wider range of voices than had previously been aired: while in the early to mid-1950s, political parties could suggest who would appear on political programmes, by the end of that decade they had lost control of that power also and broadcasters could determine the agenda and who the invited speakers would be. (See, for example, Goldie, 1977.) With the advent of cable and satellite broadcasting, the internet and a fragmented 24/7 media, the nature of the media landscape has changed radically, not only because new technologies have come on stream but also because who has access to those means of communication has changed. This is one of the most critical points that emerges from Blumler and Kavanagh's 'third age' of communication, namely, that there is 'centrifugal diversification': not only more channels and ways to communicate but it also:

> creates openings for previously excluded voices to express their views and perhaps even be noticed by mainstream outlets. It creates opportunities for would-be persuaders to seek more efficient impact by selectively focusing their communications on preferred population sectors. ... In most modern societies, then, centripetal communication is to some extent retreating and centrifugal communication is advancing. (1999: 221)

The 'centrifugal tendency' 'decentres' the political party, and it is moved away from its previously dominant position (Schudson, 1999). As Schudson has argued, in this new environment, 'no one owns politics today' and certainly not in the way that political parties owned it in the 19th century or sought to control its communication in the early 1950s. It is not a completely level playing field because the mainstream media are still very much focused on the main political parties as the key political players. Nonetheless, there are now more windows on the world than there ever were and these are being opened by a whole host of individuals, groups and organizations – some traditional, many new. As Webster has written:

> today's information networks make it impossible for politicians to maintain effective control, try as they might. The networks are simply too fluid, too leaky, too undisciplined and too rampant to allow the politicians to maintain an effective hold. (Webster, 2001: 7)

While this is not quite 'cultural chaos' (McNair, 2006), it does lead to the creation of a much wider agenda with a greater number of players taking active part than ever before.[5]

In looking at accounts of changing practices, we must take note of the interplay between political parties and media without resorting to explanations that privilege particular agents or media. In fact, and as I will argue more fully in Chapter 7, it may not be the medium itself that is the bringer of change but the rules (or lack thereof) that may be significant. So, while television did force politicians to adapt to it, the introduction of competition and commercial media, from around 1955 in Britain's case, probably had a greater impact because it altered the way politics was covered and politicians were dealt with.

These three points – changing media and practices, the transformation of political parties themselves (the subject of Chapter 3) and 'centrifugal diversification' (Blumler and Kavanagh, 1999) – are woven into the shifting patterns of political communication over the past 100 years or so. As the next section illustrates, political parties adapt to changes in media. Over time, they also learn how to communicate politics in ways that are to their advantage.

Harnessing technology: newspapers, radio and film

While the press is often overlooked in discussions of technologies of mass communication, it is important to remember that it played a significant role in the 19th and early 20th centuries as a means of political communication. Its alignment with developing political parties – either out of ideological preference and contacts, or through direct ownership by politically motivated individuals – ensured that the political messages were spread to the reading public, albeit a small one. Alan Lee has pointed out that all the metropolitan dailies published in 1855 as well as in 1870 were committed to either the Liberals or the Conservatives; the same was also broadly true of the English provincial daily press. Between 1868 and 1885, only about one-fifth of all English provincial titles were not politically committed to the Liberals or the Conservatives or to a combination of both (Lee, 1980).

The 'cadre' or 'elite' parties of the day were simply made up of the elected representatives and their direct local contacts:

> to the extent that one could speak of an enduring party on the ground, it would be virtually indistinguishable from the personal network of friends and clients of the member or his principals. (Katz and Mair, 2002: 115)

Newspaper circulation – itself a consequence of the level of technological development reached by the industry but also a reflection of costs, distribution and content – was able to cater for that public and, in the absence of a mass franchise there was little need for a wider mobilization of political support. Moreover, given the lack of competition in election contests at the turn of the century, political persuasion was a matter for a restricted public. It was only with the expansion of the franchise that a larger population was brought into the political system and had to be engaged with in ways that were different from the past.

Nevertheless, the recurring theme throughout the latter half of the 19th century was that of individual politicians and political parties trying to ensure that the press gave them some degree of allegiance. But, as Stephen Koss has pointed out, this was never a straightforward matter especially when the political nature of newspapers was seen as an obstacle to a wider circulation and robust advertising revenue:

> prudence, no less than economy ... demanded that the political press should wear its party labels more discreetly. ... Even where traditional loyalties persisted, they neither inspired nor inhibited to the same extent [as previously]. (Koss, 1984: 305)

The same pattern was observed in the US:

> The most devastating aspect of commercialization was that newspapers, once organs for the political parties, became more and more commercial and increasingly dared to be independent. The daily and weekly newspapers were becoming absorbed in commercially minded news gathering and less committed to advancing political parties. (Schudson, 1999: 177)

Even at the turn of the 20th century, political control could be detected, as could its increasingly tenuous nature:

> The *Observer*, the *Standard*, the *Globe*, and the *Pall Mall Gazette* were each receiving aid from the [Conservative] Unionist funds, sometimes as much as £10,000 a year [in the 1910s]. (Negrine, 1994: 47)

In 1918, supporters of Lloyd George helped him purchase the *Daily Chronicle*, further demonstrating the links that existed in some cases. The press barons – Beaverbrook, Northcliffe and Rothermere – though broke the pattern and began to exert their own independent spirit into their relationship with politics. Once that happened, it was clear that the press was moving outside the political control of parties. Hence, Baldwin's comment in 1931 that the press 'had power without responsibility – the prerogative of the harlot throughout the ages'. While Baldwin was attacking a section of the press for wanting to dictate party issues, the broader point of the attack illustrated the powerlessness of the politicians to dictate what the press should do, unless, of course, they were party newspapers and few of these achieved anything near the mass circulation of the commercial press.[6]

This lack of direct control over the means of mass communication could also be seen in the development of radio broadcasting. Created initially as a company but later transformed into a public service organization, the BBC sought to balance the major parliamentary political forces, although not always fairly. The exercise of balance placed the political parties at a disadvantage since they could not dictate all content (although this did ensure that they all had some access to the medium!). Despite this, as we shall see below, the parties were fully aware of the need to exploit the medium since it would give them a reach that was previously unimagined. But politicians and parties had to work within a framework established elsewhere and by others: the broadcasts they were involved in and the radio shows they contributed to were no longer fully under their control. They needed the skills, cooperation and advice of others. However, the fact that this new medium initially privileged the political classes and eased their introduction to, and use of, radio gave them an advantage which they were to lose once politics – as a topic and a profession – lost its status.

A not dissimilar pattern was to follow with television. Briefly, as we return to television more fully below, in television's first few years of development, roughly 1951–6, the BBC allowed much of its political content and the formats of political programmes to be dictated by the major politics parties (Goldie, 1977). Once competition in television was introduced with the launch of commercial television and those in television got braver in their dealings with politicians, the privileged position that politics previously had was undermined. As a general rule, if such a thing can be said to exist, the pattern would be that 'state-connected' media privilege the political world until competition forces state media to reconsider their relationship with the world of politics and, equally significantly, with their audience, an audience they had previously given limited attention to. This is part of the transition from 'party logic' to 'media logic' (Mazzoleni, 1987) that is a characteristic of much modern political communication where media pay more attention to the needs of the audience. By contrast, a new medium of communication which develops outside the realm of the state from the very start, such as the internet, does not privilege politics in the same way and leaves politics to adapt to it, rather than the other way round.

The two themes outlined above – the gradual loss of control by the world of politics over the means of communication, and the need to employ the technologies in existence since these give the world of politics access to the public – thus form part of the same equation that political parties have to grapple with, namely, how to reach voters in a changing media landscape. Arguably, a third theme was to emerge from the late 1960s onwards: with politics and politicians losing their status, the element of deference that may have given politics a privileged position, particularly in the 'state-connected' media, disappeared. Politics was relegated to rank alongside – and sometimes below – other subjects. So, on the one hand, we have evidence of a decline in the amount of political and parliamentary coverage (Negrine, 1998) and, on the other, a concern over 'tabloidisation' (Franklin, 1994).

The point to emphasize here is that political parties cannot usually afford to make choices between media of communication; they have to use them all, preferably in a coordinated way. We can see this in their use of radio and film in the 1920s and 1930s, but also in the ways in which they had planned to use television and radio in the 1950s. The development of the internet simply pushes them still further down the road of using a greater variety of media in the increasingly fragmented media world. When television was supreme and reached a mass audience, other media mattered less; when no medium is supreme and fragmentation rules, all media matter, at least a little.

Film and radio

While the relationships between politicians, political parties and the press immediately before and after the 1914–18 war were undergoing change, culminating in Stanley Baldwin's statement that the press had 'power without responsibility' in 1931, both politicians and political parties were developing different sorts of relationships with the emerging media of film and radio. The fact that all media of the day were being used *at the same time* lends support to my argument that political parties continually adapt to their environment and work with all forms of communication that are likely to give them an advantage. In a competitive electoral environment such adaptation must become the norm as political parties look for the best and most useful means to reach the mass electorate. The use of film and radio to persuade and mobilize must therefore be seen within this overall context of political parties wishing to establish their positions and to employ the available means of mass communication to disseminate their views. Very simply, politicians need to communicate with the public and each new means of communication allows them to do so more easily, but this does not mean that older means are necessarily forgotten or abandoned.

Of these two media, it is probable that the use of radio, via the BBC, was the first to be used by political parties and politicians. The BBC, it should be remembered, was only formed (as a company) in 1922, and after 1926 it became a public service broadcasting organization. At the time, it would be fair to argue, few understood the potential of radio and fewer still understood how best to use it for maximum effect. Nonetheless, the development of radio within the framework of the BBC created opportunities for politicians to talk directly to the radio audience. This was, in part, because John Reith, the BBC's first Director and later Director General went out of his way to make friends with politicians and to gain their support for the enterprise as a whole. By the 1924 general election, that is, within three years of the foundation of the BBC, the BBC had already accepted that political parties were a central, legitimate and primary feature of the parliamentary system and should consequently be given privileges in broadcasting; political broadcasts by the political parties were aired in October 1924 (Stuart, 1975). That politicians were willing to engage with radio is a measure of their prescience and awareness of its growing importance, since it was only from about 1934 onwards that 'more than half the population ... had the capacity at their fingertips to hear a single speaker ...' (Pegg, 1983: 8).

With the establishment of radio, we see how political parties – and individual politicians such as Winston Churchill – began to clamour for broadcast time even though the medium was in its infancy and few really knew how to use it to its full effect. It allowed them to reach many more members of an enlarged franchise who were not connected to political parties in traditional ways. According to Mark Pegg, local groups and local newspapers saw radio as a medium that would permit politicians to direct their messages to the public at large: 'radio was seen to be an absolutely essential aid to the traditional methods of expressing political comment or debate' (1983: 186).

Other effects of the new medium of radio signalled a change in the ways in which candidates connected to the leadership and voters connected with politicians:

> It would seem that the introduction of wireless broadcasts had at least two effects on constituency campaigning. At the 1935 election a number of candidates turned to the broadcast before going to mid-evening meetings, where they would reply to or expand on the content of the broadcasts. ... The second major effect was ... on their size. In the course of the 1935 election considerable press comment was directed to the decline in numbers attending constituency meetings. (Stannage, 1980: 178; see also Briggs, 1979)

The history of this early period in the development of broadcasting is punctuated by instances of political interference verging on almost total control, particularly during periods of crisis such as the 1926 General Strike (see Negrine, 1994; Tracey, 1977) and the BBC was still 'very vulnerable to political interference. The ideal – to use the power of the airways to nurture an enlightened, participatory democracy – was not easy to achieve in the face of pressures applied from all sides' (Pegg, 1983: 188). Perhaps a more generous interpretation of the BBC's difficulties at the time would simply point to the rapid development of a new medium which had no previous models of organization or governance to copy. In the circumstances, the first 10 or 15 years could be seen as ones in which careful steps were taken to establish the popularity of the medium and a set of practices that would then permit the organization to deliver the higher ideals. In the context of this chapter, those ideals would not only include 'an enlightened participative democracy' but also a framework that distanced politicians from the levers of control over media as would be the case under the 'fourth estate' model of the press.

Interestingly, moves towards using radio as a means of reaching the growing mass electorate/audience were taking place at the same time as resources were being put into making the most of the medium of film. As Timothy Hollins has pointed out:

> In early 1926 [Conservative] Central Office began to commission its own films. The [mainly cartoon] films produced, as with the system employed for displaying them, demonstrated ingenuity and an appreciation of the most effective method of reaching the intended audience. (1981: 60)

By the 1929 general election, the Conservative Party had '23 indoor and outdoor cinema vans available and continuously touring throughout the country' (Hollins, 1981: 59). Some of the films archived at the BFI give a flavour of these, and include *The Right Spirit* (1931) – a propaganda cartoon in which John Bull drives his car away from the 'garages of Ramsay MacDonald & Co. and Lloyd George & Co.' where he was given poor service and to 'Baldwin's Prosperity Garage, where he is given the right fuel: a mixture of Empire unity, safeguarding and reduced taxes'. (For this and other examples, see http://www.screenonline.org.uk/film/id/1196906/index.html.)

It would be wrong to conclude from these examples that each and every use of the means of communication, whether it was film or radio, was part of a longer term strategy that was well considered and well thought out. It is more likely that considerations were based on expediency and short-term thinking about what needed to be done to get messages across to the electorate. In the British context, it is not until the late 1950s when knowledge of polling and the use of public relations and advertising skills became more commonplace, that any semblance of a more coordinated strategy was to be found. In the US, one can date this to a much earlier period. (See the discussion in Chapter 4.)

Forward planning, coordination and strategizing may be part of the process of 'professionalization' of political communication that perhaps permeates the Gibson and Römmele model (2001, and see above p. 25) and it certainly points to a more knowledgeable and strategic use of media of communication post-1970. But in the 1920s and 30s, as in the 1950s with television, political parties in Britain, as elsewhere, were still adjusting to newly developed media. The onset of war in 1939 interrupted the development of radio and early developments in television. After 1945, it took less than ten years for many to realize that radio was in decline as television was emerging to dominate the landscape. With the introduction of television, political parties had different lessons to learn, including the lesson that television would transform politics itself.

Television

Television offers another good case study for exploring how politicians/political parties continually adapt to new media and what we find is not only an emerging awareness of the usefulness of television as a medium, as with radio, but also an emerging awareness of the need to learn how to use it to advantage.

Documentation in the archives of the Conservative and Labour Parties provides a glimpse of how organizers and others were coming to terms with the new medium of television. As in today's new media world of the internet, party organizers appear to have been planning ahead and anticipating the potential use of the new medium. Although in the early years of television – roughly 1951 through to 1957 – the main concern was the production of election broadcasts, there were many indications of a more general appreciation of the need to consider content and technique.

In the Conservative Party report, *Talking on Television*, (1951) one begins to find the connections between the need to tackle the new medium and the need for adequate preparation of skills to do so. It begins:

> It has been obvious for some time that no one in politics can afford to ignore Television. One million licences were sold in 1951. Allowing an average per set of 3 people, this means that the potential audience which can be reached at any time by a speaker in Television is around three million. (1951: 1)

The bulk of the ten page document offers specific advice on how one should appear and behave on television: 'some simple practical facts about Television which it might be useful for a Television speaker to know, and some points which may help him to understand the nature of the demands which Television is likely to make upon him' (1951: 2). On dress, it advises 'not to wear black or very dark clothes or show any large expanse of white'; on make-up, 'some may be required'; on 'voice and microphone', it suggests that one has little to worry about since these issues are dealt with by the technicians who position the microphones in the best possible locations. It also has advice on where to look – 'the speaker should look at [the camera] as little, or as much, as anyone does when talking to an individual in a room' (1951: 5).

While these comments – and the report itself – may appear perfunctory, it does meet its objectives of informing its readers that 'as far as the approach to the audience is concerned ... knowledge of "sound" broadcasting technique helps the speaker in Television. In every other way he has to start from the beginning' (1951: 1).

A year later, in 1952, Lord Woolton, Chairman of the Party, wrote to all Conservative MPs telling them of the facilities that the Party had acquired: 'a television studio ... Mr Wyndham Goldie, who has considerable knowledge both as an actor and producer, will be available at this studio for advice on television technique and production. The studio will be staffed by Mrs. Crum-Ewing' (Conservative Party archives, 1952/CCO4/4/250). MPs were urged to make use of them.

By 1956, Mrs Crum-Ewing announced that at a meeting with the General Director of the Party, they had discussed 'amongst other things the question of training Conservative speakers for television'. The archives also include copies of a programme for one such training day (App. 1)[7] and a list of attendees from the West Midlands region (Conservative Party archives, 1956/CCO4/7/361).

It is obviously impossible to assess how successful such events were or indeed whether the suggestions made were followed up. The memos and texts referred to above – and there are others – were produced for individuals occupying high positions within the Conservative Party organization, and their task would have been to filter down to others the suggestions, ideas or themes that had been raised. The same would be true of the documentation that one can find in the Labour Party archives. Alongside those that discuss the negotiations with the BBC over Party Political Broadcasts, there are papers that are either authored by, or include contributions from, Tony Wedgwood Benn. These are interesting because they identify the work that needed to be done in relation to the new medium of television if the Labour Party was to gain some advantage from it.

In 1953, Benn produced a report on *The Labour Party and Broadcasting* (BS/BCST/217) for the National Executive of the Party. The final report, dated 11 March 1953, was a report to the Joint Broadcasting Committee and has much in common with the draft. Halfway down the first page, section 2 on 'Broadcasting and Propaganda', it declares:

> it is doubtful whether the Party realises the full meaning of the expansion of Radio and Television audiences in the last five years. The potential Radio audience has now settled down at nearly 30,000,000 and the potential Television audience, which is growing rapidly, is at the moment almost 6,000,000. A propaganda policy which ignores this change is bound to run the risk of being ineffective. (1953: ii)

While the overall content of the report is important in itself, it is perhaps more useful for our present purposes to identify those parts of it that merit further attention. The four extracts below are comments that relate to the shift away from sound broadcasting and the need to exploit television and its potential:

- The straight Party [sound] broadcasting 'has now got a very limited value ... We aren't taking full advantage of the opportunities for dramatic presentation which Radio and Television offer. It's like issuing four pages of closely reasoned argument in small type against a coloured and illustrated glossy pamphlet. ... There are already many highly developed broadcasting techniques that are capable of adaptation for Political purposes' (1953: iiii) such as the illustrated talk, the interview and the outside broadcasts.
- As for television, it 'is far richer in potential development than Sound. The personality of the speaker and the things he has to say can have a tremendous impact, as Adlai Stevenson proved in the American Election. There is no denying the risk for a Party Leader who does this. The possibility of great success is only to be had at the risk of great failure, and rehearsal and practice are obviously important. The genuine fireside chat is not something that comes naturally, nor does the interview' (1953: v).
- On the way forward, 'the Party might find that it would have to equip itself with a certain amount of apparatus. ... Tory Central Office already have two rehearsal studios, one for Television and one for Sound. These are in regular use. So important is Television thought to be that they have recently had a special film made for

the Conservative Party on Political Television, to show to members of the Party going on T.V.'(1953: vii–viii).

- As for who should broadcast, the report was already prescient as to who was a good [professional?] performer on television: '[Christopher] Mayhew and [Michael] Foot, [Jim] Callaghan and Barbara Castle are real assets to us. We ought to do more talent spotting for our own sake. Similarly if there were a proper rehearsal studio at Transport House, Cyril Isaac could make it available to any members of the Party who wanted to practise or rehearse' (1953: viii–ix).

By 1958, a closed circuit television studio was already available in 'Transport House to provide for those politicians who need or want coaching ... [and the Labour Party was hoping] to prepare a training film on appearing on television which all those who are likely to have to face cameras will be able to see' (Morgan Phillips, Secretary of the Labour Party, 1958: 2).

Although it could be argued that the comments about television found in both archives refer, in the main, to the use of facilities, people and expertise for the production of party election broadcasts, there are also indications that the parties were investing in facilities so that anyone who was likely to appear on television could be offered help to make the most of that appearance. It should be remembered that at the time the above documents were written, television was still in its infancy and the rules, formal and informal, of political broadcasting had yet to be agreed (see Goldie, 1977). Notwithstanding that crucial point, it is important to observe that the extracts above touch on the range of techniques that those who appear on television should possess and, if they do not possess them, should learn and should use; the objective always being to reach the largest number of electors in a positive way.

Not surprisingly, such ideas and discussions were not taking place in a vacuum. The American experience informed some of those discussions (Negrine and Papathanassopoulos, 1996; Plasser and Plasser, 2002) and academics were also becoming aware of the vagaries of the medium, of what worked and what did not. David Butler's[8] work on the 1951 election is interesting, in part, because of such comments. He accused the Liberal Party's Lord Samuel 'of destroying the sense of naturalness and intimacy which can make television ... the most potent medium of mass communication'.[9] He also observed that Anthony Eden was 'pleasant and statesmanlike,' and that Christopher Mayhew employed 'a tour-de-force of television tactics' by using graphs (1952: 76–7).

In the subsequent general election of 1955, the political parties were using television more effectively and more confidently but still in a 'restrained and responsible' manner; there was 'nothing startlingly new' and the parties 'tried no great advertising tricks' (Butler, 1955) although one presumes they could have 'borrowed' from that industry. In the next general election in 1959, a more adventurous and televisual style was developed by the political parties and these were based around existing television and current affairs formats. But, by then, the political parties had lost control over the medium of television and of political broadcasting in general. The 14-Day Rule which limited what broadcasters could show and discuss was finally abandoned in 1957 (Negrine, 1999) and, more significantly, television began to develop its own ways of coping with politicians. (See also Chapter 7).

That shift was also noticeable in the US. Commenting on the 1960 presidential debates, Schudson observes that, 'before 1960 parties or candidates bought time on the networks. For the 1960 presidential debates, in contrast, the networks offered free time and thereby anointed themselves the sponsors of the nation's most important civic exercise' (1999: 234). They were in charge in a way that neither the press nor radio ever was. Political parties had to fight for publicity and the opportunity to communicate to the public, as they do with the internet.

The other point to note is that developments in television were taking place alongside the transformation of British political parties from mass-membership parties to 'catch-all' parties seeking to appeal to a large number of increasingly politically de-aligned voters. Political television, certainly in the shape of the party election broadcasts of the 1950s, was created to appeal to all rather than a section of the voting public; it does not work with the emphasis on class divisions but on unity and progress for the nation as a whole. The emphasis, it could be argued, is more on managing change and prosperity than on redistributing wealth or retaining privileges. (For examples of such broadcasts, see www.sheffield.ac.uk/journalsim/pebs.)

Over the 40 or so years in which television dominated the landscape at the end of the 20th century, it undoubtedly transformed politics in many ways. As it became the dominant medium of communication, political communication practices were centred on it and its 'manners'. Politicians could not, in reality, ignore television if they wanted to reach the mass electorate. Television became the forum of politics and played a part in transforming how politics was communicated. For example, the election on television became the 'television election' – an event taking place in the studios and constructed by the broadcasters and much less something happening out there. In this different media age of television, the political parties 'had to work harder and learn new tricks' (Blumler and Kavanagh, 1999: 212).

Whether it transformed the *content* of politics as well is another matter and takes us back to Colin Seymour-Ure's point (p. 20 above) that politics had always been 'conditioned' by the dominant media of the day. Nevertheless, there are many who have decried the impact of the media, particularly of television, on politics and have adopted the view that the media have distorted the political process and have undermined the tenets of the liberal democratic process. Against this 'apocalyptic' view, Mazzoleni and Schulz (1999) have argued that 'the increasing intrusion of the media in the political process is not necessarily synonymous with a media "takeover" of political institutions (governments, parties, leaders, movements)'. In fact, while there is much evidence of 'mediatization', namely, of how politics 'has lost its autonomy, has become dependent in its central functions on mass media, and is continuously shaped by interactions with mass media' (Mazzoleni and Schulz, 1999: 249), they argue against a view that the media have taken over politics.

The examples they cite go some way to illustrate how politics has been transformed by the media, particularly by television. These include the media's presentation of 'only a highly selective sample of newsworthy events from a continuous stream of occurrences'; the media's construction of 'the public sphere of information and opinion and [how they] control the terms of their exchange'; the significance of 'media logic' (Altheide and Snow, 1979) for understanding how media 'construct the meaning of events and personalities they report'; and 'the mass media's attention rules, production routines, selection criteria, and molding mechanisms [which] are well known in the world of politics' and to which political actors adapt their behaviour (Mazzoleni and Schulz, 1999: 215–52).

Nevertheless, they take the view that what these examples demonstrate is the ways in which media and politics coexist and adapt to one another, that is, that '"media politics" does not mean "politics by the media"' (Mazzoleni and Schulz, 1999: 252). Indeed, we could go further and point out that the reason political parties are required to learn to deal with the tricks of the trade of the media is because they are seeking to communicate to large numbers of their potential electors without being at the mercy of the media, that is, learning the ways television operates is a way of being able to exercise some element of control over it. As we shall see in later chapters, much of what prompts political actors to act in particular ways in front of the cameras – sound-bites, controlled exposure, selecting settings and so on – can be seen as a response to television's desire to dominate and represents a counteraction. This is the case if we look at how political actors learned to use the media (Chapter 5) and how New Labour reformed the governmental communications machinery (Chapter 6).

Can this perspective on the interaction of media and politics and the adaptation of one to the other in changing sociopolitical circumstances help us understand the interaction between political parties/politicians and the fragmented digital landscape? We turn to this question in the next section.

'Electronic glut' (Seymour-Ure, 1996)

If the medium of television radically changed the way politics was conducted and latterly forced political parties/politicians to adapt their practices, the post-1980s saw a proliferation of channels such that the medium of television was itself transformed from a limited system of communication to one of abundance with 24/7 media joined by the web in a 24/7 cycle of many-sided communication flows. This is the 'electronic glut'/media of abundance age that we now find ourselves in, or 'Age 3', as Blumler and Kavanagh called it: it is 'still emerging' but it is 'marked by the proliferation of the main means of communication, media abundance, ubiquity, reach, and celerity. ... New patterns and adaptations ensue for all involved in the political communication process' (1999: 213).

For those in politics, as the comment by Hazel Blears at the beginning of this chapter testifies, there is a new challenge: the challenge of how to deal with the all-consuming media *in a strategic way* yet, at the same time, *not to lose the initiative to the media*. To return to an earlier point, when television began to exert its power on politics, politicians began to learn that it too could be controlled, if not directly, then through a series of practices that limited its abilities to dictate the communication of politics. In the age of abundance, this too is a message that those in politics adhere to as they grapple with the demands of new media and the old. On the one hand, as Blears pointed out, they need to learn how to use the media to reach many disconnected citizens; on the other hand, they also need to learn how to use the media for their own ends. This is truly a process of professionalization.

How they will do so will depend on many factors, including finance and ingenuity, but there are already signs that political parties are engaging fully with the web; there are websites for individuals and parties and websites not dissimilar to politicized web-television services; there are blogs and webcams, there are links for members of political groups and there are links for non-members and so on. The combinations are many and the possibilities are endless. The ways in which parties use the web is not central to this chapter but the fact that they do use the web is (see also Chapter 8). Equally important is the fact that they use the web alongside other technologies old and new, ranging from posters through film to television and so on. The more integrated all these different uses are, the better the communication campaign, but the more integrated, the more centralized the communication strategy. Or, to put it the other way, the 'cartel party' inevitably seeks to dominate the channels of communication and to create a strategy for its communication needs.

What is obvious, though, is that the new media cannot be ignored and must be dealt with. In the words of Stanley Baldwin (1929), 'the whole organisation, the political organisation of a party, has to adapt itself to the modern condition of electioneering' (quoted in Hollins, 1981: 62).

Summary and conclusion: adaptation, transformation and professionalization

The central theme of this chapter is that political parties continually adapt to their environment. This includes to the 'new' media whenever they appear and develop. In lending support to this argument, this chapter has used a number of historical examples – the press, radio, film and television – to further develop that point and to attempt to move away from other accounts that privilege particular technologies or use particular labels to historicize the material.

But in adopting these positions, this chapter has placed the emphasis on the idea of adaptation, that is, of adjustment to new conditions, rather than of transformation, that is, a marked change in circumstances, because there is often evidence of continuity, for example from radio broadcasting to television broadcasting. There is evidence of discontinuity also, for example the growing professionalization, or the greater emphasis on more strategic communication, that could be seen as a transformation, although this is a transformation that has come about because of changes in approaches to dealing with the media rather than changes in media per se.

Of the media considered in this chapter, it is the medium of television that has perhaps forced the greatest amount of change, to the extent that one could perhaps see it as transforming the nature of political communication. The reasons for this undoubtedly include the combination of the audio and the visual in one form – bringing together, in a sense, experiences of film and radio – and, at the same time, the development of a competitive media environment that brought about a different way of dealing with politics and politicians. (This is discussed in more detail in Chapter 7.) Whether the internet will be as transformative is discussed in Chapter 8.

Finally, all politics is 'conditioned' by the major media of the day and the interplay between media and politics that takes place within any time period gives rise to different phases in a complex relationship between major institutions in modern society. As I shall argue more fully in Chapter 4, it is important to note how parties and media adapt constantly to one another and that in that longer term process of adaptation relationships are forever being negotiated and renegotiated. And one of the reasons why those relationships are always in flux is that political parties – like media – change their organizational make-up and act in the face of media, rather than simply respond to changes in media. This is the subject of the next chapter, Chapter 3.

The Transformation of Political Parties: Organizational Change and Communication Technologies

3

Introduction

The study of political communication in Western democracies inevitably focuses on the interaction between politicians and the media and the interplay between two quite different worlds: the world of media and the world of politics (see Cook, 1998). The previous chapter explored the context of that relationship by highlighting the significance of different means of communication and the ways in which political parties adapted to them. One of its key themes was that political parties respond to changes in communication technologies and in communication practices; they do not simply react to their surroundings. Whilst newer technologies always present challenges, the political party that wishes to survive and thrive must take these on board and exploit them to its advantage. The use of the web by a whole host of politicians in the 21st century is evidence of this general point.

But political parties have their own complex histories and those histories also help us to understand how they use new communication technologies. Whilst Chapter 2 explored the interplay between political parties and the media through the lens of the media, this chapter seeks to reverse the viewpoint and explore the relationship between the two through the lens of the political parties. Rather than seeing the different media as creating different forms of campaigning, this chapter will argue that different forms of campaigning might also be a consequence of the changing forms of the political party.

The aim of this chapter is to offer a broadbrush account of how and why political parties have changed over the past 100 or so years, and to examine how these changes have also taken account of changes in the ways in which parties communicate with their members and the electorate more generally. Whilst parties have not restructured themselves because of new means of communication, when they have restructured themselves that process has involved some attention being paid to the requirements of communication. New means of communication, most notably the press or television, did not bring about changes in the structure and organization of political parties; rather, new means of communication have become incorporated into the organizational make-up of political parties and have required – or been given – different degrees of attention, depending on their importance as a means of communication with the electorate. In this respect, political parties are no different from other organizations in that they continually adapt as change takes place around them, as information flows into them and as the communication landscape around them changes. The latter becomes a critical consideration when the means of mass communication become the only means to communicate with the electorate at large, that is, when political parties no longer have a mass-membership base.

In reviewing these transformations in the make-up of political parties from mass-membership to 'cartel' parties, this chapter will argue:

1. That it may be best to explore the transformations in the organizational make-up of political parties as part of the process by which they seek to adapt and meet the challenges of the present and to create the future of their choosing. It is an uneven process and one of adaptation and change.
2. That it is wise not to privilege one factor over any others as change comes about as a consequence of a whole range of factors. This is particularly important in the context of explanations of change which privilege technologies, for example television or the internet, as key motors of change. Communications media – be it film, television or the internet – are usually incorporated into the armoury of political parties rather than dictate their organizational form.
3. That we need to have an understanding of why parties go through changes in order to have a better grasp of how those processes have, in turn, impacted on the nature and content of political communication.

In order to develop these three points, this chapter will use a number of detailed historical examples to show how political parties – like other organizations – continually seek to adapt to their environment. Transformations, in other words, often mask smaller step changes that, in themselves, may be of significance. Within these transformations, we can begin to appreciate how political parties have come to learn to deal with the emergence of different technologies of communication.

Political parties in the late 19th century: a background sketch

Political parties, like all other organizations, are continually facing change and the need to adapt to that change. Whether that change comes as a result of a new, enlarged franchise, or new ways of thinking or election defeats, parties have to adapt to their environment as best they can. In his work on political parties, Bob Self has argued that the 'emergence of a mass electorate and stricter methods of controlling corruption and coercion demanded the adoption of new forms of party structure and novel methods of electoral mobilization in order to enable party leaders to appeal directly to the people for a mandate founded on political legitimacy' (Self, 2000: 2). To lend support to his argument, Bob Self gives an example of changes in party practices that were the consequence of the enlarged electorate brought about by changes in electoral law in the 19th century. As a direct consequence of an enlarged franchise from about 2.5 million in 1868 to 7.9 million in 1891, he has argued that:

> parties were obliged to devise cheaper and more effective means of wooing, winning and mobilizing voters through new organizational structures and novel forms of propaganda and appeal ... existing organizations were transformed from cadre[1] (or elite) parties into something akin to mass membership bodies. (2000: 21)

One of the features of political parties during this period was 'the growth of powerful centralized and centralizing party bureaucracies, to control and direct the party in the country and to provide a link between the constituencies and the parliamentary leadership' (Self, 2000: 21). A point also made by Dennis Kavanagh:

> by the 1880s ... organized political parties, the modification of campaign techniques to meet the needs of a growing electorate, and the decline as candidates of social leaders in favour of party regulars, were discernable characteristics of the electoral scene. In sum, national party campaigns were emerging in response to legal and cultural changes. (Kavanagh, 1970: 6; see also Rush and Cromwell, 2000)

One interesting example of such attention to organizational and electoral matters can be found in the study of the Conservative Party organization in the 1870s. In his book on E. J. Gorst, Conservative Party agent from 1870 to 1874 and from 1880 to 1882, Feuchtwanger makes a number of comments about his work that indicate both the importance of organization for securing electoral victory and also its crucial role in connecting the central party organization, and its leaders, with its constituencies and potential supporters. According to Feuchtwanger, Gorst represented a new style of party management in contrast to the 'traditionalists amongst the party managers [who] continued to cling to old methods and ideas' (Feuchtwanger, 1968: 106). This change:

> was simply a reflection of the general political circumstance: to convert the recently enfranchised electors required more systematic organization, and without such conversions the Conservative party could not return to office. … The expectation of Disraeli [party leader] and others probably was that the affairs of the party would now be run much more methodically and professionally, and by someone who understood the problems posed by the new borough electorate. (1968: 114)

Three features of Gorst's work emphasized the importance of organization as part of a strategy for electoral success. The first to note is that Gorst collected in 'a methodical way' (Feuchtwanger, 1968: 119) vast amounts of information about constituencies and constituency organizations. This enabled him to advise the party leadership on its electoral prospects as well as on the health of the party more generally. Secondly, Gorst brought together the Central Office and the National Union of the party, which, in effect, merged the organizational and propaganda arms of the party. Thirdly, in becoming part of the party's Central Committee – formed after the 1880 election defeat that brought calls for 'some serious steps to improve the organization' of the party (Feuchtwanger, 1968: 143) – Gorst and the Committee created a framework in which the central party organization would monitor constituency organizations and advise on improvements.

In an age when the *mass* media did not yet exist – provincial newspapers very much dominated the landscape (Lee, 1980) – the organizational structure of the political party was one of the principal ways in which communication with party members and the electorate could take place. Not that the task of obtaining favourable press coverage in the small but influential *political press* (Koss, 1984) was ignored – Gorst helped the Conservative party take over a newspaper business that 'was in effect a Conservative news agency for provincial newspapers,' (Feuchtwanger, 1968: 120) – but that other means were perhaps more important in ensuring that local party associations, which were not directly controlled by the central party organization, continued to give it their support. Nonetheless, the spectre of the press was always there. Stephen Koss noted that at the first meeting of the National Union of Conservative and Unionist Associations, with Gorst in the chair, one of the aims 'promulgated was "to increase and multiply the influence of the Conservative press throughout the United Kingdom"' (Koss, 1984: 184).

The problem for political parties lay not so much in the desire to exert control over the press, but their increasing inability to do so as newspapers became more aware of the need to lessen traditional forms of political coverage in favour of other more commercially beneficial material. 'The essential difference', Koss writes, 'between a full-fledged political journal in 1900 and its equivalent, say, in 1865, was the relative decrease in the amount of explicitly political material contained. … More significantly, the balance of coverage shifted' (1984: 431). The coverage of Parliament and politics was basically downgraded.

Whilst the account of Gorst's work may not be typical of the general experiences of other political parties or of the Conservative Party in other periods, it usefully illustrates three points that run through this chapter and this book, more generally. The first point is that political parties do go through changes for a whole host of reasons, for example election defeats, changing sociopolitical circumstances and so on. These changes do not come about because of the nature of the media landscape and are not forced upon political parties as newer media come on stream. However, and this is the second point, when parties do go through changes, whether it is the Conservative Party in the 1880s or the Conservative Party in the 21st century, those changes incorporate some consideration of how to improve the party's 'profile' in the media. And, third, because political parties have rarely had direct control of the media probably since the late 1880s, the task of gaining media attention increases in importance and value. All three points underscore a similar objective and that is reorganization for the purpose of becoming more electable or, in modern parlance, organizational change and 'rebranding' for the sake of electoral success.

... into the 20th century

As the 19th century gave way to the 20th century, and as a result of forces that lay outside the control of political parties but which the political parties could not afford to ignore, one begins to see changes taking place. These included changes in the electorate and in political and economic conditions, but they also included developments in the means of mass communication – gramophone, radio, film and, much later, television – and developments in propaganda techniques (Taylor, 1999), public relations and public opinion polling.

Political parties also began to change at both a national and local level. The parties began to organize on a national basis to gain large numbers of members. They became mass parties and better organized and governments were 'formed as [a] direct result of general election[s]' (Kavanagh, 1970: 13). At the national level, the role of the leader was probably enhanced by the use of the medium of film and radio as a means of political communication (see Chapter 2), and at the local level, local organization began to matter more. Prior to the introduction of universal male suffrage and any female suffrage, local Conservative associations, for example, were mainly concerned with registering votes. But as the franchise expanded and social and political change was beginning to take place, their role changed. As Stuart Ball has pointed out, in the period before the First World War, local Conservative associations were merely 'local registration societies, and their yearly work revolved around the electoral roll and the battles in the revising courts'. But this changed in the 1920s as these societies became larger 'with social, propaganda and campaigning function(s)' (Ball, 1992: 264).

Changes in the organization and roles of political parties and their constituent parts were taking place alongside changes in other aspects of early 20th-century life that were to have quite significant impacts on not only the future organization of political parties but also the means by which they would communicate to a widening electorate. Developments in technologies of communication – for example the gramophone record, film and radio – forced politicians, particularly party leaders, to deal with them and to use them as best they could. Early efforts might have been amateurish in as much as any incursion into a new territory is bound to show up the absence of wisdom regarding how new technologies work best but they were, nonetheless, good indications of how newer ways of communicating with the electorate were gradually being infused into party political work (see Chapter 5).

Alongside development in technologies of communication, some consideration was also being given to the question of whether the lessons of propaganda[2] learned during the 1914–18 war could be applied to politics (L'Etang, 1998). In due course, developments in propaganda techniques, public relations and public opinion polling during the interwar period were to begin to transform the way political communication was being conducted and political parties began to employ outsiders and new ideas to propagate their positions. In fact, newly emerging ideas in the 1920s and 1930s about propaganda, publicity and public relations were initially used within the context of commerce and business but it was not long before they were applied to politics. As Stanley Kelley Jnr. wrote in his 1956 study of the emerging professionalization of public relations in the US, there was a 'tremendous increase in the volume of business publicity around the turn of the century' which subsequently moved into the world of politics. According to Kelley:

> the Roosevelt Administration [in the 1930s] had set up new publicity divisions and expanded old ones, hired more newspapermen than were working for the newspapers, retained commercial advertising agencies to promote its programmes, and created and enforced procedures for the dissemination of official news. ... propaganda became not only a tool for promotion but a way of governing. (1956: 15)

The intersection of politics with commerce, evidenced in Kelley's comments regarding the Roosevelt administration, significantly transformed political activity from an untutored experiential-based approach to an evidence-based, professional activity. A point that did not escape Kelley: as 'business [though one would soon add political organizations and governments also] began to make more complex demands of its propagandists, the practices of propaganda became more and more a task for specialists' (1956: 25).

The importance of publicity, propaganda, public relations and the new technologies of communication were beginning to be appreciated in both business and politics in the era between the two World Wars. Kelley (1956) testifies to its place in politics on the American scene and there are examples from Britain which show a similar appreciation of its importance. The Conservative Party distributed recorded speeches of its leaders on gramophone records at the turn of the 20th century,[3] and all the major political parties used film and radio to publicize their politics between the wars (Cockett, 1994). As always, some led the way in professionalization of their work with the media, whilst others very much lagged behind (or never caught up); Herbert Morrison, leader of the London County Council in the 1930s, 'depended on professional advertisers and public relations men to advise him on how best to promote the LCC and the work of the Labour Party there.' In the 1937 local London election, 'a team of advertisers, public relations men and journalists, sympathetic to Labour' was recruited to work in a voluntary capacity (Donoughie and Jones, 1973: 208–9).

Other examples from this period help to sketch an environment in which there was a growing awareness of the importance of propaganda and public relations techniques and their use within the newly emerging technologies of communication. As Jacquie L'Etang has argued, the:

> evidence in [the journal] *Public Administration* suggests that by the 1930s there was, within central and local government, an understanding of the importance of good public relations to facilitate smooth administration. Achieving 'understanding' between the populace and local government began to be seen as of intrinsic importance to the job of administration and to the improvement of democracy 'to build up public understanding and appreciation of the services rendered to them and thus obtain goodwill'. (1998: 417)

Furthermore, the 'dissemination of information and more proactive campaign initiatives necessitated the allocation of posts and … by 1930–31 twelve government departments were employing around 44 people on publicity or press work' (L'Etang, 1998: 419–20). The growth of the documentary movement in the 1930s, with its interest in film and education, further underlines the theme that ideas about the use of new communication technologies were circulating and being applied in different contexts.

The effectiveness of those techniques was less easy to judge since research into public opinion was not very well advanced. In fact, it was not until the mid- to late 1930s that advanced techniques such as using samples as a means of assessing mass public opinion came into their own. The Gallup polling organization, a prime mover in this field, for example, was only founded in the early 1930s (see http://www.gallup.com/content/?ci=1357). Once such techniques became commonplace and trusted – as always, first in the US and later in other countries – political parties inevitably made use of them to position and define themselves.

These individual examples, coming as they do from different sectors of activity, are suggestive of an awareness of the need to deal with politics in a way that was different from the past: political leaders would now need to consider *how* to talk to the electorate since the speech from the pulpit did not work so well on film or even radio; they might want to consider what they said since alternative positions might be available via radio as well as in the press; they might even want to consider employing those who had learned how to communicate with and persuade the public. In these ways, and others, there may have been a growing appreciation of the need to woo voters, to persuade and mobilize them through the means of communication rather than relying only on the organizational structure to achieve one's objectives. By the beginning of the post-1945 era, therefore, British political parties could hardly avoid the conclusion that it was becoming important to pay attention to organization *and* publicity, the two pillars on which electoral success was built.

Political parties post-1945: organizing for success

By the mid-1950s, and not many years after the launch of the BBC television service, members of both major political parties in Britain had made moves to organize themselves so as to meet the challenge of television (see Chapter 2). But it was fairly obvious that publicity, as well as polling information and advice, was of little use unless the party organization was in a position to exploit it. While both the Conservative and Labour parties were aware of the need to organize and publicize, it was the former that made most of the necessary changes, leaving the Labour Party, in the words of Harold Wilson[4] in 1955, still at 'the penny-farthing bicycle' stage in a jet-propelled era (*Socialist Commentary*, 1965: iii).

As will be argued more fully in Chapter 4, in the early 1950s and under the Chairmanship of Lord Woolton, the Conservative Party was 'completely reorganized … in the process also vastly increasing the power of Central Office' (Wilson, 1961: 93) and professionals in advertising and publicity were introduced to help the Party. Reorganization continued when Lord Poole took over as Chairman in 1955 and, in due course, the Conservatives emerged as a well-organized and successful electoral party. The need for good organization – of all aspects of a political party's activities, of which communication was only a part – is a central feature of Lord Windlesham's analysis of the Conservative Party in this period, and he offers an interesting contrast with the fortunes of the Labour Party:

> The Conservative propagandists of 1957–9 left behind them a blueprint for future political organizers. The first lesson of their experience was that effective political propaganda depends on effective political

organization. If in this period a Tory propagandist grew gloomy or depressed, he had only to contemplate what was happening in the Labour Party. As Mark Abrams [the Labour Party's polling adviser] recalled, 'Perhaps the most important reason why the Labour Party failed, in the late 1950s, to engage in public opinion surveys was that the exercise could have led nowhere. The Party simply had no machinery that could have taken survey findings and used them to help shape effective political propaganda. Here lay the greatest contrast with the Conservative Party'. (Windlesham, 1966: 59–60)

In Mark Abrams' view the Labour Party simply did not have the organizational structure that would have enabled it to exploit many aspects of modern campaigning. And so, whilst the Conservative Party was able to make the most of its organizational structure and the skills of outsiders, the Labour Party was unable to establish any coherence in its own set-up.

What accounts for the difference between the two major political parties and what does this tell us about how parties deal with a changing sociopolitical environment? It was certainly not a lack of ambition or vision on the part of (or parts of) the Labour Party that held back change. Harold Wilson's 1955 report, 'Our Penny-Farthing Machine', (see *Socialist Commentary*, 1965) on the problems of the party organization makes clear that the deficiencies of the party were well known and obvious. The problem was how to implement a programme of change, since 10 years later, as *Socialist Commentary* (October 1965) pointed out, despite the changes that had taken place in the early 1960s and the election victory of 1964, there remained some fundamental weaknesses in the organization of the Labour Party.

Its comments on Harold Wilson's 1955 report – and its insistence that more change was desirable – emphasized the overwhelming need to modernize and professionalize the party as a whole so as to transform it into the sort of modern party that would be able to use a range of resources and skills to enhance its electoral position. In this respect, the 1965 *Socialist Commentary* report readily acknowledged that things had changed since the 1950s but it pointed out that more had to be done. To paraphrase one of its key messages: a modern Britain needed a modern party.

Three features of the report are worth highlighting and these begin to illustrate the differences that it felt separated the two major political parties at that time. The first is the plea for review and adaptation. The second is the theme of modernization. The third is the call for professionalization, particularly in the context of the media. In all three areas the report is replete with examples of how things could be better structured to make use of people and information. The first two are of interest because they place the need for change in context:

> The world of today is, in comparison [with the 1910s], almost unrecognizable. The rise in living standards and the spread of education are perhaps the most important factors of change. These, combined with the revolution in technology and communications ... have created new outlooks and demands in the electorate. Behind them both Transport House[5] and most local Labour Parties trail along – in methods and attitude a couple of generations out-of-date. (*Socialist Commentary*, 1965: iv)

The challenge was how to deal with these changes and how best to organize in order to maintain the party's position. So, for example, rather than abandon the grass roots – 'one cannot visualize a political party without local branches – there would be no link between leadership and members; it would be all central organization and no soul' (*Socialist Commentary*, 1965: v) – it felt that the real task was how to improve local organization and make it work for the party.

But organizational considerations go beyond matters of structure and personnel. What is equally important is vision and strategy and of understanding change and its possible consequences. Better organization must be complemented and supplemented by intelligence for both policy-making and electoral purposes. It is in the latter context that the *Socialist Commentary* report addresses the question of publicity. In essence, the report called for a better and more professionally coordinated approach to publicity and public relations. It noted:

> After 1962, there was still a good deal of suspicion of the new methods but the Party grasped the fact that if publicity is to be engaged in at all, this must be done professionally; it must take advantage of all the appropriate media. But two basic weaknesses remained: there were still too few staff ... and the coordination ... was poor in some cases. (*Socialist Commentary*, 1965: xviii)

And, as always, the Party could look over its shoulder at the opposition and see how much better off they were; at the height of the 1964 election Labour 'employed ten publicity people' and some support staff, the Conservatives 'employed 24 publicity men' and 28 support staff (*Socialist Commentary*, 1965: xviii); the Labour Party provided 'some' coaching and training for television, The Conservatives had videotape for coaching and a videotape library (*Socialist Commentary*, 1965: xix) and so on.[6] As the authors of the *Commentary* pointed out in their introduction:

> In microcosm these [problems] ... reflect the attitude of the Party in general to the tools and amenities of the modern age. We are suspicious of them as we are of professionalism in the Party HQs staff or Agency service. Up and down the country cosy squalor and amateurism are our main hallmarks. ... but confidence in our ability to modernize Britain will be strengthened if we can show determination to modernize ourselves thoroughly. (*Socialist Commentary*, 1965: iv)

However, the task of modernizing the Labour Party – and henceforth modernizing all aspects of it – was hampered from the late 1950s onwards by turmoil and internal debates around its socialist heritage and the debates around Clause 4.[7] The significance of these debates was noted at the time by Samuel Beer since it created an 'intellectual crisis' and a need for rethinking:

> as nationalization and planning failed as instruments of economic control, administrators turned more and more to the mechanisms of the market. This collapse of the old ideological premises created problems not only for managers trying to increase productivity, but also for party leaders trying to write a manifesto and for socialist intellectuals trying to restate their beliefs so that they would fit the facts and give coherent direction to party and government. (Beer, 1997: 320)

Three successive defeats in the 1950s – in 1951, 1955 and 1959 – made it more conscious of the need for change but, as *Socialist Commentary* (1965) readily pointed out, even those defeats still left the Party somewhat amateurish. Its performance in the 1964 election was judged good but the theme of the report is essentially that it could, and should, have done better.

In many ways, one could argue that it was not until the 1990s that one could support the claim that the Labour Party had fully modernized itself and begun to reflect the concerns of the contemporary era. But in doing so, the party gave up its attachment to its founding principles rooted in early 20th-century labour history and it began to reflect the needs of a party that had to find success in a broader set of constituencies than had originally been its traditional base. It had to become the 'catch-all' party (Kirchheimer, 1966) that sought to represent the interests of many constituencies rather than of a traditional base of support (the working class and so on). It also had to use different means to reach these new potential supporters and to use them more imaginatively and professionally than hitherto. That is why the role of the professional experts employed by the Party from the 1980s onwards is so critical; the Party had changed significantly enough in structure and organization that it was able to make use of those specialists who could help refashion it (see Chapter 4). It was not that professionals/experts had not been used before, but that their role had been too limited and too secondary to make any impact on the Party as a whole.

Indeed, as political parties became more centralized and more tightly run and controlled by the leadership, changes made to them begin to reflect and lend support to the needs of those in charge, primarily those leading the party in Parliament. As Katz and Mair have argued, the changes that have taken place in the organization and structure of political parties have seen 'the ascendancy of the party in public office' (that is, in Parliament) over the party in central office (that is, head office) and the party on the ground (that is, membership): 'party organization in Europe has gone beyond the catch-all period and has entered a new phase, in which parties become increasingly dominated by, as well as most clearly epitomized by, the party in public office' (Katz and Mair, 2002: 122). In that process of change, the importance of political communication cannot be overemphasized, for what we have now come to appreciate is that once the party 'in office' becomes the party – for there are very few members, constituency associations are quite strongly directed from the centre, local media are of limited importance – it is only *through* the national mass media that it can communicate. More than this, it is only *in* the national mass media that it exists as a national and coherent entity.

If one wishes to argue that there has been a transformation and professionalization of political parties post-1945, then one would point not to the emergence of new technologies of communication nor to greater organizational expertise but to the confluence of a centralization of political power in the party 'in office' – although for 'party in office' one could read 'leader's office' – and a heightened role for political communication in setting the agenda and channelling political power. That, if nothing else, is one of the lessons that comes out of New Labour's victory in 1997 and, perhaps more critically, the 2007 Conservative Party's rise to popular power which was built on the tactics and strategies developed by New Labour two decades before. The change brought about through New Labour's tactics affected not only matters of organization, but media practices and government communication strategies (see Chapters 4–6).

New Labour: the 1997 election and all that

It is difficult to make sense of the 1997 New Labour Party victory without having a good grasp of the events leading up to that fateful event. This is not the place to reproduce a summary of the many accounts of New Labour's victory (see, for example, King, 1998; Shaw, 1994; Wring, 2005) but it is important to draw attention to a number of points that have a direct bearing on the general discussion in this chapter.

Very briefly, since Chapter 4 offers a more detailed discussion of these points, the work of the Shadow Communications Agency in the late 1980s and the beginning of the 1990s entrenched the idea that the Labour Party needed modernization if it was going to have any chance of winning power again. The Labour Party had lost four elections – in 1979, 1983, 1987 and 1992 – and many put forward the argument that it was still too strongly associated with its past – its links with the unions, nationalization, dissension and so on – to be trusted as a sound future government. More critically, it needed to find a new set of messages for it to connect with the changed circumstances of the 1990s. The 'project' that Philip Gould and others embarked on was to modernize it, to change its public image to make it look as if it could govern and to make it look electable again (Gould, 1998a).

Gradually between roughly 1983 and 1994, old policies and positions were abandoned in favour of new policies as the Labour Party repositioned itself. And, as the Conservative government entered a period of crisis after its return to power in 1992, the Labour Party began to move ahead in the polls. But as a modernization project, Gould accepts that it stalled under the leadership of John Smith (leader 1992–4). Tony Blair's election as leader of the Labour Party after John Smith's sudden death in 1994 unlocked, as it were, the whole process of change and led to the birth of New Labour.

New Labour came with new policies based on new principles and it established itself as a party that could be trusted and could be elected to government. In his review of the election, Anthony King has written that the polling 'evidence suggests that the [election] campaign was largely irrelevant. ... Labour would probably have won an election at any time from the late summer of 1994 onwards; it would certainly have won at any time in early 1997, even if there had been no campaign at all' (King, 1998: 81). Whilst the evidence does support that conclusion, it is also worth noting that the Labour Party advisers used the years preceding the campaign to establish the Labour Party as a new and credible party. In other words, King's conclusion is valid as long as one recognizes that the party's success was built on its success in changing the voter's perception of what the party stood for. Two different questions follow on from this. First, was New Labour a creation of professional advisers? Second, what was so significant about the campaign run by the professional advisers that it achieved such notoriety? In answering both questions, it is possible to begin to see the dramatic change that New Labour brought to the way election campaigns, government communication and politics were organized.

As to the first question concerning the role of professionals in the party, from the evidence at hand, it is perhaps easier to argue that the advisers simply fed into a process that was already taking place. The lost elections of 1983 and 1987 offer a background to the desire for change, as the discussion above described. But the modernization project carried on into the 1992 election although it stalled under the leadership of John Smith. Under Tony Blair it gained momentum. The fact that the process did stall under Smith shows how political considerations – personalities, principles and traditions – mediate the power of the professional advisers. In Blair, the 'modernizers' found someone who saw the need for change in the same way that they did, and who was willing to move ahead as fast as they did (or faster) (Gould, 1998a).

The other point to note is that for the change to take place, it was critical to have the right organizational structure, the right staff and the right communication strategy. In this respect it is interesting to note that the 1987, 1992 and 1997 campaigns were run away from the party's head office, so symbolically creating a new locus of power away from the traditional party base (in 1997 it was run from the Millbank complex); and, as Gould also acknowledges, rebuilding Labour required not only a new set of principles but also a 'new campaigning organization' (1998b: 6). The campaign was 'structured around a warroom in which all campaign operations and all campaign personnel were in the same physical space; opposition activity was constantly monitored; attacks were instantly rebutted; dialogue with the electorate was constant. From top to bottom, voter feedback was built into the system' (Gould, 1998b: 7).

The extent to which a sea change came about with Tony Blair – but with key foundations set under the leadership of Neil Kinnock in the

1980s – comes out strongly in a speech by Charles Clarke, one-time adviser to Kinnock and Blair and later a minister under Blair. Recalling the discussion surrounding Blair's bid for the leadership of the Labour Party, Clarke highlighted:

> Tony's assertion [was] that the absolutely central factor in determining the outcome would be the attitude of the media. So the media had to be the target of his campaign. ... In practical terms it also had some notable outcomes. Most important, it was the central driver of the need to create 'New Labour', a device to distinguish the post-1994 Labour Party from all that had gone before. At one stroke, it removed the media narrative of 'winters of discontent' and miners' strikes, 'loony left' councils and factionalizing Deputy Leadership election contests. Shadow Budgets and state controls and introverted and isolationist foreign policies were consigned to history, of no current relevance. ... Tony Blair's ... conviction [was] that modern politics inevitably takes place in a media environment which politicians need properly to comprehend, and then to seek to influence. (Clarke, 2007)

The centralization of the campaign and the skilled use of professionals enabled the Labour Party to come to power after many years in opposition. The significance of New Labour's successful strategies can be seen in the fact that David Cameron (Conservative Party leader, 2006–) has taken a similar route; cajoling the media, using it, playing to it to great advantage in a way that resembles, although some say copies, the hallmarks of the strategies built by the likes of Philip Gould, Alastair Campbell and Peter Mandelson (Hitchens, 2007).

Yet as things became more centralized and more leader-directed, the role and nature of political parties inevitably changed from parties with constituencies to parties existing, surviving and inhabiting a world that often seemed disconnected from the world of the electorate. Part of that change – or transformation – is summed up in the discussion of the 'cartel party' (Mair, 1998), a discussion that brings together three core elements in the study of political communication, namely, political parties, the electorate and the connecting bridge, the media.

From the mass-membership party to the 'cartel' party: political communication in the 21st century

In reviewing the changes that political parties have undergone in the post-1945 era, one is struck by the fact that one of the greatest pressures for change was an election defeat or the prospect of further defeats. As Stuart Ball has argued, 'developments ... in organization [for the Conservative Party] since 1900 have resulted either from electoral defeats, as in 1906, 1911, 1948–9, 1965–7 and 1975–9 [and 1997–2005!], or from the changes in the electoral system in 1918 and 1928' (Ball, 1992: 297). But behind these defeats – and the same applies to the Labour Party post-1945 – lies the story of a changing sociopolitical environment which was itself beginning to create its own pressures for change: 'between 1957 and 1964 doubtful voices began to be heard within the [Conservative] organization, pointing to a decline in support ... the failure to recruit the "young marrieds" of the 25–40 age group, and the problems of an ageing membership' (Ball, 1992: 299). These themes were not unfamiliar to the Labour Party and its own internal enquiries into the likelihood of the party ever winning power again after its own defeats in 1951, 1955 and 1959. More critical, for both parties, was how to maintain a level of support from within an electorate that was becoming less partisan or traditional in its voting preferences.

If the 1950s and 1960s still saw a reasonable symmetry between class allegiance and voting behaviour, that symmetry was to break down in subsequent decades and this posed an enormous problem for political parties because they could no longer rely on a base of supporters. By the 1980s, for example, less than half of the electorate strongly identified with a particular party, down from around three-quarters in the mid-1960s, and post-1970 the share of the vote of the two major political parties was about 75% of votes cast compared with 90% in the 1950s and 1960s (Lynch and Garner, 2005). Membership, a key indicator of party strength and allegiance, was also in decline (although the picture was the same across Europe) (see Table 3.1).

The causes of that increasing volatility, and membership decline, were much more difficult to identify. Changes in income, working and living conditions, the growth of consumerism and the rise in living standards all certainly contributed to a changing electorate. As living standards and conditions changed, the key class-based fault lines of traditional politics no longer mattered in the way that they used to. Similarly, as the ideological differences between Left and Right diminished in the face of improving conditions of living generally, the way politics was conducted also needed to change. Political parties had to accept that as conditions and sociopolitical circumstances changed, they too would have to change. Hence the debates in the early 1960s, 1980s and 2000s within the Labour

Party on the way forward (Clarke, 2007; Shaw, 1994; Wring, 2005) that have been mirrored in more recent times in the Conservative Party which, having lost three successive elections in 1997, 2001 and 2005, also needed to ask itself if it was ever going to gain power again. And if it did want to win power again, what changes would it have to make to itself and its policies after such a long period out of office? Would it have to become less ideological in its orientation, as New Labour had done? Would it have to vacate its traditional 'low tax, hard on crime' image? Would it have to accept as givens the changes made by New Labour? And was its fate, like the fate of many modern political parties, to become a 'catch-all' party (Krouwel, 2003) that appealed to a large mass of electors and to different and varied constituencies rather than to a particular – and declining in numbers – group of members?

Table 3.1 Total membership of British political parties, 1980–2006

Year	Electorate	Party membership	Party members as % of electorate
1980	41,095,490	1,693,156	4.12
1989	43,180,573	1,136,723	2.63
1998	43,818,324	840,000	1.92
2006	44 million (approx)	532,000	1.20

Sources: Mair, 1998: 16; figures for 2006 from Woodward, 2006a, 2006b

The attractions of 'catch-all' parties appear obvious: when traditional cleavages such as class and religion are no longer determinants of political behaviour and when ideological divisions begin to matter less, political parties may find it necessary to appeal to non-traditional supporters so as to widen their base of support. But in doing so, political parties inevitably eschew strong ideological positions in favour of positions with broad electoral appeal. Consequently, political parties cease to connect strongly with their – admittedly declining – traditional base of support, and vie with one another to represent the mass electorate. Differences between the parties, once sharp and clear, become little more than differences concerning which party is better able to manage the economic and sociopolitical environment. Radical alternative visions of society are abandoned in favour of a more managerialist approach to it (Kirchheimer, 1966).

In this new political environment, the role of the voter/citizen is reduced to choosing between political parties that are more similar than dissimilar. However, the role of the political party in this environment becomes much more complex: does it follow the public in order to win power, or does it seek to manipulate the wishes of the public to maintain its position? Each of these positions creates different ways of acting, different ways of interacting with voters and different ways of making policies. This is, in part, one of the discussions underpinning the literature on political marketing (Lees-Marshment, 2001; Scammell, 1995, 1999) and it usefully illustrates the modern dilemma for political parties: they have to listen to the voters/citizens but do they have to follow what voters/citizens desire or should they guide or lead the desires of the voters/citizens? In both cases, what happens to the ideological traditions of the political party?

More significantly, when membership plummets political parties cease to exist as mass-membership parties with vibrant local branches, and election contests are increasingly conducted via the means of mass communication because these are the only means of reaching the mass electorate. This has several consequences. First, it tends to further centralize and give a national character to the nature of the election campaign. This also impacts on any communication from the political party to voters (and members) more generally. Second, it probably privileges those who claim to know how to reach the 'floating' voters. Indeed, Larry Sabato has argued that in the US 'the decline of political parties created opportunities for consultants ...' and that other factors, such as demographic changes, migration and so on helped to contribute to their rise (Sabato, 1981: 10–11). Whilst this point may not apply as strictly to the British scene, it is nonetheless true that the use of professionals has increased over the past 30 or so years. The third consequence is that it creates a version of a political party that is no longer a mass-membership party that is connected in an organic way with a traditional base of supporters but is more of an 'electoral-professional' party, that is, a professionally run political organization with tenuous links to a (declining) membership base but organized in such a way as to meet the challenges of regular contests for power.

As Peter Mair describes it:

as the age of the amateur democrat has waned, and as the less grounded and more capital-intensive party organizations have come increasingly under the sway of professional consultants, marketing experts, and campaigners, they have clearly improved both the pace and the extent to which they can adapt to changes in their external environments. These may not be attractive parties, especially in the eyes of those who mourn the passing of the golden age of the mass party; they may even be seen as quite unrepresentative parties; but, in these terms at least, they are certainly more effective. (1998: 11)

But Mair (1998) goes on to draw a further distinction between the 'catch-all party' with its professionally run, mass-mediated campaign and the 'cartel' party where the political party has detached itself even further from its membership base and become incorporated into the state itself and to an extent funded by the state (see Table 3.2). Such parties are not only run professionally but politicians themselves treat politics as a profession: they are increasingly drawn from a particular set of occupations and, in many cases, from the world of politics itself (see Chapter 5). In respect of communications, modern parties – as Table 3.2 indicates – have gained privileged access to state-regulated channels of communication, mainly public broadcast services. For example, in many European states, established and major political parties are automatically granted free airtime or airtime at reduced costs. Such privileges are not normally granted to smaller political parties who usually have to meet certain qualifications (Plasser and Plasser, 2002). As for other media, although they have to compete for access to these, the political parties have such a long-established and legitimated place in the sphere of politics and in national life that it could also be claimed that they have privileged access to these by comparison to less established political groups (Schlesinger and Tumber, 1994).

In these accounts of the transformation of political parties from mass-membership parties to 'cartel' parties, we can begin to grasp how their changing organizational make-up also takes into account some consideration of how to use the means of mass communication available to them. As the constituency level loses its traditional power as a recruiting and mobilizing agent, more and more resources are pumped into the national, media-directed campaign. Put differently, the fewer the foot soldiers of the party, the more intensive the media-directed campaign at national and sometimes local level. Equally significant is the fact that as a centralized and leader-directed party, it is the political party as represented by the party in Parliament that gains and not the political party as an organization. The repercussions can be severe, for as Katz and Mair put it:

the growth in organizational resources ... has tended to be to the advantage of the parliamentary party. Moreover, the resources which remain within central office appear to be increasingly devoted to the employment of contractual staff and consultants, and to the provision of outside expertise ... More specifically, the gradual replacement of general party bureaucrats by professional specialists may act to 'depoliticize' the party organization ... (2002: 125)

Table 3.2 The models of party and their characteristics

Characteristics	Elite/cadre party	Mass party	Catch-all party	Cartel party
Time-period	19th century	1880–1960	1945–	1970–
Degree of social-political inclusion	Restricted suffrage	Enfranchisement and mass suffrage	Mass suffrage	Mass suffrage
Principal goals of politics	Distribution of privileges	Social reformation (or opposition to it)	Social amelioration	Politics as profession
Nature of party work and campaigning	Irrelevant	Labour-intensive	Both labour-intensive and capital-intensive	Capital-intensive
Principal source of party's resources	Personal contacts	Members' fees and contributions	Contributions from a wide variety of sources	State subventions
Party channels of communication	Interpersonal networks	Party provides its own channels of communication	Party competes for access to non-party channels of communication	Party gains privileged access to state-regulated channels of communication

Source: Adapted from Mair, 1998: 110–11

One can see these changes taking place gradually from the late 1950s onwards. In the mid-1950s – and still in the era of the mass-membership party – television had just been established. As that decade came to a close, television was well on its way to establishing itself as a mass medium. Its use in the 1959 general election shows how the political parties grew to understand its practices and this knowledge was to increase with every subsequent election (see Chapter 2). Gradually, one could therefore argue, the means of mass communication took over as the best way of communicating policies and positions. Traditional means of communication such as posters, canvassing and leafleting were not abandoned but they were seen as of lesser importance than the 'television election' and the television contest that was taking place in the living rooms of voters.

As political consultants and advisers came to recognize the need to think of the electorate not as a mass but as composed of distinct and varied constituencies each with their own profiles and needs, more targeted election practices were to be employed in election contests. Constituency campaigning, which emphasized local elements and therefore mediated the national campaign, became common practice in political campaigns from the 1990s onwards but it did not override the national campaign. As with canvassing and leafleting, it did not erode other practices but fitted into a more complex mosaic of electioneering techniques with changed orientations to the electorate from 'propaganda' through to the 'marketing' of political parties, as is well illustrated in Table 3.3 (and also Tables 2.1 to 2.3).

Two aspects of Table 3.3 need to be emphasized. The first is the growing prominence of consultants as campaigning techniques evolve and become more complex. This is dealt with at greater length in the next chapter but it underscores a simple point made earlier to the effect that political parties can often find it more cost-effective to call in expertise when they need it to deal with particular technologies or techniques. The second point to note is the distinction made between different concepts of 'campaign communications'. The distinctions between 'selling' and 'marketing' are significant – and we return to them later on – and they highlight the need for parties to engage in longer term strategic thinking and planning about where they stand and how they can communicate ('sell') themselves and their positions to an electorate that is less partisan than it used to be. Political parties must continuously rethink how best to communicate and one of the things that has become abundantly clear is that one cannot expect to win an election without considerable pre-planning; pre-planning, in this instance, means not simply arranging for the odd publicity event but a concerted effort at 'marketing' the political party.

Table 3.3 Three stages in the development of election campaigning

	Stage 1	Stage 2	Stage 3
Technical developments			
Campaign preparations	Short-term; ad hoc	Long term	Permanent campaign
Resource developments			
Campaign organization	Decentralized	Nationalization, centralization	Decentralization with central scrutiny
Agencies, consultants	Minimal use	Growing prominence of 'specialist' consultants	Consultants as campaign personalities
Thematic developments			
Campaign communications	Propaganda	Selling concept	Marketing concept

Source: Adapted from Farrell and Webb, 2002: 104

Running through much of the above discussion is a reflection on the changing form of the political party and its response or adaptation to changing environments, be they political or technological. Moreover, political parties take from their environments or adopt those things that they find useful for their longer term survival and prosperity. I argued earlier that developments in propaganda, public relations and polling bled into politics in the 1920s and 1930s and, in the same way, in the 1970s and 1980s knowledge gained in cognate areas such as marketing and management infected politics. At one point in his work, Stuart Ball observes that the Conservative Party responded to by-election defeats in the 1980s by drawing 'on the language of the worlds of business and advertising: modernization would be achieved through "campaigning" and "management" techniques, with new technology blazing the trail to increased efficiency and productivity' (1992: 301–2). This comment echoes to a considerable extent the talk of 'modernization' and 'professionalization' that we find in Feuchtwanger's analysis of E. J. Gorst's work for the Conservative Party a century earlier (see p. 47 above).

The point to stress here is not simply that there are continuities as well as breaks, but that political parties – as organizations – adapt to their environment. They incorporate new things, including new media, new ways of thinking and of doing things, in order to retain their positions as successful organizations and/or to gain advantage. Consequently, that they adapt is unsurprising since not adapting leads to oblivion, but in adapting they also change and, as we have seen, that change can lead to something radically different to what had gone on before. How different may depend, though, on the points of comparison that are used: which is why attempts to quantify levels of professionalization are likely to be of limited value. In their work, Gibson and Römmele (2001) sought to establish a way of making judgements concerning the levels of professionalization of different political parties. They set out 'four key factors that make a party more likely to adopt professionalized campaigning' that included such things as level of resources, party ideology, level of centralization and its primary goals. To this, they added a dependent variable made up of an index that was intended 'to capture the basic elements of professionalized campaigning' in various elements, for example the extent to which the parties used particular forms of technologies such as direct mail, computerized databases, email sign up and so on (2001: 38–9). But these are time-specific elements and will, in due course, be overtaken by other technologies and other uses of still other technologies. It cannot be possible, therefore, to make judgements relating to levels of professionalization that apply across time, for what may have been the height of professionalization in 1997 might not be so in 2007. Yet at both moments, the parties in question might have been seen as highly professional for their time. Similar criticisms can be levelled at work that tries to make judgements regarding the professionalization of political parties themselves that does not take full account of large scale occupational changes, for as all occupations become professionalized so too will people working within them (Negrine, 2005).

Summary and conclusion

In the Introduction to this chapter, I suggested that it is best to explore the transformations in political parties as part of the process by which they seek to adapt and meet challenges. In that process of transformation, I further suggested that no single factor should be privileged over others. New technologies of communication, often seen as a cause of change, are usually only parts of larger forces at play and become incorporated into the armoury of political parties rather than dictate their organizational form. Finally, I suggested that once we have a grasp of the processes in play, it becomes easier to understand how those processes have, in turn, impacted on the nature and content of political communication.

The examples discussed above – whether drawn from the late 19th century or from more recent times – lend support to these comments. I have argued that changes in the social and political context made political parties, as organizations, aware of the need to redefine their role and positions; changes in technologies of communication, as well as techniques of communications, became embedded in those processes of change. By the end of the 20th century, though, it is possible to argue that communication had become quite central to the pursuit of political power; not simply in terms of communicating policies to an electorate but, and more significantly, by influencing and controlling the flow and direction of communication from the centre. This, it could be further argued, would not have been possible unless political parties had become organized, centralized, leader-directed and focused on achieving political power, that is, had taken on the form of either the 'catch-all party' or 'the cartel party'.

Two final points need to be made and underlined. First, that the changes in the nature, structure and organization of political parties – including as a consequence of a changed sociopolitical environment – have a knock-on effect on those things that political parties need to do to sustain themselves, namely, fighting elections to continue to survive. The professionalization of communication is one of those things. Furthermore, as politicians become professionalized – 'not only with regard to an income directly related to their electoral office and a full commitment to their political career, but also with regard to the separation from their social background and the loyalties devoted to it' (Best and Cotta, 2000: 8)[8] – they can be placed on a trajectory away from the more 'amateur' organizations and electoral processes of the past. Herein, one could argue, lies the importance of figures such as E. J. Gorst, Lord Poole and the sponsors of the New Labour 'project'; they create the organizational form that underpins and, at the same time, privileges the role of the politician. The professional politician, in this respect, is a product, and producer, of a professional party organization and it is in his/her interest to ensure its continued existence.

It follows, and this is the second point, that such things as new technologies of communication, although not secondary, are part of the puzzle of change. They should not be privileged but placed within the overall context of change. More critically, they are not themselves motors of change; there is no reason to think that television did any more to alter political parties than did the enlargement of the franchise, for example. To privilege television, or the internet, is to mistake cause and effect. The transformation and professionalization of political communication should be understood as a part of the whole process by which political parties are forced to engage with their changed environment.

The Transformation of Political Parties and the Use of Professional Advisers in the Communication of Politics

4

Introduction

Chapters 2 and 3 offered general overviews of the intersection of, on the one hand, developments of technologies of communication in the lives of political parties and, on the other, a way of understanding the ongoing transformations in the make-up of political parties. Those chapters hinted at the use of professional advisers by political parties to further their ambitions, whether these lay in the field of communication or in creating better and different organizational structures. This chapter will develop these points more fully by exploring in some detail how a variety of professional advisers have come to play an ever more important role in the lives of political parties, especially in respect of electoral contests. If anything, professional advisers have become increasingly central in the conduct of politics and in political communication. As Magleby et al. (2000) have pointed out, the 'rise of candidate-centred campaigning' in the US has created a situation where 'formal party organizations and normal citizens ... increasingly found themselves on the sidelines watching individual candidates wage increasingly sophisticated campaigns' (2000: 8). One could similarly argue that in Britain, as in the US, the weakening of political parties as mass membership organizations and the greater centralization of power around the leadership are factors that have led to the growing importance of professional consultants to help run centralized and professionalized election campaigns (see also Plasser and Plasser, 2002).

As with other chapters in this book, the historical context is important. Although one is now accustomed to discussions of the role of paid professional advisers in the conduct of elections (see Mancini, 1999; Plasser and Plasser, 2002), there is evidence to show their use in US elections in the 1920s and of their use in Britain, as elsewhere, somewhat later. As important as these historical developments are, equally important was the overlap of communication and publicity practices in commerce with the world of politics. One way of looking at this historical background is to argue that developments in the means of communication and in knowledge concerning their uses, as well as developing knowledge about the means of mobilization and persuasion in marketing and propaganda, nudged political organizations towards those with the skills to enable them to reach the ever-widening and ever-changing electorate. As Stanley Kelley Jnr. concluded in his 1956 study *Professional Public Relations and Political Power*, 'technological advance has made political communication a highly technical, if not a professional, field' (1956: 104). Moreover, as those skills themselves developed and became more specialized, different sets of professionals began to play a variety of demarcated roles in the conduct of political communication. Consequently, and in due course, political parties – as well as other organizations – became reliant on a host of professional advisers for the purposes of communicating with their publics, and professionals became more important for political parties. As Harris observed:

> The polltaker who is knowledgeable about politics will inevitably be invited to sit on strategy meetings, mostly as a resource but also as a man of balanced judgment. (1963: 7)

Who are the professionals?

But who are these professional advisers and how can they be distinguished from others who play a part in the political process and, more specifically, in political parties? The term 'professional advisers' – henceforth in this chapter 'professionals' – will refer to those individuals who have specialist and/or technical skills that have been acquired usually outside the world of politics and which are then employed in a political context. The term could be applied, for example, to an expert in public opinion polling whose expertise is then solicited by a political party for its own ends; it could also be applied to someone who would advise on dress and demeanour, or on overall campaigning strategy. The growing complexity of the field of the professional is well illustrated in Dennis Johnson's work. He has suggested that professionals can be grouped under three headings: strategists, specialists and vendors:

> In the top tier are the *strategists*, the key consultants who develop the campaign message, communicate it to voters, and provide strategic advice and support throughout the campaign. ... In the second tier ... are the *specialists*, who provide essential campaign services: fund-raising, candidate and opposition research, media buying, voter contact, initiative and referenda legal services, petition and signature gathering, and speech writing. ... The third tier of consultants is comprised of *vendors* who supply campaign products and services: website developers, voter files and mailing list firms, campaign software and computer services, print and promotional materials, media tracking, and other services. (Johnson, 2000: 37–42)

The significance of this division will become clear later when this chapter discusses the role of professionals in political parties, but its identification here is useful because it shows the ways in which developments in knowledge, techniques and media create specialisms and further sub-divisions within specialisms. It also illustrates the different levels of responsibilities that different professionals might have: some work at a level close to the political centre, others are merely functionaries. In the study of political communication, the focus of interest is primarily on those who play strategic roles within political parties or who use research skills to enhance their strategic roles. The focus is not on those who, in Johnson's words (above) 'supply campaign products and services'. Crucially, professionals are rarely permanent, full-time employees of a political party; it is more usual for such professionals to be employed for the duration of, say, a campaign and they can thus be distinguished from full-time political party employees (or 'party bureaucrats'). (See Mancini, 1999 for a full discussion of these points.)

In the course of exploring the growing involvement of such professionals in political communication, three related themes will emerge and these point to certain continuities in the organizational life of political parties, continuities that essentially derive from their desire to gain power amidst a constantly changing sociopolitical and communications environment. The three themes can be summarized as follows:

- A constant desire amongst those in charge of political parties to improve their electoral strength usually through a process of organizational restructuring and centralization of activities. Without a suitable organizational framework, no organization can fully exploit the skills of professionals.
- A readiness amongst political parties to take advantage of all available technologies of communication and to exercise some means of control over how they are used for political communication. Sometimes this 'readiness' is less than it should be: in his book *Making an Impact*, Harvey Thomas, a media professional who was used extensively by the Conservative Party in the 1970s and 1980s points out that the party had 'gathered together a superb voluntary team of some of the UK's top communicators for both the 1983 and 1987 General Elections, [but it] could not find any strategic use for them' (Thomas and Gill, 1989 130). Would this still be the case in 2008?
- A tendency to employ, or seek help or advice from those who are skilled in the many aspects of communicating to the public, be they journalists, public relations agents, polling agencies or advertisers. The more 'mediated' the political communication process, the more likely that such 'outsiders' will be employed in order to provide expertise across a wider range of areas. Importantly, the position of such advisers within a political party and within the political process is rarely uniform. As Martin Harrop has argued, in Britain such professionals have occupied 'a role that is more subtle and varied than commonly assumed' (2001: 68). Nonetheless, employing such professionals is often seen to give political parties an extra edge in the competitive political environment.

Before this chapter moves on to a more detailed analysis of the developing role of professionals in the transformation of political communication (and of political parties), it is worth pondering why their use has created such a wealth of concerns and such dismay and why they are often feared.[1] The answer probably lies in the belief – not always unjustified – that such professionals, versed as they are in their own particular techniques of persuasion, somehow distort the essence of politics and that their activities have a malign effect on the political message, its construction and its communication. Put differently, that the attention given to the form the political message should take – whether it is on a poster or in a television broadcast – and even sometimes to who should deliver that message impacts on its content. In these ways, the substance or content of politics is therefore inevitably altered in some undesirable way. Lord Windlesham pointed to this risk in the 1960s:

in political communication as well as in commercial advertising the way in which a message is presented may alter the effect it will have, those who have a professional skill in methods of presentation may come to influence or even determine the form and content of the political message as well as the way in which it is presented. (Windlesham, 1966: 53)

Such concerns have, if anything, become more acute as professionals have taken on a more central role in the lives of political parties. Chris Powell, of advertising agency DDB London 'and one of those central to modernising Labour since the 1980s' has gone so far as to claim that 'Philip Gould [New Labour's polling adviser] took advertising and used it to permeate the way the whole party operated. The way people presented themselves and spoke; the use of focus groups. The big change of the past 20 years is that the processes of advertising have become very influential in everything New Labour and then [David] Cameron is doing' (Branigan, 2006).

If the substance of politics is conceived as being totally separate from how it is communicated, then these concerns are fully justified. But if one adopts the view that the content of politics and how it is communicated are inextricably linked (see pp. 18–20 above), then it is possible to argue that those who are involved in the communication of politics have always paid some attention to the techniques of communication. Where the conduct of contemporary political communication may be distinguished from that in earlier periods is in the extent to which newer techniques, including those of manipulation, persuasion and presentation are becoming integral to it. As Walter Lippmann pointed out in his seminal book *Public Opinion*:

The creation of consent is not a new art. It is a very old one which was supposed to have died out with the appearance of democracy. But it has not died out. It has, in fact, improved in technic, because it is now based on analysis rather than on rule of thumb. And so, as a result of psychological research, coupled with the modern means of communication, the practice of democracy has turned a corner. A revolution is taking place, infinitely more significant than any shifting of economic power. (1922: 158)

One of the other key points that will emerge in this chapter is that many of the changes in the way politics has been or is being communicated can be usefully seen as part of the process of adaptation of political parties to their environment, and that these changes are not specific to any particular era. The use of outside professionals is a reflection of a desire, implicit or explicit, on the part of political parties to deal with change: change in practices and structures, change in the ways in which individuals and groups see things and define what works and what does not, as well as change in economic, political, technological and cultural landscapes. Those who make claims to facilitate and manage that change are the professionals to whom parties and governments constantly turn. In the context of political communication they are the opinion pollsters, the political advisers, the advertisers, the trainers of politicians, media employees (journalists, broadcasters, film makers), and sometimes also academics who offer advice to political organizations based on their working experiences, usually in non-political environments. Each, in their own way, claims to offer insights into how the electorate behaves and what needs to be done to gain their support. In the much larger picture of how governments communicate, each can also offer advice on how to sustain governments in power; in the context of pressure and lobby groups each can offer insights into how to advance arguments, and so on. (Davis, 2002) It is, in other words, a transformation built on a series of incremental adaptations over decades and, in the context of a rapidly changing sociopolitical and communications environment, no organization can afford to ignore the potential for change.

A contemporary example will illustrate this point: as the internet grows in importance, political parties, governments and others will turn to those who have the skills to run and design web pages, blogs and related outputs, in the same way that their predecessors turned to journalists or broadcasters to assist them to write content or make television programmes. Although technological advances have made political communication a highly technical and professional field, as Stanley Kelley had observed in 1956, he was also acutely aware of the fact that changes in news values and news priorities would force politicians to turn to those who knew how to use the media to obtain coverage (1956: 103). Something, in fact, that was already apparent in the late 19th century, as Michael McGerr notes in the context of both a changing newspaper system and a changing political environment, so that 'party managers no longer thought primarily of educating the people with didactic literature; more and more, these men saw their main function as obtaining as much space for their candidates as possible in the newspapers' (1986: 159). Perhaps significantly, at the turn of the 19th century the formerly titled 'literary bureaus' were re-titled 'press bureaus' and then 'publicity bureaus', moves which reflected the adoption of business publicity techniques in politics (McGerr, 1986: 159).

Michael McGerr's work illustrates in a simple yet insightful way how professional roles in political publicity changed from the late 19th century onwards and how practices in one field, business, were taken up in another, politics. That process of a transfer of skills and knowledge is clearly important for understanding how professionals have come to play such a significant role in politics since they have essentially taken on the duties of persuading voters to lend their support to particular candidates, duties not very different from those who seek to aid businesses to prosper. It comes as little surprise then to note that more recent explorations of the changing world of political communication have turned to the business of marketing as a source of concepts and ideas for understanding political party campaigning (Scammell, 1999). In other words, in the process of adapting to their environments and seeking to gain power, political parties will draw on any skills and tools that will give them a competitive edge.

Transforming political communication: Political parties and communication professionals

In the late 19th century, political parties began to organize themselves into coherent and coordinated bodies. In doing so, they began to acquire more distinctive characteristics as bodies that could take charge of campaigns, candidates and political programmes. Consequently, they were better able to direct campaigns and, in the process, take on board those who could help them achieve their objectives. At first, one must presume, that help was offered voluntarily but, over time and as specialisms began to develop, it is likely that professionals were paid for their services.

The precise moment when such a transition took place is difficult to pinpoint, but there is evidence that in the US paid professionals were employed in campaigns from the 1920s onwards (Kelley, 1956). It is likely, though, that candidates for political office did make use of some assistance – probably of a voluntary nature – in the conduct of campaigns before then. According to Michael McGerr, one US governor running for office in 1874:

> directed a tightly knit organization that used circular letters to reach down to loyal personal representatives in each township across New York. Through polls of the entire electorate, these men identified the undecided and independent. To capture their votes, the organization tried to cultivate a sense of personal contact with

the candidate. Party workers visited each wavering voter and left behind pamphlets on Tilden [the candidate], copies of his speeches, and issues of Democratic newspapers. (1986: 71)

The use of voluntary help in the conduct of campaigns is a common and traditional method of building support and one can also see it in the example of John Gorst and the Conservative Party in the 1870s. (Feuchtwanger, 1968) There is also evidence that at the turn of the century there was a growing effort to organize the political party and its constituent parts in order to maximize its effectiveness as a mobilizing force (see Ball, 1992). The attention to organizational matters is particularly important in competitive election environments where electors are no longer necessarily tied to any particular individual or party, and where seats are increasingly contested and not decided by the absence of alternatives (Caramani, 2003).

It could be argued, though, that those who helped political parties in the late 19th and early 20th century were essentially working in a voluntary capacity and, perhaps more critically, they were still very much part of the political organization and working under its direction. But by the 1920s, and in part as a by-product of the psychological and propaganda techniques used in the First World War as well as the publicity and public relations lessons learned in commerce, many of the same techniques were being applied to the world of politics, at least in the US. According to Kelley, in the 1920s and 1930s, the firm of Whitaker and Baxter was working with a variety of corporate clients *and* politicians. The firm's work was usually informed by a common set of practices which included treating every campaign 'as we would if we were merchandising *commodities* instead of selling *men* and *measures*', (Kelley, 1956: 39, original emphasis) and the testing of issues and campaign themes by, amongst other things, opinion polling (Kelley, 1956: 39–51). Professionals in those fields of work were thus developing skills and techniques outside, and independently, of the world of politics but could then be employed within that world.

In some ways, one could find parallels in the British context. In the 1920s, there was also an awareness of the growing importance of expertise in the conduct of politics. J. C. C. Davidson, who became Chairman of the Conservative Party in 1926, apparently suggested 'using advertising agencies on a professional basis to design and formulate the slogans, posters, and leaflets that were the common currency of election campaigning during the inter-war years' (Cockett, 1994: 556). He had also expressed a wish 'to apply the lessons of the Great War to the organization of political warfare' (Cockett, 1994: 548).

That skills and techniques derived from commerce, psychology, advertising, management and so on were becoming increasingly useful in the world of politics can be illustrated by the example of the use of public opinion polling in the 1930s. As the understanding of sampling and polling grew, it became possible to measure public opinion in a robust, rigorous and efficient way. As these new skills and practices developed – the use of sampling, using small groups for studying opinions, moving from looking at what people thought to what motivated them – different ways of looking at mass opinion could be exploited to advantage. Although, as Mark Abrams pointed out, 'no attempt was made to extend the techniques to the study of political opinions until Dr Gallup's poll came to Britain in 1938' (1963: 9). By which time those techniques had already begun to take root in the US where the Gallup Poll was established in the early 1930s. (Abrams, 1963; Kelley, 1956: 28f.; L'Etang, 2004: 30–1; Mayhew, 1997; Schudson, 1999: 223–8).

Few of these developments, it could be argued, could be fully exploited unless political parties had the funds to pay for them and were sufficiently well-organized to make the most of them. Without funds, experts could not be employed (but could obviously volunteer help and advice); without organization, the fruits of the experts' knowledge could not properly be exploited. These points are well recognized today just as they were in the past: Stanley Kelley quotes a Hiram Jackson in 1910 arguing that to run a successful campaign one needed 'money, organization and "a publicity bureau in charge of a skilled and competent newspaper man"' (Kelley, 1956: 28). In 1962, Mark Abrams made very similar observations: 'the three instruments of electoral victory' were a 'first-class public relations department', 'central office organization, and finance' (1962: 4–5).

The use of *paid* professional outsiders – outsiders in the sense that they were not full-time employees of the party and were being employed for specific tasks of more than a specialized technical sort by a political party – can thus be seen to represent a step change from what had gone on before. Free and voluntary advice from experts had probably always been given (and usually accepted) but payments for such services began to establish a complex relationship between the professionals and the political parties. The professionals would almost certainly claim that they know how best to run election campaigns but it is the political party that employs them and it is the political party that has ultimate responsibility and authority over what has to be done. Neither work in a sociopolitical vacuum: the professionals may be conscious, for instance, of a party's ideological compass, the preferences of the leadership, the political climate; the party leaders, too, may be conscious of the overall political context but also of the need to do battle and to succeed, since failure would mean losing power and prestige, amongst other things. There are, in other words, many different ways in which the relationships between the professionals and those in political parties work themselves out. Chris Powell, quoted above p. 73, suggested that some professionals are very influential but, equally, others would eagerly point to their limitations: in the 1997 election campaign, John Major (Prime Minster, 1990–1997) 'vetoed a poster campaign painting Tony Blair as untrustworthy, believing it was too personally negative' (Branigan, 2006). As later sections of this chapter will show, those relationships are both complex and varied.

We can get a glimpse of these forces at play – principally organizational imperatives and the use of professionals – in the histories of both the Conservative and Labour Parties in the immediate post-1945 period. What these examples show is not only the increasing attention paid to issues of organization per se but also the use of experts and professionals within political parties in the pursuit of electoral success. The most controversial aspect of these developments was the possibility that the use of professionals by political parties would somehow alter the make-up of parties themselves by making them no more than electoral machines detached from any meaningful body of supporters.

The Conservative and Labour Parties in the 1950s: the importance of organization and the use of professionals

In the course of reorganizing Conservative Central Office in the 1950s, Lord Woolton made 'professional advertising and public relations men … key figures in the Central Office, rapidly improving techniques and strengthening reliance on a manipulative approach to politics' (Wilson, 1961: 94). Woolton, for example, appointed Toby O'Brien in 1946 as a public relations consultant to the party and he was put 'in charge of publicity' (Marquis, 1959: 344). Although O'Brien's role seems to have been one of establishing good relations between the press and the party, (Pearson and Turner, 1965: 227–9) he represents an early example of a professional from outside the party – albeit someone who also wanted a political career – hired to help the party position itself in the country.

Other changes, discussed more fully in Chapter 2, show how both the main political parties were aware of the need to meet the challenge of the newest means of communication through the use of professionals in communication techniques. The Conservative Party set up studios and training programmes[2] and the Labour Party was being propelled into the future by Tony Benn who observed, in 1953, that television:

is far richer in potential development than Sound. The personality of the speaker and the things he has to say can have a tremendous impact, as Adlai Stevenson proved in the American Election. ... The possibility of great success is only to be had at the risk of great failure, and rehearsal and practice are obviously important. The genuine fireside chat is not something that comes naturally, nor does the interview. (Benn, 1953: v)

In the case of British political parties in the 1950s, those employed by the party or giving advice to the party – be they producers, consultants, actors, or radio producers – worked within the confines of the party. Their role was quite limited. Even the advertising firm Colman, Prentis and Varley which was used by the Conservative party to organize its advertising campaign in the 1949, 1951 and 1955 elections remained on the outside: advertisers were not part 'of a long-term programme of ... image-building. When the [Conservative] party was returned to power in October 1951 the advertising stopped; *the importance of long-term campaigning was not then recognised'* (Butler and Rose, 1960: 18–19, emphasis added).

By the mid-1950s, the political use of television in the US had already undergone something of a transformation with the development of television political spots. The political consultant Rosser Reeves is credited with researching and creating a series of political ads on behalf of Eisenhower. (See http://www.pbs.org/30secondcandidate/from_idea_to_ad/, accessed February 2008.) Whether the American experience played a part in the development of political communication in Britain in the 1950s is a question that requires its own study although the evidence suggests that British political actors were aware of what was going on overseas. What is certainly clear is that political broadcasting in Britain developed more slowly and in a more restrained way until the late 1950s (see, for example, Cockerell, 1989; Goldie, 1977). In these quite different circumstances – and with a very different regulatory regime for the mass medium of television[3] – it may be that there were fewer ways in which television could be exploited to the full: political communication had to be conducted within a strict regime of political broadcasting to get the message across to the electorate and use of the more traditional media of press, posters and manifestos remained of some importance. These factors did not diminish the need for better organization; it simply meant that better organization would contribute to some forms of political communication (for example press advertising, teaching of skills in the use of television) more than others (for example controlling the TV image and flow of news).

At the 1959 election, it would appear that things were beginning to change – at least for the Conservative Party – in the way election contests were being conceived with greater devotion to better organization and with more intensive use of advertisers. Lord Windlesham's analysis of the Conservative Party in this period illustrates both the organizational advances made by the Conservatives and also the poor state of its main rival, the Labour Party:

> With a businessman's belief in professionalism, not always found in political organizations, he [Lord Oliver Poole, party chairman since 1955] employed professional public relations men to supervise publicity and Press relations. … It is worth noting that, with the exception of television broadcasters, the Conservative Party made little use of party members volunteering to lend their professional skills to the cause, preferring to raise money to pay established companies whose continued existence and reputation were a surer guide to competence. (Windlesham, 1966: 51)

The Labour Party also used 'outside assistance' (Windlesham, 1966). In 1962, John Harris, 'a young newspaperman and protégé of Hugh Gaitskell … built up a professional team in Transport House and was taking regular advice from a panel of consultants including Dr Mark Abrams [the opinion poll specialist] and a number of Labour supporters from leading London advertising agencies' (Windlesham, 1966: 247). Clive Bradley, another professional with publishing experience, also worked with Harold Wilson in the run-up to the 1964 election. (Personal interview, 2006). By that point, though, it was becoming clear that the Labour Party had moved ahead of the Conservatives and created a successful model of an electable party.

A number of factors helped to account for this change. The first was the election defeat of 1959, the third defeat in a row for the Labour Party. The second was the response to that defeat, which emphasized the need for change in politics as much as structures. The third factor was that the Labour Party began the process of change soon after the 1959 defeat so that by 1962 it had created an organizational structure that brought together advertisers and researchers in order to exploit the lessons of research in the pursuit of power.[4] Significantly, the publicity group began to feed findings into 'general matters of tactics and presentation' (Butler and King, 1965: 70). In fact, the work of Mark Abrams was considered vital for the publicity efforts of the Labour Party: he had prepared a document 'by the autumn of 1962' – that is, two years before the election – based on a 'sample of 1,250 voters in marginal constituencies'. This document not only considered the nature of 'uncommitted electors in uncommitted constituencies' but identified them as 'the target voters' that the party had to persuade and mobilize. Such information fed directly into Labour's publicity efforts in the run-up to the election (Butler and King, 1965: 68–70).

The difference between this structure and that of the Conservatives was highlighted in the study of the 1964 election: Labour's publicity advisers were 'an integral part of [its] election planning. Neither Colman, Prentis and Varley … nor the various pollsters who worked for it were regarded as performing more than ancillary services …' (Butler and King, 1965: 91). A fourth, and related, factor was that the Conservative Party, having been in power since 1951, was suffering from a lack of direction, whereas the Labour Party 'was remarkably unquarrelsome in 1963–64, and its propaganda effort was not upset by internal party wrangles' (Harrison, 1965; see also Rose, 1965: 378–9). Such an 'integrated' organizational model – a publicity organizer aided by professionals (usually, but not necessarily only, volunteers), feeding into a campaign committee, and under the control of the party leader – has some interesting parallels with the 'Mandelsonian' model of the 1980s and 1990s (discussed below). In other respects, it highlights two issues of interest here:

- The first is that it is possible to argue – on the evidence drawn from the above examples – that the better organized a political party becomes, the greater the likelihood that it will seek to exploit expert/professional (outside) help.
- The second is that in the 1950s and 1960s, the outside experts employed by the political parties worked under the direction of both political actors (for example party leaders) and paid party officials. They did not direct the nature or content of campaigns, although there were often fine distinctions to be made between the formation and the communication of policies. This obvious tension was probably one of the reasons why the Labour Party was more reluctant to use all available means to court voters, but *not* using all the modern means available was not always an option. As *Socialist Commentary* pointed out, if publicity was to be 'engaged in at all, this must be done professionally; it must take advantage of all the appropriate media' (1965: xviii).

By the mid-1960s then, the political parties in Britain as elsewhere were drawing on a range of skills that were becoming widely available outside the parties themselves, such as in the worlds of advertising and public relations. As we have seen, the use of such experts and professionals to run press and poster campaigns and to help produce the party political broadcasts was reasonably well established by the late 1950s (Harrison, 1965: 172–9). Just as advertisers were beginning to exert their influence on the sale of goods, so politicians were becoming aware of the application of advertising and, more generally, public relations skills to the field of politics. Its use in the US and then in the British political context therefore comes as no surprise; if anything, the surprise is that it was used so little in the immediate post-1945 period, something that could be explained by a number of factors that made the British context different from the US: the short duration of election campaigns, the absence of a constant series of elections that would permit the development of a profession of political consultancy, the prohibition against paid television and radio political advertising, and a certain ideological aversion to anything that either smacked of sale and/or Americanization. In such circumstances, it was only the press (and posters) – and to a much lesser extent the party political broadcasts – that could really be used as media for political advertising and mass persuasion, although one could clearly become sophisticated in *how* they were used.

If the 1950s and 1960s saw the intrusion of professional communication experts – mainly advertisers, broadcast specialists and polling organizations – the 1970s saw a continuing interest in ways in which to improve campaigning strategies. Advertising was used very effectively by Saatchi and Saatchi during the 1979 campaign and the then Tory leader, and later Prime Minister, Margaret Thatcher was given professional advice on how to speak and how conferences should be staged (Thomas and Gill, 1989). According to Rathbone:

> The Conservative election campaign in 1979 was professionally planned and executed; perhaps it was the most professionally run Conservative campaign ever. The party hierarchy was aware of the need for professional research (both quantitative and qualitative), for proper analysis of that research and for sophisticated use of the information so gained in the planning and execution of the pre-election and election political propaganda. (Rathbone, 1982: 43)

Conservative party advertisers were directly linked, via Gordon Reece the party's Director of Public Relations, to the 'controlling group' of four, chaired by the party chairman. They were 'able to see virtually any relevant piece of information [they] wanted concerning party policy or party research' (Rathbone, 1982: 11). Labour, by then and in direct contrast, had multiple centres of control and direction, and no real strategy. (Delaney, 1982) The fortunes of the two main political parties appeared to see-saw between extremes of success and direction and exhaustion and defeat.

New Labour: laying the foundations for a new campaigning template?

If the 1979 defeat of the Labour Party showed up the strength and professionalism of the Conservative Party, the 1983 election defeat further confirmed the parlous state of the Labour Party. It had entered the 1983 election period having done little public opinion research and there had been little forward planning (Grant, 1986). This, one could argue, may have been no more than a reflection of the political turmoil that it was itself undergoing. But change had to come if Labour was to consider itself electable again. As Eric Shaw records:

> Along with many others, Neil Kinnock [then Labour leader] was struck by the contrast between Labour's campaign and the sophistication and professionalism exhibited by the Tories and a total overhaul of its approach to campaign and communications was an early priority.

> In 1985 … all campaigning and communications functions were brought together within a single body, the newly established Campaigns and Communications Directorate into whose hands control over the conduct of media relations was vested so that it could operate as the clearing-house for all contacts between the Party and the media. In October 1985 … Peter Mandelson [a television producer and researcher] was selected as Director of Campaigns and Communications. … In a report to the CSC [Campaign Strategy Committee] … he urged an 'even greater disciplined communications and expertise in projecting key policies to target audiences' and called for:

> - an agreed communications strategy;
> - cohesive presentation of our message through the full range of media;
> - publicity material which is better and is used more often;
> - and proper use of outside professional support. (Shaw, 1994: 54–7; see also Gould, 1998a)

Mandelson's recollection of his arrival sheds light on the level of disorganization: 'You had party machinery and personnel without leadership, management or purpose, which needed to be professionalized. You had a communications operation which was wholly discredited and demoralised' (Gould, 1998a: 44).

The Shadow Communications Agency (SCA) was seen by Philip Gould (himself a professional political pollster) as a unit that would 'draft strategy, conduct and interpret research, produce advertising and campaign themes, and provide communications support as necessary' (1998a: 55). The SCA research – qualitative as well as quantitative – was fed into the campaigning process and into the party as it embarked on the process of modernizing itself in order to make itself more relevant to the Britain of the 1980s and 1990s.[5] It was 'largely a volunteer team of advertisers, headed by Philip Gould and Chris Powell, and was essentially an addendum to the Director, to whom it reported' (Butler and Kavanagh, 1992: 46). At its first formal meeting were members of advertising agencies, advisers from the MORI polling agency, market researchers, political consultants, party officers/employees (Peter Mandelson, Patricia Hewitt from the leader's office) and politicians (Gould, 1998a: 57). In the run-up to the 1987 election the American political consultant Joe Napolitan also 'started to help Neil Kinnock (the Labour leader)' (Gould, 1998a: 162). There were regular presentations to a range of committees on which politicians sat but, by and large, the SCA contributed to the broader strategy and provided a flow of information for the campaigning team.

Accounts of the life and work of the SCA suggest that it managed to provide the sorts of insights – always supported by research – that would enable the party to begin the process of modernization. It was a part of what a modern political party that sought electoral victory needed. But did it initiate policies or merely implement policies decided elsewhere? Butler and Kavanagh suggest that 'the policy review was initiated from the top of the party. It was not a response to demands from the grass roots.' And they generally cast doubts on accounts that portray the SCA as the motor of change, preferring to see it as providing the ammunition that party modernizers could then use to initiate change (1992: 53–4).

Without doubt, the SCA did play a very important role in the run-up to the 1987 election, but it faced greater problems in the run-up to the 1992 election (which Labour also lost). By then, Mandelson had left (in 1990) and changes in the Directorship of the Campaigns and Communications Group, and internecine warfare between members of the Labour Party, left it more dependent on key players and more distant from the leadership. Gould claims that the SCA 'hardly' saw Kinnock in the six months prior to the 1987 campaign but 'huge amounts' once the campaign had started (1998a: 146–7). In these circumstances, it is difficult to give a proper assessment of how the SCA linked up with the Labour Party, the leadership and key players within it. Equally difficult is any attempt to measure its influence, as different accounts offer somewhat different interpretations. For example, Eric Shaw suggests that 'the formation of the committee [the Campaign Strategy Committee to which Mandelson and the SCA would report] was motivated by political as much as campaigning considerations as Kinnock intended to use the new body to short-circuit the NEC [National Executive Council of the Labour Party] and thereby reduce the role and its still influential left-wing contingent' (Shaw, 1994: 54–5). Similarly, whilst the SCA was 'closely involved' in the policy review process post-1987 – 'the polling foundation upon which the party's modernisation was built' (Gould, 1998a: 84) – the review itself is credited with being the idea of Tom Sawyer, a trade unionist and General Secretary of the Labour Party (see Gould, 1998a. 88–9).

These accounts, and others, give rise to different interpretations. On the one hand, they can contribute to the view that the SCA had hijacked the party and that it was simply offering 'magic means of winning elections that ultimately ignore political realities' (Gould, 1998a: 157). On the other hand, the qualifications offered in some of the accounts stress the manner in which the SCA – and advisers more generally – fed into a much bigger and more complicated political organization, an organization in which personalities and policies jealously competed with one another, and an organization that often ignored the work of the SCA. But it is difficult to escape the conclusion that it worked – as did other advisers – within a political organization where questions of political purpose and policy were paramount. The SCA, in other words, could not take the leadership in a direction in which it did not want to go. However, and this is also an argument that can be put forward, the leadership in the run-up to both the 1987 and 1992 elections appears to have been reluctant to grasp the full implications of the SCA research. Had that research been taken on board, the 'modernization' of the Labour Party would have happened earlier; that it did not happen earlier reinforces the view that wider political and personality considerations impacted forcefully on the information fed into the process.

The organizational changes introduced in the 1980s and carried through into the 1990s, alongside the major review of policies, began to transform the Labour Party but that process was perhaps only completed after Tony Blair took over the leadership in 1994. By then, and with the John Major government rapidly losing public support, New Labour was on its way to victory. Its organizational structure and tactics allowed it to focus its activities of converting disenchanted Conservative voters, on targeting key and marginal seats (for example Operation Victory, Operation Turnout), using new techniques to target voters and opinion leaders (for example phone banks, rapid rebuttal, the internet) and, more generally, adopting strategies that would enable it to get its message across to voters in a clear and simple way. Success in 1997 was repeated in 2001, again aided in part by the weakness of the opposition. With no credible opposition in 2001, it was unlikely that New Labour was ever going to lose the general election. And, in both these elections, research for the purpose of electoral advantage was integrated into the party organization (see Cook, 2002).

The campaigns fought by New Labour in 1997, and to a lesser extent the elections of 2001 and 2005, can be seen as the templates for contemporary elections. The Party had created a structure that achieved success and delivered a style of politics that suited New Labour's circumstances and its need to recreate itself as a trusted party. It allowed for a centralization of power under the control of a party leader, and for a level of coordination of activities across the country that many could only dream of. So, it is not surprising to note that others have now adopted some of the practices. For example, the Conservative Party has now begun to exert greater control over its constituencies in order to ensure that there is a uniformity of practices that will be to its advantage.

After the 2005 election defeat, the Conservative Party changed its leader – yet again – but this time to a younger leader, David Cameron. Cameron was often likened to Tony Blair, in part because of his youthfulness, but also because he appears to have adopted the same style of politics, a personalized style which is full of rhetoric and fine words but which is often criticized for being low on substance. At the heart of Cameron's campaign is an adviser, Steve Hilton, who learned his trade at an early age and who appears to have modelled his operation on that of New Labour's Peter Mandelson in the 1980s. His profile is particularly interesting because it shows not only the part played by advisers but the growing professionalization of advice for party leaders: 'at the age of 22 Hilton was a campaign coordinator for John Major in the 1992 election. He became the link man between the party and the advertising agency, M&C Saatchi. Maurice Saatchi then recruited him to the agency … After Labour won in 1997, Hilton[6] founded a "social marketing agency" called *Good Business* … Before the last election [of 2005] he tried (unsuccessfully) to be selected' for a safe Tory seat (Barnett, 2006).

When Hilton was appointed, it was rumoured that he was 'the highest paid adviser in the history of the Conservative Party, earning £150,000 more than Cameron himself and almost £100,000 more than the Prime Minister' (Barnett, 2006) but this was probably not as large as the 'up to £475,000' alleged to be paid to Andy Coulson, the Party's new Director of Communications, who was appointed in May 2007. Three points make this appointment relevant in the context of this chapter. The first is that Coulson was a journalist and an ex-editor of a tabloid (*News of the World*) so was thought to bring much-needed media handling skills to the party. Parallels with Alastair Campbell, also a journalist, were obvious. The second was that, unlike Campbell, Coulson was seen to have tendencies towards the Conservative Party rather than the allegiance that made Campbell so distinctive (Robinson, 2007). The third, and more general point, is that both these appointments signal the leader's efforts at building a key strategic publicity and communication team at the centre of the party and one occupied by consummate professionals.

The centralization of the Cameron campaign and its direction by a skilled professional – not unlike Labour Party strategies in the 1990s – made it possible for the Conservative Party to present a new face and a new profile to the electorate. But, as with the Labour Party and Labour Governments, it has also raised questions about the power and influence of the unelected outsiders who work in the shadows and who serve the centralized power structure. These questions surfaced throughout 2006 and 2007 as the press focused on the influence of one of the Party's major donors, Michael Ashcroft, and his advice that fewer key marginal seats should be targeted in order to achieve victory (Ashcroft, 2005). As his role in election planning became public, questions about the influence such individuals have were once again being asked. Have such individuals taken over? Have party bureaucrats been displaced? Have politicians lost control over parties? Have political principles been abandoned? The next section offers some thoughts on these questions.

Parties and professionals: the nature of the relationship

In trying to establish the nature of the relationship between political parties and professionals, the starting point must be to acknowledge that it would vary from period to period, professional to professional and party to party. A point made as far back as 1963 by Louis Harris, the polling expert:

The role of the polls and the polltaker will vary, depending upon the professional employed and the candidate involved. A polltaker may go so far as to serve on the candidate's strategy committee as a professional advisor, privy to all the key decisions made, he may only be called in for special consulting from time to time, or he may simply provide some sort of written report of his survey, without any personal contact with the candidate or his campaign staff. (1963: 3)

In the British context, and given that general elections take place every four or five years, the pattern seems to be that political parties employ the services of outsiders rather than employ them within the party as permanent full-time employees. This would certainly be true of the professionals who provide services only during election campaigns – the *vendors* of services, in Johnson's terminology (2000: 27–42) – but it would also be true for the *strategists* and other *specialists* who play a more important role pre- and post-elections.

Sometimes the positions, and fortunes, of these advisers become inextricably tied up with those of the politicians they serve – Blair and Campbell for example – but there are probably several advantages to these sorts of arrangements. One advantage is clearly that of minimizing costs. Hiring or using advisers full-time would be expensive in itself and there may be few such professionals who would seek to devote all their energies – and the resources of their own organizations if they are experienced heads of polling or marketing agencies – to one client. Another advantage is that outside professionals can be used to establish campaigning units separate from the party's general organization and usually working to the leadership; the traditional party organization can thus be bypassed. A third advantage is that such arrangements allow for both change and continuity – one can hire and fire advisers much more easily than one can permanent staff and they can be used to reinforce the fact that the political leadership remains the dominant partner in the relationship.

Such organizational structures also ensure that politicians and party bureaucrats work in conjunction with experts/professionals but usually retain overall control of election strategies, for better or worse, more so when politicians and party bureaucrats themselves have some knowledge of aspects of political communication. This had already emerged by the 1960s, as Lord Windlesham noted:

Whereas professional politicians normally will have obtained their skills as a result of experience inside political organizations, professional publicists more often will have obtained their skills as journalists, advertising or public relations men outside political organizations. [Although the distinction should allow for] a considerable overlap, ... [between] 1957 and 1964 responsibility for the overall supervision of governmental public relations was entrusted to a Cabinet Minister with some professional experience of political communication ... (1966: 243)

A recent example of the potential difficulties that lie in the path of such relationships comes from the Conservative Party's election campaign in 2001. Whilst the data collected for that party's campaign pointed in one direction, key people in the party overlooked the data or imposed their own interpretation on it. As Andrew Cooper, the party's then opinion researcher, observed in his account of the 2001 campaign, 'the overwhelming information collected was "ignored"' (Cooper, 2002: 2). (The John Major example quoted above, p. 78, is another).

One other point to note about advisers in the British political context is that, by and large, they are politically committed and some even become politicians, for example Peter Mandelson, Patricia Hewitt and Charles Clarke, while others continue with their work but remain allied to particular parties, for example Philip Gould and Maurice Saatchi. A younger generation of advisers may be less committed: the Conservative Party's short-lived marketing director, Will Harris – he stayed in post a mere nine months – had voted for Tony Blair in 1997,[7] though David Cameron's adviser, Steve Hilton has been with the Conservative Party for well over a decade. Andy Coulson, the new Director of Communications, was described as 'a classic Conservative voter who was swayed by Blair but never by Labour' (quoted in Robinson, 2007)

If there is an aversion or antipathy to the use of experts/professionals, it is an aversion that grows out of a fear that they are leading the political party rather than lending it their support, skills and knowledge. This can be seen in the reluctance of the Labour Party to embrace the 'new tools' of polling and advertising in the early 1950s but that reluctance was clearly overcome in due course (see Wring, 2005). In many important respects, then, political parties are rarely averse to using new means of communication or persuasion to gain electoral advantage. The way they have embraced the internet is a good example in support of that point.

A final point to make in relation to experts and professionals is that the nature of the relationship between 'insiders' and 'outsiders' has oscillated over the past half century. Harrop has suggested that in the immediate post-war period, campaign professionals, principally advertisers, were called upon to help the political parties (mainly the Conservatives) to advertise their policies, but that in the mid-1960s both advertisers and pollsters became more acceptable within political parties, although their role 'remained ancillary' (2001: 61). From 1965 onwards, one begins to see a more fully integrated campaign being run with campaign professionals almost at the heart of all activities, with either campaigns under the direction of advertisers (for example Saatchi) or under the full control of the party (for example the 'Mandelsonian' model). Equally significant for Harrop is the fact that different eras have seen different types of professionals being favoured: in the 1960s and 1970s the opinion pollsters, in the 1980s the qualitative researchers and the advertising agencies vying for ascendancy. From the 1990s onwards, the changes are taking place, according to Harrop, *within* the political parties with the parties once again calling in help from outsiders. This conclusion finds some support in Kavanagh's study of pollsters in British politics. Although he concludes his 1996 paper by arguing that 'the private pollster's role has failed to expand' and the role is 'rarely part of a party's strategy team' (1996: 111), he accepts that the 'new generation of politicians' – his paper predates Blair's premiership! – and a different organizational make-up for political parties, for example centralization, may be opening up a new chapter in the history of professionals in British politics (1996: 113).

Developments within the Conservative Party throw much light on the above discussion and lead one to conclude that significant changes were taking place: each new leader – William Hague, Iain Duncan Smith, Michael Howard and David Cameron – saw a restructuring of the party and their favourite advisers brought in: Maurice Saatchi came in with Michael Howard but was displaced by Steve Hilton under David Cameron as a new style of leadership and party was being created. In this process of change, the party was well aware that it had to re-create itself in a new way in order to challenge the Labour Party for power and to appeal to voters long displeased with it. Unfortunately for David Cameron's Conservative Party, voters were by then fully aware of the 'new' Conservative Party but put this down to a change of style rather than a change of substance. An ICM poll conducted in April 2006 – some six months after the election of the new leader – found that 40% of those sampled agreed either a lot or a little with the statement that 'David Cameron's leadership is more about spin than substance'. Only 28% disagreed either a little or a lot with that statement (ICM Polls, 2006). Just as political parties and professionals come to acquire new knowledge to mobilize and manipulate voters, so too do voters acquire new knowledge that often helps them see through those activities!

Professionals and political parties: political communication transformed?

If the lives of politicians and professionals have now become inextricably linked and the fortunes of the former are in some measure related to the work of the latter in ways that are more obvious and apparent than at any time in the past, does this represent transformation in the conduct of political communication? Or does it represent no more than an extension or an evolution from what had gone on before?

I have argued that there are moments in the past 100 years when one can identify experts – voluntary and paid – giving their services to political parties or politicians. That expertise may not be as sophisticated as that found today but it would have been considered as sophisticated in its own time. For their part, political parties have in the past also sought out the help of professionals to help them achieve their objectives. As Wernick has pointed out:

> the transformation of electoral politics into a public relations game is a long-term process which has had structural causes. Not only has this process been propelled, at key moments, by the wholesale borrowing of techniques from the sphere of commercial marketing. It has also responded to long-term changes in the socio-cultural character and composition of the electorate. In both these respects, moreover, what has ultimately pushed it along is *the competitive logic of electoralism*. (1994: 142, emphasis added)

Does this history suggest that a transformation has taken place? Inasmuch as paid professionals have now become indispensable in the electoral process, one can argue that political communication has moved away from being something that one dabbled in and had a 'feel for' to an activity that requires careful and strategic thought and planning. The examples of Philip Gould, Alastair Campbell and Steve Hilton in the British context and Stan Greenberg, James Carville and Frank Luntz in the American context suggest that there is now a coterie of specialists that are becoming embedded in the political process – and in the political process internationally (see

Plasser and Plasser, 2002). These are truly professionals and to the extent that they are professionals one could make a case for saying that what we see is a professionalization of political communication and a realization that no contemporary election could be conducted without their help.

But we need to see these developments alongside changes in the structure and fortunes of political parties. Arguably, these developments might have less of an impact – and there may be less of a need for specialists – if parties had partisan supporters by the millions. It is only when parties cease to have an organic linkage with members and cease to be truly representative of a significant and extensive constituency that they have to hawk their political wares to not only a less committed public but a less interested one as well. If political parties are parties in search of voters – akin to businesses in search of customers – it would seem that those who are able to successfully market the product are likely to find places at the centre, or very near the centre, of operations.

Can the process of change be reversed? Given the nature of the political system – and the nature of political parties within that system – it is unlikely that significant changes will take place. Differences between political systems will always be apparent as different practices and rules apply, for example with respect to funding, the sale of airtime and so on, but the overall trend will not change. If anything, it is likely that the process of professionalization will become even more pronounced and that professionals will continue to play their part in the way leaders are made visible, party programmes are shaped and voters are persuaded and mobilized. As Kolodny and Dulio (2003) have pointed out:

> Rather than seeing the proliferation of consultants as a sign of party decline, we argue that their presence is actually a next step in party evolution. If political parties are meant to contest elections with the hope of gaining power (by winning office), then the parties must help their candidates remain electorally viable in whatever way they can. We believe this is further evidence of a political party adaptation to increasingly specialized campaign needs. (2003: 740)

It could also be evidence of the ways in which bringing professionals into the centre of political parties may alter their relationships with their supporters and members. It certainly raises questions about what methods of campaigning are best suited for victory.

Political Actors: Transforming Practices

5

Introduction

Previous chapters have explored the questions of adaptation, transformation and professionalization of political communication at the level of the political party but the changes that have taken place at that level cannot be seen in isolation from changes that have taken place, or are taking place, at a more local level or at the level of the individual politician. The aim of this chapter is to explore how individual political actors have also changed in the course of the past century, although there may be different considerations to take into account depending on the nature of the political system in place.

In political systems where political parties are no more than loose labels that are attached to individual candidates, it is possible to argue that individuals standing for office trade on their personalities and abilities – although usually aided by a plethora of helpers. Candidates standing for national office in the US enter into a competitive race that pits them against one another for funding, attention and advantage. In the course of the competition, though, they learn from their advisers and consultants how best to behave, address their audiences or pull their thoughts together. Even at lower levels of the political hierarchy – at Congressional or Senate level – individuals competing for office engage in a competitive race and their advisers help them make the most of their personalities and skills in order to make them more professional in their approach to campaigning and the prospect of winning.

In political systems such as in Britain, where political parties do matter and still offer the best route to office, the individual personalities and skills of candidates matter much less. Apart from the key positions in any political party, such as that of leader or deputy, and sometimes that of prospective ministers, candidates for office tend to be seen by voters as party members first and individual personalities second. In most circumstances it is usually the national voting pattern that determines the level of success at local constituency level rather than the personality and skills of the individual parliamentary candidate.

However, as political parties change their organizational make-up – becoming more professional, more centralized, more strategic – this can have a knock-on effect on the individual candidate. As a party becomes a more professional campaigning organization, it may require its candidates to become equally professional in their campaigning work. A party may also become more aware of the need to direct all aspects of its work at the local level from the centre in order to organize for victory. In the process, it may begin to ask more of its candidates; rather than ceding control, the party heightens the level of centralized control. When David Cameron's Conservative Party wanted to introduce an A-list of candidates with a high proportion of ethnic minority and women candidates, it signalled an increase in the power of Conservative Central Office over traditionally largely independent constituency party offices (Wintour, 2006).

But in this accelerating process of professionalization and the centralization of power, the demands on the individual candidate also changed: candidates could no longer be amateurs; they had to be professional in their approach to all their speaking, campaigning, canvassing and presentational activities. The point here is that just as political parties have been going through change, candidates standing for parliamentary seats have also changed – or been forced to change – how they approach their political work. Compare, for example, the experiences of British MP Julian Critchley[1] in the 1950s with those of contemporary candidates. In his memoirs, *A Bag of Boiled Sweets*, Critchley (1995) tells the story of how he was interviewed by the Conservative Party's vice-chairman in charge of candidates. In what turned out to be a fairly chaotic process – the vice-chairman confused Julian Critchley's parents with the parents of someone else – Critchley was put on the party's list of candidates without any particular or further scrutiny. Reflecting back on his experiences, Critchley noted that in the 1990s:

> someone in my shoes would be obliged to spend two hundred pounds of his own money in order to attend a weekend 'course' … where he would be put through his paces. I went on one such undertaking in the early eighties … Fifty aspirants were obliged to write essays, debate among themselves, deliver five-minute speeches on unrelated topics, and display a command of table manners … (1995: 65)

The extract is a rich example of how things change over time and how individuals also need to adapt to change. Julian Critchley makes the point that he did not have to attend any weekend courses unlike today's prospective MPs but, from the political party's point of view, today's MP is expected, almost required, to be much more prepared for the role: more prepared in the sense of having been 'trained' to a level to cope with the cut and thrust of politics and media in the 24/7 culture. Indeed, one of the major political parties even offers a 'Campaigning Diploma' which is open to all members and which includes sessions on media, targeting, and other campaigning techniques (Labour Party, internal communication, 2007, sent to author).

If ordinary members are encouraged to take such training seriously, candidates for parliamentary seats would need to become even more familiar with these techniques. They would need to have a good grounding in how to develop their message, with public speaking and speech writing, and with campaigning in a more strategic and integrated way than ever before. And because the political party expects more from its candidates and more integration with the centre of the party, the candidate of today is rarely left alone and if they are standing in marginal constituencies they are even more likely to be closely scrutinized. In the run-up to the 2005 election, Dr Liam Fox, co-chairman of the Conservative Party, introduced an 'audit' of candidates in marginal seats with candidates 'ordered to submit a weekly email to central office outlining their plans'. Dr Fox wanted 'to see each candidate's diary, outlining every visit they plan to make and a copy of every press release and speech' (Watt, 2004).

That change – from a more relaxed and informal process of selection to a more intense, better organized and more rigorous one – is the theme of this chapter. It will look at the ways in which political actors, principally MPs and parliamentary candidates, have become more 'professional' in their approach to their work with the media. The extent to which this has brought about a transformation in political communication is explored in the final section of this chapter.

Transforming the candidate: what does it mean to be a professional?

The reminiscences of Julian Critchley (above) are instructive because they alert us to the days before the development of television as a mass medium; to the days when television was still only available to a small percentage of the population. Yet, as Chapter 2 shows, political parties were already waking up to the prospect of television and to the need to develop in candidates and MPs a range of skills that would make them work successfully with this new medium. In his television documentaries *Live from Number 10*, Michael Cockerell (Cockerell, 1989) has usefully drawn our attention to Winston Churchill's inability to get the 'hang' of television. He had mastered radio – a medium of his generation – but he never was able to use television to good effect. A not dissimilar point could be made in respect of an earlier generation of politicians: in the election/political films of the 1930s, Ramsay MacDonald adopted a style of presentation more suited to the public meeting than to the medium of film; it was too static, too oratorical and had few of the qualities of the medium of film (http://www.screenonline.org.uk/film/id/1192584/index.html).

By the 1960s, and with television becoming *the* mass medium for politics, potential prime ministers could not afford not to know how to use television. By and large, most succeeded (Harold Wilson and Jim Callaghan in the 1960s and 1970s), although Edward Heath (Prime Minister, 1970–4) was less at ease with the medium. The 1980s and 1990s brought forth a crop of political leaders such as Margaret Thatcher and Tony Blair who were very comfortable in front of the cameras. The advent of the internet and a new way of communicating politics to the public will test the current generation and offer new challenges to newer politicians, just as it has already done for those seeking electoral victory today: Clinton, Sarkozy and Cameron are all dealing with this newest of technologies in their own ways and seeking to blend the right level of informality and sincerity for a medium that has its own language and grammar.[2] (See Chapter 8 for a fuller discussion of the internet.) Whilst the generational analysis of politicians' use of the media is undoubtedly useful (Seymour-Ure, 2003), some of the above examples also suggest that there are numerous factors at play when considering how politicians come to use particular media. One of these is that different individuals may have different abilities or capacities when it comes to media use. Some may be 'naturals' – at ease, comfortable – others may not. Those comments notwithstanding, the key point that this chapter seeks to stress is that with the mediatization of politics – increasingly centred around forms of audio-*visual* communication focused around television and the internet – it is imperative that one should know how to use the visual media of communication. It is no longer possible to go into an election contest as an amateur, unable to use the media to good effect, unable to communicate ideas speedily with maximum clarity, unable to control the context of the communication. No modern leader could survive without those skills, no candidate could either. In these circumstances, being 'a natural' is a great advantage but it may not be enough, and if one is not 'a natural' at handling the media of communication then one has simply to learn how to be at ease with the media. In the age of mediated politics, learning how best to communicate is elevated into an essential and necessary requirement and not just a desirable skill. That, in brief, is an indicator of the transformation of political communication at the individual level.

What, though, is being transformed and how does one measure or denote the process of transformation? At a basic and simple level, one could imagine someone who had absolutely no media skills whatsoever being taught how to use particular forms of communication or the media in general. In the 1950s, Winston Churchill, as Cockerell (1989) has shown, tried to learn how to use television but was never quite able to do so. With television still in its infancy and Churchill in his twilight years, he probably could get away without learning how to use it. For the purposes of election broadcasts, the party used the telegenic and suave looking Foreign Secretary, Anthony Eden. In any case, in the 1950s many felt that power emanated from Westminster and not from the media. As David Butler wrote in connection with the television broadcasts in the 1955 election:

> The vast majority of leading politicians in the last half-century could, if they had taken to it young enough, undoubtedly have learnt to project themselves on television in a competent and sympathetic way. The fact that one man may be a little more successful than another at this special aspect of public relations is unlikely to have great effect in the atmosphere of Westminster, where political reputations are really made and lost. (Butler, 1955: 64)

Changes in world politics in the past fifty years have had an impact on domestic politics, and Westminster is less the crucible of power that it once was. Whilst it does still possess powers and remains an important location of power for domestic politics, much activity has gravitated elsewhere and much political discussion now takes place around the television studios of a plethora of services rather than in the Chamber of the House of Commons. As Richard Rose has documented, recent prime ministers have tended to spend less time in the Commons than their predecessors and they make fewer interventions and fewer major speeches (Rose, 2001: 130–7). In so far as reputations can be made and lost in Westminster, this may only be true today if those moments are captured on television or YouTube!

If politicians from the mid-1950s onwards, like Churchill and Macmillan (Negrine, 1999: 113), had to accept that television would change what was required of them, they also had to accept that what journalists expected of them was also going to change. In the 1950s when the attitude of journalists in general was somewhat less adversarial and brusque than it is today (Day, 1975: 4–5), someone in high office would be prodded very gently about his/her plans and policies. Prime ministers or ministers did not have to face a barrage of questions from a hungry and hostile press pack (see Cockerell, 1989: Chapters 1–3; see also Day, 1989). Practices and forms of behaviour that were commonplace then were clearly not acceptable in later decades and over the past 50 or so years the adversarial exchange relationship between the media and politics has changed so significantly that a whole new set of skills has had to be learned by both journalists and politicians. Journalists have had to become more forensic in their examination of statements and less ready to take for granted what is offered. They too are regularly in the spotlight! Alongside this, there is a measure of robust disregard for the status of the politician verging, some would say, on rudeness. Possibly as protection – or is it a cause of media behaviour? – politicians have had to learn to defend themselves, to neutralize attacks and to develop strategies that protect them from the intrusiveness of journalists. This is not the place to either justify or excuse the actions on either side of the media–politics fence. (See Lloyd, 2004, for a detailed discussion of this issue.) The point to note is that as far as political actors are concerned, it is now no longer possible *not* to be careful about the media, *not* to be aware of one's own vulnerability and *not* to learn how to protect oneself or present oneself in a favourable light.

It is interesting to reflect here on the experiences of MPs who sat in Parliament in the 1960s and 1970s. When interviewed during the course of research into the growing media professionalization of MPs,[3] many pointed out that they had no training in media matters or felt that they had not needed any. Those that did have some training referred to 'half-hour sessions at Central Office' or 'one lesson' or 'a couple of hours with a professional journalist'. This was not because there was no training on offer. As we have seen in Chapters 2 and 3, once television became available in the early 1950s political parties quickly set up training facilities for MPs. The only conclusion that one can draw from this, is that media considerations were much less of a priority than they were to become from the late 1960s onwards.

The changes that have taken place in both media and politics since the late 1960s have not been restricted to technologies or political parties. They have also had consequences for individuals: the individual politician is much less likely to be an amateur – an innocent, untutored, unknowing subject – and more likely to be professional at media handling – a savvy operator who is wary of the media but can nearly always spot a media opportunity. In the mediated world of politics, it is often the political actor's interface with the public via the media that matters and is used to measure the professionalism of the politician more than their skills with constituents, their personal qualities, or their organizational abilities. The fact that most politicians now have web pages is testimony to their belief that maintaining high visibility and connectedness with their constituents is important for their profile and, hence, their election prospects.

Whilst the media are of increasing importance in political life, this does not necessarily mean that the media are of increasing importance in the lives of *all* politicians in *the same way*. For backbench MPs, for instance, media work may have less significance than debates, bills, interventions and constituency work in general. MPs acknowledge the importance of the media – and of the local press in particular – but the *relative* importance of the media when compared with other aspects of their working life is more difficult to determine. Michael Rush's study of MPs (Rush, 2001) makes very few references to the media, so if the media are important, then it is probably as an adjunct to the life of the MP – something one does following on from other things and not something that one continually obsesses about. As we shall see below, MPs will often make claims for the importance of the national and local media but, in practice, will not always engage with either to any significant degree. The same is true of their web presence – some MPs have better websites than others, just as some make better use of the interactive facilities of the web than others.

Prospective parliamentary candidates, on the other hand, will see the media – again, the local media in particular – as of great significance, because they need to gain publicity so as to enhance their chances of winning votes. However, outside the three to four week election period itself, prospective candidates, even if they have been selected months in advance, lack any real legitimacy and find it difficult to get the sort of publicity they crave. Their need for publicity is greatest at election time; past the election – if they have lost – they cease to be of interest to the media and tend to disappear from local constituencies, although they often reappear to fight seats elsewhere. Unlike the sitting MP, then, the candidate seeks different sorts of publicity at different times. The media, for its part, sees the two sets of players quite differently and so treats them differently (see Negrine, 2005).

If backbench MPs and candidates spend much of their time thinking about the local media, government ministers spend much of their time thinking about the national media, including television – a national media that is far more adversarial, demanding and precocious than its local counterpart. Ministers, in contrast to backbench MPs and candidates, operate at a very different political level altogether and need to pay greater attention to all the national media, although they also have a greater number of advisers to both shield and promote them.

These three groups of political actors, separated as they are by considerations of seniority and responsibilities, have different needs and hence enter into different relationships with different media. Whilst most would argue that they all need to develop skills to deal with and manage the media, how and why they do so varies depending on the seniority and status of the candidate, MP or even minister. Nevertheless, all politicians would now accept that they need to act in a professional way with respect to the media, as will emerge as this chapter explores in greater detail the way candidates and backbench MPs deal with the media.

What does professionalism mean? This can best be understood as developing at least a 'basic competence in news management techniques' (Schlesinger and Tumber, 1994: 84). To act in a 'professional' way, and to be a 'professional', would be to display a range of skills for handling the media and an ability to use 'modern' communications, unlike the 'amateur'. As Jay Blumler has observed, those 'who are less attuned to the media sphere are discredited as *amateurs* out of touch with the modern world' (1990: 104, emphasis added). By implication, inappropriate use of the media would be tantamount to lacking professional skills.

So, what has to be learned and why does it have to be learned? The four sets of quotes below give a good overview of the reasons, and of the skills behind the training programmes that political parties increasingly urge their candidates to attend. The first three quotes come from three different media experts and media trainers involved in the Labour Party in the 1980s and early 1990s. They not only offer an insight into what has to be learned but also why the Labour Party had to learn these lessons: it had been pilloried for far too long by the press and it could no longer afford to ignore the need to deflect criticism and to paint a more professional, united, electable and proactive picture of itself. (See Chapter 3 for a full discussion of this background.) If that meant silencing critics and supporters alike in the interest of the Party, so be it.

The fourth quote is much shorter but displays some of what emerges in the first three quotes. It comes not from a national figure or a media trainer but from a prospective parliamentary candidate who was learning that certain ways of acting vis-à-vis the media produced positive and beneficial results. Underpinning all these extracts is the sense of transformation that was taking place in the way political actors were being taught to think about and deal with the media.

The first quote appears somewhat trivial but illustrates some useful lessons:

> *we took photos of Neil [Kinnock, Labour Party leader, 1983–1992] shaking hands with all the candidates. And we'd just line up fifty candidates in a row and I couldn't believe the number of chaps who'd turn up looking absolutely terrible, hair all over the place, bald pates, you know. There [we were] covering them up, combing their hair for them, it was unbelievable. [We were] doing the same thing with candidates in 1987 so they hadn't got it. [By 2001] we had a proper make-up department in the Green Room at Millbank Media Centre. So that's just symbolic really, you can just see the change.* (Special adviser. Personal interview)

The views of the media trainers are more considered and more incisive:

> *[There was a growing view that] people just decided they had to deal with journalism as they'd been losing out, … and that if you had a press officer and a press office you could actually get a jump-start …* (Media trainer 1. Personal interview)

> *[In] my experience, candidates and Ministers have always been very conscious of the importance of the media. I think the difference between now [2003] and then [1980s] is that they are less in awe of the media. In 1989, the media was something that was outside our control and that you were nervous about because you didn't feel it was entirely in your gift. That was one of the things we were trying to teach them in media training: that the interview is not something in which you are powerless. There is a question about who is dictating how the interview goes and that isn't a given when the interview starts, and I think nowadays that's much more understood by candidates and Ministers that the interview is there to be taken control of and having an interview is not something in which you are a passive player.*

[When I arrived in 1989/90] presentation was getting better but there was no control-freakery about this. The strong line from the Party was, 'we're not telling you what you have to say, we're doing this training course in order that you are better at communicating what you want to say'. It wasn't about, 'this is the line', which it very much is these days. (Media trainer 2. Personal interview)

At the local level, the experiences of one prospective parliamentary candidate neatly summed up what media trainers seek to achieve, namely, a view that 'what you need is an active management of the media ...' (Parliamentary candidate. Personal interview.)

From these extracts it is clear that the objective is to learn how to manage the media *in your favour* and not to let the media take the lead and allow things to spin out of control.

But can all the techniques of the skilled or professional communicator be learned? Most probably, yes, although it is worth recalling an earlier point that some may be more at ease with the media because they have either an intuitive understanding of how the media work or experience of media work, or both. A good illustration of the former comes from the 1930s in the advice Sir Patrick Gower, a civil servant working in Stanley Baldwin's private office, gave to Baldwin on how to use the medium of radio:

> it seems to me that many of the talks have been too formal. They sound like speeches delivered in a hall rather than talks to people sitting in their armchairs at home, and I have always held the view that the more personal, intimate and friendly these talks can be, the greater the influence they will exercise. (Quoted in Cockett, 1994: 559–60)

As for the latter, working in the media or cognate areas such as public relations can lead to an understanding of how the media work and that knowledge and those skills can be transferred into the world of politics. Such people often take on the role as either formal or informal media 'trainers'. Two notable examples include the Labour MP Tony Benn, who was a BBC radio producer before he became an MP and started to pay attention to the Labour Party's media activities in the 1950s, and Roger Ailes, a television producer, who later worked for Richard Nixon in the 1960s US presidential elections (McGinniss, 1970: 57).[4] Similarly, the television studios set up by the major British political parties in the 1950s, as discussed in Chapter 2, were run by individuals who knew how the media worked and could then give advice on how to work with television.

More generally, though, the media have colonized so many of today's professional activities that many people in professions such as law or higher education who come into contact with the media often become familiar with their practices in the course of their work. In fact, the need to understand and learn how to use the media rears its head in the unlikeliest of quarters: even universities now run regular 'media events' for academics. As a regional agent for one of the main political parties observed, the nature of the communications industry, PR and 'the rise of lobbying companies' have all 'produced more people who are then inclined to go from that into representative politics' (Personal interview). The general media colonization of other professions has thus contributed to the creation of a new breed of aspiring politician who possesses varying levels of media skills. These observations contribute to the more general discussion as to whether modern politicians are emerging increasingly from a narrower range of 'facilitating' occupations and professions, so creating a breed of professional politician (see Best and Cotta, 2000; Cairney, 2007; Rush, 2001).

It is thus not unusual for today's aspiring politician, especially if they have a professional background of some sort, to be aware of the importance of the media and their careful management. In the study of the media skills of MPs and prospective parliamentary candidates referred to earlier, we found that 14 out of 15 prospective parliamentary candidates who stood in the 2001 election had some experience of dealing with the media prior to their selection as prospective parliamentary candidates. A similar pattern was found in the background of MPs elected in either the 2001 or 1997 Parliament: of the 28 interviewed in the course of that research, 5 had been journalists, 10 had been at some point advisers to either voluntary or political groups, and the rest had been local councillors. This latter group is important because local councils often provide an introduction not only to the world of politics but also to the world of the media and media relations. Our research also suggests that MPs from earlier generations were less likely to have as many media-related experiences as contemporary MPs or candidates although a few had journalistic experience or had been councillors. A trawl through the CVs of newly selected candidates will more than likely confirm the extent of their media-saturated backgrounds. To confirm the point, one only needs to look at David Cameron's CV after Eton and the University of Oxford to see both the narrowness of his work experience and the depth of his media skills:

1988–92	Conservative Research Department, Head of the Political Section
1992–3	Special Adviser to the Chancellor of the Exchequer
1993–4	Special Adviser to the Home Secretary
1994–2001	Director of Corporate Affairs, Carlton Communications Plc
2001–	MP for Witney
2005–	Leader of the Conservative party

What media experiences do aspiring politicians in the 1990s and 2000s bring to the world of politics? Four broad categories of experiences can be identified and these reflect the extent to which media elements are part of the background of aspiring political players. These are by no means mutually exclusive categories but are broad enough to cover the different routes that individuals travel in their careers before becoming candidates in local constituencies. These include:

- A background in journalism.
- Working for or with politicians:

  I think my formal title was Senior Political Assistant. My job was to write press releases for [politician] to maintain a relationship with the newspapers so that we were getting stories in, and then develop relations with the local parties. (Personal interview)

- Working for the local council:

  I started off in politics in 1994, standing for the Borough Council ... as a candidate at that sort of low level we were given basic media training for the council candidates. We would be given basic advice on how to prepare a press release, that's the main thing, and also how to conduct ourselves in radio interviews, and how to try to identify media opportunities which we could then use. (Personal interview)

- Other work-related activities:

  As an NHS senior manager, I did a number of PR courses; [later I] became national media spokesman for Oxfam. (Personal interview)

The nature and depth of those experiences obviously vary and it would be wrong to suggest that all the individuals in the study were completely at ease in their media work or in dealing with the media. What the familiarity with the media shows, though, is that by the time they enter politics, such individuals most probably have an idea of the importance of the media and the importance of developing strategies to deal with them. Indeed, one could go further and argue that the transformation in the world of political actors lies precisely in this area and that what was once a desirable quality is now an essential one.

A media 'trainer' who worked for one of the main political parties in the 1990s put this change into a broader picture of what was happening in the world of politics:

If we go back to 1990, I think we were just getting over the cusp of moving from representational politics being an amateur game into a professional game. We were just beginning to see people coming up as PPCs who'd never done anything else before. They might have worked for a Trade Union for a bit but it was always that they were going to be a candidate for parliament. … One of our stock interview questions was 'Have you ever had a real job?', and I think in those days it was something you were slightly embarrassed about. We've now got to the point where nobody's embarrassed about that at all anymore. You come out of University having been in Labour Students, you go and work for an MP, you might go and work for the [a policy institute] for a bit, you aspire to being a Ministerial special adviser, and then you get your seat. (Media trainer 1. Personal interview)

Such skills are never enough to guarantee success. Prospective parliamentary candidates are usually an unknown quantity with fairly low profiles and their fortunes are usually affected by the fortunes of the political party nationally. When the political party is doing well, candidates benefit from its fortunes; when it is not, the candidates suffer. Yet, to have a chance of success, candidates must establish themselves and this means working very hard to create a profile. By contrast, sitting MPs have many advantages, not least the established media links and, consequently, the established profile. For both, it is the local rather than the national media that are important, since it is the local media – and the local press in particular – that cover their constituencies, the source of their electoral success. Significantly, a politician's relationship with the local press and other media differs greatly from the adversarial exchange relationship that operates at the national Westminster level: there is not the same degree of animosity and opposition that one finds at the national level. In order to explore how political actors are now learning to handle the media, it is therefore important to distinguish not only between national and local media but also between candidates and sitting MPs. The next section will focus on the prospective parliamentary candidate and the impact of the transition from candidate to successful MP on the relationship with the media. Chapter 8 will consider how the internet changes those established relationships between the MP, the constituency and the 'mainstream' media.

From amateur to professional: transforming prospective parliamentary candidates

How does the invisible recruit become transformed into the confident, astute and ubiquitous politician? What are the stages that take him or her from someone with no 'name recognition' to a regular face on the pages of the local newspaper or on the regular news programme? How does one try to position oneself as a viable contender? As one candidate put it:

> *The challenge I had to overcome was that with a majority of nearly 12,000, the incumbent was able to present my challenge as of little consequence, that is, a mere irritant rather than a serious chance of winning. So my image and demeanour was to try and present myself as a credible candidate who had a real chance of winning the seat.* (Personal interview)

This extract illustrates a more general point that candidates are often selected to fight constituencies only a short while before an election and so find it hard to establish themselves in the local media and in the minds of the local electorate. They have little time to build up a profile and to be seen as credible candidates. This partly explains why parties sometimes try to select candidates well before an election is due in order to provide the candidate with the opportunity to build a profile in the local constituency. However, since candidates are at this stage without an office or an income from constituency politics much of what they do is done voluntarily. Nevertheless, from the point of view of candidates, their task is to establish themselves, make an impact and ensure that they gain the support of local voters. Those who are 'local' clearly have an advantage over those who are 'parachuted in', but both categories benefit or suffer from the state of their political parties nationally. And the parties try to make sure that the candidates develop appropriate media handling skills so that they can build a profile:

> *There are more opportunities for [candidates] to have training, but we tend to provide it ourselves and not on a formal course-style basis, but training is available to anybody who wants more help in dealing with the media, either on an individual basis or in groups of candidates. For example, we might get all the candidates in [the county] together to discuss handling the media, to look at what we are achieving in terms of media, and how we could make it better.* (Party official. Personal interview)

Most candidates take part in training opportunities, although special attention is often paid to those in marginal constituencies where small changes in voting patterns can easily affect the outcome:

in 1995 when I was selected, and I would say that for the greater part of that period, I had no formal training from the Labour Party and only skeletal advice in the '97 campaign. In 2001 it was different. ... In this region, the BS seat was considered to be the one that could be grabbed, and the second seat that received support was [my constituency]. As a result, the regional press officer did put opportunities my way that I hadn't always had in 1995 to 1997. That included the opportunity to do some television ..., some access to radio and some help with statistical and other information that actually gave reinforcement to local stories on issues like policing, health ... but it wasn't regular and sustained briefing of a parliamentary candidate by any stretch of the imagination. It was very ad hoc, and quite often we had to chase the region. Now I don't know if that's any different for a sitting Member, but it was better in 1997 and in 2001 but hardly robust media support for a candidate, unless I suppose, you got in the mire over something. (Personal interview)

There were often criticisms of such training because of its inadequacy and inappropriateness for the situation that prospective parliamentary candidates find themselves in:

Although there is media training, I'm not sure it's all that effective. You can have media training and what you like in front of the TV camera and that's important, but for most candidates it's totally irrelevant, you're not often going to be in front of the TV camera. When you are in the Shadow Cabinet then you can start worrying about it. (Personal interview)

Despite such criticism, it is important to emphasize three points. The first, and more general one, is that at each election the provision of training gets better in the sense that it builds on and enhances what has gone on before. As the candidate quoted above pointed out, things changed for the better between 1997 and 2001. If one looks at the larger picture, one can also observe that the Labour party's media training was very perfunctory in the early 1990s compared to what it became later (personal interview). The second point, and it is a related one, is that all the political parties now see media training as a vital part of what candidates have to experience. This underlines the importance they attach to gaining publicity and using it effectively. The third and final point is that parties constantly review the provision of training and in the process further 'improve' what they have to offer. The respondents from the Head Offices of the three main political parties interviewed in the run-up to the 2005 general election made a point of stressing how the provision of training was constantly under review. For example, one said:

> We're going to run the training a different way [for the 2005 election]. There will be a series of training modules where account holders can buy into a course that they want. But also we will identify the training needs of the individual, so we will create a much more rounded person by training them up in the certain aspects rather than trying to define a finished product, and a lot of that will be media training dependent upon the seats we go to. It is very clear to us that certain candidates will get a lot of media attention because they are in certain key seats; it's just one of those things, coaching and training will be encouraged more there. (Senior party officer. Personal interview)

Another said:

> We have moved away from offering blanket training, blanket targets ... We will steer away from one standard. ... We are trying to individualise it [and] the [regional agents/coordinators] are there to monitor and see what shape the campaign is in and where more effort is needed. (Senior party officer. Personal interview)

The 'one size fits all' template fails to address anything more than a general awareness of media-related issues.

Despite the growing importance of the media in politics and the growing awareness of the media in the lives of candidates for election, it is still worth stressing that the media play only a part in the whole election strategy of candidates at local level. British electoral political communication, like electoral political communication in other Western democracies, is essentially of a national character. The political parties compete against one another in the media at the national level and candidates who have to fight in local constituencies can do little to buck the overall national trend. This does not mean that they can do nothing, but that what they can do takes place within a much bigger contest and they have to find ways of establishing themselves not only as credible candidates but as candidates whose concerns are local and deeply felt. This explains, in part, the strategy of the Liberal Democrat Party which puts the emphasis on placing candidates in constituencies well before an election and engaging in forms of local politics as a means of alerting voters to the existence of someone who lives in and cares for the local community. Whilst the media are clearly crucial in establishing those credentials, other dimensions of local politics and campaigning such as canvassing, good local organization, meeting local dignitaries and so on are never far behind.

So, whilst attention is paid to the media as a way of generating publicity, even in the 21st century the basic lessons of electoral competition and the 'foot soldiers' of political parties remain important for they are the points of contact between the party candidate and the individual voter. Party organizers are aware of the importance of such activities and of good organization; more so today, given that the circulation of the local press is in decline and that local broadcast media rarely fill the gap. Such activities might not buck the national trend but they could be critical in tightly fought contests or useful as a means of establishing a presence in a community. In this respect, while the provision of extensive training marks a transformation from what had gone on before, in other respects there are many similarities between the activities of the modern MP and one from three or so decades ago. The means of communication have changed radically in that period but the basic principles of how to get elected are still very similar. This is particularly true when we consider what contemporary MPs do, and those in the recent past did, to obtain publicity and to get themselves in the public eye.

From candidate to MP

If a prospective parliamentary candidate wins a seat, he or she finds that the relationship with the local media changes rapidly and radically. Firstly, the media become more attentive:

> Yes [the relationship with the local press] has to some extent [changed]. I think there's a more instant natural receptivity, a more natural instant willingness to listen to what you have to say or to take the call, and moreover you're expected to have a view on things. ... Well that didn't used to happen to the same extent when I was a PPC. (Cons. MP, elected 2001. Personal interview)

Secondly, the media becomes more of an accomplice than an adversary:

There is a feeling, I would say, that the local press get on much better with local MPs, maybe because there is a common goal hopefully and what we found is the Labour MPs in particular are keen on promoting the city in Westminster, and we think that is a good thing. (Journalist, north of England. Personal interview)

Recalling how one minister had got into trouble with the national broadcast media, a journalist explained that *'he wouldn't have had that problem with us, and I think he would have felt protected by us, that we would have stuck up for him, and I think we probably did on that occasion'*. (Journalist, central England. Personal interview)

Whilst other journalists would probably not phrase things in this particular way, the way local journalists work and the evidence collected in the course of this research does suggest that local journalists more often than not act as recipients, or conduits, of information. Many of the MPs interviewed in the course of the research reported, for example, how they had developed strategies that enabled them to get their stories, almost unaltered, into the local paper. These strategies give us an insight not only into how MPs learn to use the local media but also into how the local press, and local journalists, work. The strategies also reveal the fairly limited political role of the press in the local community. They are mostly based around a set of practices that create favourable circumstances for getting stories into the local media, and the local press in particular. These practices include:

- Getting to 'know' the local media and journalists (both local and those based in Westminster who provide coverage for the local paper).
- Knowing what they require in respect of local news stories, human interest stories, national concerns morphing into local events/ stories, and quotes.
- Knowing how to get the story to the local press, for example email with attachments. The better the material sent, the less effort required by the journalist to alter it prior to publication.
- Being organized, prepared, able to communicate clearly and simply.
- Being always available.
- Knowing one's audience (reporters, local voters and so on).

One candidate described his experiences in 2001:

We had a local daily newspaper which I found absolutely critical. I think a weekly newspaper would have been very, very different, but because they were daily they had space for political articles and were willing to follow current issues, which in a weekly you don't get.

I compiled a directory for myself of the [media's] fax numbers and of their email addresses and I set myself the task of putting out two or three press releases every single week to them on whatever topic: current affairs, local issues primarily. They were always much more interested in local issues than they were in national issues, and even if you tried to do a national story you always needed to do a local angle, otherwise it wouldn't get covered. And, I just followed that up by phoning them. They very rarely picked up stories simply from a press release, but if I went into their office or phoned a journalist that I knew that would often turn into a story. [Personal contact] was the most important thing to be honest. Phoning journalists always proved more effective than simply broadcasting to them via a fax or an email. (Personal interview)

On the whole, local politicians – and others – need to remind themselves that journalists working for local newspapers (and other news media) have a greater degree of freedom to decide what is 'newsworthy' particularly when the medium is a monopoly. If it is the only source of news in town, so to speak, it will be hungry for news, more so if it is a daily or regular news outlet. On the other hand, it being the only source of news in town puts pressure on local politicians to make sure that their news items fit in with the news medium's agenda and preferences, including political preferences.

There are two other points that need to be made alongside the above. The first is that it would be wrong to suggest here that MPs from an earlier generation were not knowledgeable about how to use the local media, then mainly the local press. While the aspiring politician of today is constantly being made aware of the need to learn how to manage the media, the MPs of yesteryear could also use the local press and many had developed their own strategies for doing so, although the nature of the local media was very different even as recently as the 1970s. Local news media today are, by and large, politics-free zones; they cover less politics than they used to and they are less inclined to pursue politicians than they used to. That change is captured in the quote below from an MP who first entered the House in the 1970s, and it contrasts neatly with the quote above relating to 2001:

When I was first elected for [Town] in 1970, the press used to come to us. ... The big change is that you now have to go to them. They were in fact, prepared to come and see you, prepared to listen to you and they wrote the story. Now, of course, you have to write the story that you want for them so that they are now the listeners and you are the journalist, if I can put it that way, and I think that's altogether bad, quite frankly. (Personal interview)

What binds MPs from the recent past with contemporary MPs is not only the appreciation of the local media in the election contests – although even here there are reservations about how useful they are – but also their more critical role between elections. Whilst election contests are in progress, the local press and media now tend to adopt a fairly impartial attitude towards all the candidates which means that no one candidate gets very special treatment. There will be some variations in coverage but these will not be so blatantly obvious that they enrage any of the political parties to such an extent that protests become the order of the day (Negrine, 2005). That being so, the value of the local press and media can be seen as limited in spite of all the attention they get, from media trainers right down to candidates who wish to build up a profile.

Where the local media do come into their own is in respect of building a profile for the sitting MP, a profile which may be of use when the next election comes around. The experiences of two MPs, one from the 1970s and one from 2003 are instructive:

In the election campaign itself, of very little importance at all ... because they were concerned with, much more with, the national issues ... [and] ... once the election was called they basically used to allocate to every candidate an equal amount of space during the course of the three weeks of the campaign, on an entirely neutral basis, ... The value of the local media was not in the election campaign itself, it was in the long time I was always in Parliament, ... when they would report basically whatever you did or said provided it had, particularly if it had, some local significance. ('Old' MP. Personal interview)

I ... don't particularly bother with the national press. I suppose you might think to send something to the national press, but no, the local press, local media is really what we are interested in. The thing for me as a new MP is getting my name into people's conscience basically, and you know I am the MP and people recognise me and you just have to keep doing that. ... it probably takes 10 to 20 times of people seeing your picture and hearing your name before it registers, so we just try and get something in every week, at least once a week. (Sitting MP. Personal interview)

Whilst the above set of practices is based on the experiences of interviewees, the extent to which it is scrupulously adhered to is another matter altogether. Generally speaking, the local political reporters identified a whole range of practices that covered both those who were supremely active and successful in generating publicity but also those who did almost nothing. And once reporters began to reflect on the activities of the MPs covered by their respective newspapers, it became clear that MPs were far from uniform in the way they dealt with the media or sought publicity. If anything, the reporters' reflections highlighted the variety of skills possessed and the fact that the local press very often played a secondary role in the lives of local MPs. For example:

I took a straw poll in the [newspaper's] office to find out various opinions. The general conclusion [amongst the reporters] is that they [the MPs] could all do a lot better. Some are better than others at being proactive. The best ones we have are LL [a minister] and MM [a minister] and, from my point of view, NN who does very very well indeed by personal contact. NN contacts the office regularly by email. OO has to be chased all the time. If I want something out of OO I have to find him. I don't recall very often in the last few years that he has approached us with anything. PP we hear very little from. He will send the odd fax, but we don't get much supply. LL is more likely out of the six MPs in the area to phone you with a story or a reaction. MM and NN phone directly also but LL phones the most. NN (or their office) contacts by email. (Journalist, eastern England. Personal interview. See also Negrine, 2005)

This reflects not so much a disdain for the local media as a sense that there are other things to do and that the local media, although important, are not always the highest priority. Except, that is, when there are assistants and helpers who may be able to deal with the media on your behalf, something which happens in many of the offices of MPs today.

Summary and conclusion

The above discussion has focused almost entirely on the activities of MPs and candidates in local constituencies just after the 2001 general election and, in some cases, in anticipation of the 2005 election. At the time, the most important forms of local communication were the 'traditional' ones: the local press and local radio. Regional television – Britain does not really have 'local' television – covers too wide a geographic spread to be of great importance to an MP, although it has its uses for raising his or her regional and national profile. The internet and emails, web pages and blogs were still in their infancy inasmuch as they had not yet become part of the fabric of either national or local politics. Moves were being made in that direction but it was not something that was widespread, or as widespread and commonplace as it was to be in 2008.

Have these newer forms of communication altered things so significantly as to require a complete reassessment of the key arguments developed above? The short answer is probably 'no' and for three main reasons.

The first and most obvious answer relates to the take-up of the internet and its global character as opposed to the character of the truly local press or radio. Whilst it may be interesting to find out about a Sheffield MP, as someone living in a Leicester constituency I cannot do very much with that information. In that sense, the local media remains of significance in the context of local politics since it is also highly unlikely that in a medium-sized city which has a local newspaper readership of, say, 300,000, that many voters are going to look at their candidates websites!

Second, just as media 'trainers' had to familiarize aspiring politicians with the ways of television in the 1950s, much more so in the 1960s and 1970s and still more so in the 1990s, they continue to do so, but have added the internet to their arsenal of election campaigning. In other words, newer media are added to the existing forms of communication and are used as, and when, necessary to get messages across to the public.

Third, politicians, aspiring or otherwise, make use of old and new media to get their messages across when the need to do so arises. In this respect, it would be wrong to see one medium completely replacing another; in practice, political actors use different media in different ways to ensure that their messages get across, their profiles are raised and their comments find a wider audience. The objectives remain the same even though the precise mix of media alters from one period to another and from one context to another. It is not surprising, therefore, that in the 2005 general election the media and campaigning mix was not very different from what it had been a decade earlier: canvassing, leafleting, local press/media coverage, knocking on doors, (small) meetings, shaking hands in shopping centres and so on.

These reasons should not be taken to mean that the internet is unimportant. It may be of less value during election contests than local media but, just as the local press is important for sitting MPs during the life of a parliament, the internet allows the possibility for a conversation with voters and local media alike. An MP's website – now de rigueur for all MPs – will let constituents know what is going on and how to reach the MP, but it is also a useful source of information for the local media. One of the MPs interviewed in 2003 had gone so far as to strike a deal with his local paper that it could download any text or images it wanted without seeking prior permission!

It may be that, in time, the internet grows in importance but it is difficult to imagine it as a regular source of political information for constituents. That is why the 'old' local media still have a place in local politics. The problem for political parties and MPs – and indeed constituents – is that the local press is in decline and, as we have seen above, less keen on politics than it has ever been. The consequences for the conduct of elections in the future is significant: will the national mediated election become even more critical as the local becomes no more than an extension of what happens elsewhere, and where will we find information about our locality?

Future politicians will no doubt be completely au fait with how to manage the media, including how to create a website and blog, just as in the past they picked up new skills when these were needed. Unlike the situation in the past, perhaps, there is now more expectation of preparedness and competence in these skills. This is the transformation that has been central to the discussion in this chapter. Parties can no longer expect their candidates to be truly inspired amateurs with a love of politics. Too much is at stake; which is why political parties nationally are more organized than they ever were, and more dirigiste than they ever were. In this, the new technologies undoubtedly help them achieve their objectives, namely, ensuring continuous communication with candidates and control over candidates, as well as the newly acquired skills of targeting constituencies, emailing supporters and so on. At the local, individual level, though, the new and old methods somehow manage to operate next to each other:

I guess the kind of techniques that we're using can be seen as being more professional, but in many respects the things that I was doing as a non-target seat parliamentary candidate, were the things that had been done for decades, using the local media, knocking on doors, producing my own material, obviously using more high-tech techniques, better photos and what have you, and in the 2001 Election email was an amazing revelation really. I think if you were to take a target seat … you would just be bowled over by the professionalism as with any target seat. … It's just a hive of activity – you're targeting, the segmentation, the messages – but if you go back to where I was standing, very little had changed, I would argue, from an historic perspective, for at least a number of decades, and the one thing that changed in 2001 was with email, and with the extranet, that suddenly you were presented with all of your leaflets, designed for you. I can very easily see 5, 10, 15 years down the line, computers have improved, you've got the whole constituency on a database, segmentation, and sending out letters and targeting people will become easier and easier and easier, and it seems that the technology is speeding up the process of being more professional …
(Candidate. Personal interview)

Transforming Government Communication

6

When you are in Opposition for 18 years, as we were, there was a tendency (because this is the way that Opposition works) that you believe the announcement is the reality. ... I think for the first period of time in Government there was a tendency to believe, as it were, that the same situation still applied. It does not, in fact. For Government the announcement is merely the intention; the reality is what you have to go on and deliver on the ground. I think ... doing it this way, making sure that we have more ministerial statements, making sure that we try and find new ways of reaching out in direct conversation with people is a way of overcoming what is perceived, I think, often unfairly, as issues to do simply with news management. (Prime Minister Tony Blair, 2001)

Introduction

In democratic political systems, it is taken for granted that governments – and here one includes the whole apparatus of government and its administration – will communicate with their citizens in some way or other. At the most basic level, governments need to communicate information to citizens: information about safety and security, health and education, and a whole range of seemingly apolitical concerns. But governments are about more than the transmission of apolitical information, say, the need for 'flu jabs. Governments come to power with principles, policies and proposals. These could include proposals for reforming schools or hospitals, road pricing or taxation, and governments need to communicate these also. Whilst the first type of information may be deemed to be essentially apolitical and hence uncontroversial, the second type of information is anything but; it can be a matter of controversy as it becomes embroiled in an

117

altogether more complex and highly charged political process where oppositional groups contest claims and outcomes, costs and consequences. As this sort of government information becomes mediated and mediatized (Mazzoleni and Schulz, 1999) it becomes a subject of scrutiny and debate.

It is possible to argue, therefore, that one of the transformations that has taken place in the conduct of political communication has been the realization that governments, at least if they wish to be in charge of their own destiny, can no longer take a disinterested approach to the generation, production and dissemination of information. Governments, in other words, must exercise some measure of control not only over how information is produced but also how it is communicated to the public. This is one side of the coin that Tony Blair is referring to in the quote at the top of this chapter; the other side, though, is the sense that such activity can be perceived negatively. But achieving some sort of balance is critical and never easy, also something acknowledged by Blair.

The fact that governments – and it is now truly all governments – have arrived at such conclusions shows the extent to which techniques of public relations have infiltrated all aspects of public life, alongside an understanding of the inherent dangers.

The speed with which such techniques have been incorporated into public life has been dramatic: it is, for example, a mere 30 years between the Conservative Party's innovative use of Harvey Thomas, a public relations/events producer, to stage Mrs Thatcher's appearances at its conference in the 1970s (Thomas and Gill, 1989) and the slick, colour-coordinated, technically sophisticated events of the 21st century. In that period, much has been learned about what 'works' and what does not, how best to stage events to exploit settings, styles and personalities and how best to craft messages and image. What has been learned is a critical part of what Mannheim calls 'strategic political communication' which:

> incorporates the use of sophisticated knowledge of such attributes of human behavior as attitude and preference structures, cultural tendencies, and media-use patterns – as well as knowledge of such relevant organizational behaviors as how news organizations make decisions regarding news content and how congressional committees schedule and structure hearings – to shape and target messages so as to maximize their desired impact while minimizing undesired collateral effects. (1994: 7)

Whilst many of these practices, at least in an embryonic form, can be traced to the early 20th century (see, for example, Kelley, 1956, and the discussion in Chapter 4), there are strong indications that the contemporary 'management of political information' differs in important respects from this earlier period. One indication of this is the 'sudden growth' (Davis, 2002: 19; Miller and Dinan, 2000; see also Jones, 2006) in the public relations sector in Britain from the 1970s onwards which has increased both its density and penetration into all aspects of public and private life; another is 'the intensity and the degree of professionalism with which it is conducted by all social actors, from terrorists to trade unions, and prime ministers to pop stars' (McNair, 2004: 327).

The reminder that 'all social actors' are now engaged in the management of information draws our attention to the fact that it is not only governments who are engaged in such activities: corporations, civic movements, trade unionists and the like are now adept at managing public communication in what Davis (2002: Chapter 6) calls our 'public relations democracy'. Not only are such bodies now more likely to employ people to undertake these tasks but the necessary knowledge to carry them out is probably so widely dispersed nowadays that nearly everyone has learned some of the basic skills of effective communication.

Seen in this much broader context, it becomes easier to understand the changes that have taken place in recent years across the full range of public relations and communication professions. Put simply, the interrelations and interconnections between communications activities in commerce and political communication permit both personnel and practices to move across thin membranes that do little to keep them apart: advertising personnel 'colonize' politics, public relations personnel intermingle with journalists, journalists move into public relations and so on, as on a Möbius strip. An example of such networks came to light when Google announced its intention to play a part in American politics. It emerged that it had:

> hired Rachel Whetstone to head its European communications and public affairs team in London. A former political secretary to Michael Howard [former leader of the Conservative Party] ... Her partner is Steve Hilton, Cameron's [leader of the Conservative Party 2005–] head of strategy ... Whetstone is also a founder of the PR firm Portland, which Google uses in Europe. The head of Portland, Tim Allan, is a former deputy to Alastair Campbell [Blair's spokesperson in the 1990s] and knows his way around the corridors of power as a lobbyist for BSkyB. (Wray, 2006)

Aside from the implications of such relationships for the health of a democratic polity, the movement of personnel between commerce and politics (and media) can give rise to a situation where the public becomes no more than a target for information managed by like-minded, politically astute, media-savvy professionals. This, and the media's culpability in the processing of managed information, is the subject of the concluding part of this chapter.

The first part of this chapter will outline some of the changes that have taken place in the past 50 or so years that can be taken to represent a transformation in the ways in which a range of bodies communicate with the public. By drawing attention to this broader context, it will become easier to understand why – and how – governments from the 1980s onwards became more conscious of the need to manage their communication activities in a proactive and professional way.

The second part of this chapter will examine the ways in which the New Labour government of 1997 overhauled the communications infrastructure of government. In effect, the New Labour government brought about a major change in the way that politics and the communication of politics was conducted at the Westminster political level and also in the way that it was covered by the media. The importance of New Labour and its approach to communication cannot be overestimated, since it did bring about a transformation in the communications infrastructure. This not only reflected a desire to 'professionalize' the service but also to ensure that it could be driven – from the top down by a 'new style' of Prime Minister (Rose, 2001: 3; see also Seymour-Ure, 2003) – to deliver the agenda for change.

But the new infrastructure also gave rise to a paradox in modern political communication. On the one hand, it saw the widespread use of an allegedly new type of professional communicator ('spin doctor' or 'special adviser') in the governmental machine, yet, on the other hand, it also saw an increase in media interest in, and increased critical comment on, the practice and content of government communication (for example 'spin'). As Brian McNair has argued in his review of 'spin' and the media in the period 1997–2004, 'the regularity with which spin and PR-related stories emerged in the UK's mainstream news media meant that the activities of political PR practitioners were rarely far from the top of the domestic news agenda' (2004: 326). What was initially a success story, in time became a critique of a government per se!

The primary theme of this chapter, then, is that changes in the communication of government information in the British context have accelerated in recent decades as governments have had to confront more ubiquitous media. Those changes can, at times, be likened to transformations, as new refined practices and ways of looking at communications issues have become embedded. Once those changes have taken place, it will be argued, it becomes difficult to undo them. Indeed, it is a moot point as to whether those who follow would ever want to undo them. This explains, in part, why the current juncture (2008–9) in British political communication is so fascinating: will the major changes brought about by New Labour since 1997 be undone by a successor government? And, if not, what does that tell us about the nature of political communication in the modern era?

The secondary theme of this chapter is the extent to which changes brought about since New Labour came to power in 1997 represent a transformation per se rather than a greater professionalization of practices that have been in use in previous decades. As with other chapters in this book, it is important to explore not only the present configuration of forces but also the broader historical and political context so as to have a better understanding of the significance of change.

Managing communication

Since the 1970s, there has been growing academic interest in the fact that professional advisers have taken on significant roles in the process of mediating communication to a wider public. Whether the interest lay in the actions of those who played a part in the communication of politics – the advertisers and consultants who came to play a role in election campaigns such as Saatchi & Saatchi in the 1970s, or the plethora of advisers who helped Richard Nixon in the 1968 presidential election (McGinnis, 1970) or those who played a part in corporate communications (see Gandy, 1982) – the underlying theme that was being exposed to the light was the strategic and professional way in which information was being managed.

One of the early excursions into this field of study was Oscar Gandy's work on 'information subsidies' in the US, and the:

> attempt to produce influence over the actions of others by controlling their access to and use of information relevant to those actions. This information is characterized as a subsidy because the source of that information causes it to be made available at something less than the cost a user would face in the absence of the subsidy. ... The journalist

receives a direct information subsidy, and the target in government (or elsewhere) receives an indirect subsidy when the information is read in the paper or heard on the news. (1982: 61–2)

The extent to which such activities had become commonplace in government and elsewhere is well documented by Gandy and there is a degree of awe in the face of the data that he produced, for example, 'at least 3,300 government workers whose principal goal is the generation of public information', and 'the flood of information [emanating] from government agencies' (1982: 73–4). But it is the underlying themes of the study that have a contemporary feel to them, namely, the fact that 'public information specialists, or "flacks," ... have gotten considerably more sophisticated in their use of public media channels to deliver an agency's message' (1982: 78).

Whilst Gandy was principally chronicling changes in the US, it is clear that similar changes were taking place in Britain. According to Davis, 'the corporate PR industry expanded at unprecedented rates in the 1980s', so much so that 'over the five year period, (1979–1984) it became the norm rather than the exception for top companies to use PR' (2002: 23). While the labour and trade union movement as a whole is comparatively much weaker than the corporate sector, there are strong indications that it too has began to appreciate the importance of PR for the purposes of advancing its cause and of the need to employ PR professionals to make its case (Davis, 2002, Chapter 6).

At the governmental level, there is also some evidence to show the increased attention given to communication activities. Figures quoted by Aeron Davis give the advertising budget of the Central Office of Information (COI) – the British governmental body in charge of expenditure on advertising – as £27 million in 1979 but £150 million in 1988, whilst its spending on advertising was £44 million in 1979 but £85 million in 1988 (2002: 20; see also Newton, 2001). The Phillis Review put the 2003–4 figure at £230 million (2004: 9). These increases must, however, be seen in the context of an explosion of media outlets and an expansion in governmental activity, but it is nonetheless fairly obvious that expenditure on advertising in all its forms has increased. In 2006, the *Daily Telegraph* (Wilson, 2006) revealed that 'the Labour Government spent £154 million on advertising over the past 12 months' and that 'Whitehall is the country's third biggest advertiser ... only Unilever and Procter & Gamble managed to outspend the government.' The same report also suggested that there were now '3,200 press officers and other PR staff in Whitehall, government departments and agencies' (Wilson, 2006). Although this figure has been disputed – it includes press officers as well as PR staff who work in government agencies that operate separately from government – and the report has been criticized for implying that all the staff work directly for government in an overt or covert governmental and political ('spinning') capacity, the trend seems obvious: more effort now goes into communications activities, more staff are dealing with communications activities, and more money is spent on those activities.

A number of reasons may account for the increases both in expenditure and staff. An important one is undoubtedly the changed nature of the media landscape both in terms of its round-the-clock character but also in terms of the proliferation of outlets. In 1990 Britain, there were only four terrestrial television channels to supply with news reports, press releases and interviewees at set and fairly regular time periods; a mere 15 years later, there were five terrestrial television channels and a number of 24/7 digital services (BBC News 24, Sky News, ITV News, CNN) and numerous web outlets. A second possible reason that may go some way towards explaining *some* of the increased expenditure suggests that governments use publicity in a political way and for their own benefit rather than simply for the purpose of informing citizens. For instance, there have been claims that expenditure on advertising campaigns has been politically motivated inasmuch as some of it has taken place in advance of elections. In a BBC *Panorama* programme transmitted in 2002, claims were made that expenditure on recruitment for nursing, for example, was tinged with political motives and could be seen as implicitly supporting the government's position in respect of the health service. (*Panorama*, 2002) While such claims can obviously be countered – as they were – they are suggestive of the way in which expenditure can often have political overtones.

A third reason why expenditure on communications-related activities has increased is that New Labour increased the number of special advisers, from around 30 in the mid-1990s to 74 in 2006 involving an expenditure of some of £5.9 million (Hansard, 2005–6). In a related way, the number of staff in the Number Ten office had also increased quite substantially (see below, p. 140). A fourth reason could be that governments and government agencies are generally responding to the increase in PR and communications-related activities that is taking place across all sectors of business and industry. As other organizations professionalize their communications activities, governments and government bodies have to do likewise. Given that 'the expansion of public relations activity targeted at governments' (Miller and Dinan, 2000: 13) took place in the 1980s and after, it follows that governments had to respond in kind. One can speculate, therefore, that the view held by many in the early 1990s that the governmental communications machinery was 'not fit for purpose' reflected the lack of progress on modernizing the service and bringing it to the operational level existing outside government prior to New Labour taking office in 1997. (See below, pp. 125–30 for a discussion of this point).

Whatever the precise reasons behind the increased numbers of professional communication workers in government as elsewhere, there is enough evidence to argue that from sometime in the 1980s onwards it became commonplace to devote more attention to communication as part of policy-making, governing and public advocacy. It may not be a coincidence, therefore, to observe that the emergence of the 'new phenomenon' – the so-called 'spin doctor' – has been located in this period (Sumpter and Tankard, 1994). Not that 'spin' as the 'attempt to ensure that information is understood and interpreted in a way in which the person conveying it desires' (Seymour-Ure, 2003: 150) is anything new. It was merely a coincidence of factors – leaks by individuals, overzealous partisan lobbying on the part of ministers, overblown assessments of their roles, self-promotion – that made it both newsworthy and lamentable. And the more it was written about, the more it acquired the quality of something unspeakable and pernicious, to the point where everything was seen to be spin and/or the result of spinning. As Lance Price, a one-time New Labour spin doctor, observed, 'in politics … spin became synonymous with every sort of news management and manipulation whether legitimate or not (Price, 2006: xxvi).

However, if we step back from the view of 'spin' as something inherently bad and reprehensible, what we have is a broadbrush representation of a changing communications machinery, both outside government in the corporate world but also inside government. Other sectors, such as higher education, have also taken a leaf out of the books of the communication specialists and have sought to promote themselves in all sorts of ways. Which university, for example, has not wrestled with updating its image, is not creating a new corporate identity, creating a uniform public visibility and so on. Why they have done so is a bigger question that deserves its own study (see Wernick, 1994) but the underlying intent is the same as in government or the corporate sector: to control and so create a public profile that is positively received and garners the support of the intended customers, be they consumers, students or voters.

New Labour and government communication: controlling and managing the process

In retrospect, it is clear that when New Labour first took office in 1997, it failed to appreciate the deep significance of the distinction in respect of media practices between being in opposition and being in power, as the statement from Tony Blair at the beginning of this chapter illustrates. Whilst in opposition, it ran a very professional media operation: it was focused on the task of gaining power and it was run as a tight, efficient organization that would not be deflected from its primary objective of getting New Labour elected. This is clearly underlined in Philip Gould's comment that Unless you handle the media well, you cannot govern competently.' (Philip Gould, quoted in Rose, 2001: 6). As Richard Rose observed: 'In Opposition Tony Blair had created an "organizational weapon" to transform the Labour Party, and he brought to Whitehall a command-and-control strategy for Whitehall' (2001: 39). But transferring that organization from opposition to government was a much more problematic task than had originally been assumed and for two very different reasons.

The first reason has already been touched on, namely, that the task of running a government is very different from being in opposition. Governments are more active, are buffeted by events, and are populated by individuals who are both colleagues and competitors. Things, in other words, are less easy to control and efforts to control are likely to prove counter-productive as the controversies over government 'spin' clearly show. Furthermore, attempts to show that the government is constantly acting can also become problematic as the signals and signs of activity can soon lose all meaning. Tom Clark, a former government adviser, described Blair's approach to services as 'at times … hyperactive and divisive. His great fear was that voters would not credit the government with steady improvements in health and education. Controversies were whipped up simply to show that something was being done.' (2006).

The second reason why transferring the 'organizational weapon' into office was problematic, relates to a government's structures and procedures. In the British political system, there is a permanent, 'impartial' Civil Service with its own staffing, procedures and history. Incoming governments have to find ways of working with this structure and the personnel within it. Importing into government a combative and politically motivated organization such as New Labour's communications operation in Millbank, London, would pit the traditional system of governance – impartial service, loyalties to individual Ministers and so on – against a government that sought to bring about political change in its own way. The tension between the two were/are difficult to reconcile as testified by the ongoing controversies over government special advisers (and spin doctors) that have dogged New Labour since it came to office in 1997. (See, for example, Blick, 2004; Franklin, 1998; Jones, 1999; Phillis, 2004).

But identifying the problem of transferring one style of organization into another as essentially a clash of cultures minimizes what is perhaps more significant about New Labour's coming to power and its communications strategies and requirements. New Labour, whilst in opposition, had learned to operate – that is, use, manage, manipulate, control – the media and to act and react to the requirements of the contemporary media landscape in a way that could not be matched by the then existing Civil Service machinery. For an incoming government intent on reform, a Civil Service that lacked professional communication skills could become an obstacle to driving through the government's agenda. According to Seldon, 'Whilst still in opposition [Alastair] Campbell [who became Prime Minister Press Spokesman in 1997] had formed a poor opinion of the Government Information Service (GIS) … he thought the GIS was insufficiently active in anticipating the demands of a twenty-four-hour news media' (2005: 301). It was also generally not up to the job of enabling a government to meet its communications objectives, objectives that were inextricably linked with its policy objectives since policy and its presentation were no longer seen as separate. New Labour, in other words, could not avoid reforming, and transforming, the Civil Service information machinery.

If we place these considerations alongside one another, we can better begin to understand the changes in New Labour's communications management strategy since 1997. There was a strong desire to reform the communications infrastructure of government so as to create an efficient, proactive organization that could also respond to prime ministerial steering. This led to the setting up of the inquiry into the Government Information Service (GIS) and the subsequent 1997 report (the Mountfield Report). The reforms that came about and the overzealous actions of some of those in charge of New Labour's communications strategies produced their own (adverse) reaction. Managing the media became a subject of intense concern, along with 'spin' and those 'special advisers' who were reputed to 'work in the dark'. In order to meet and deal with the whole raft of issues and controversies that came to the surface as a direct outcome of the communications strategy, a committee was appointed to look at the issues and recommend changes. The report that followed – henceforth the Phillis Committee report (Phillis Review, 2004) – was generally well received and it now sits alongside a myriad of Parliamentary and other reports and commentaries on 'special advisers', 'spin' and government communications.

Whether these reports and commentaries are merely the outcome of a process of convulsive change is perhaps a less interesting question than the expected 'what if' one: if the changes introduced by New Labour have been so problematic – controversial, distasteful, dysfunctional, anti-democratic, coming out of a culture of control and centralization and so on – will they all be undone? Or, as is more likely, will subsequent governments only tinker with the system once they have recognized that change has taken place for specific and possibly even sound reasons and that, ultimately, one does not really wish to go back to practices that are out of place in the contemporary technological and sociopolitical environment.

While it is impossible to answer this question – at least not at the time of writing in 2008 – one of the underlying themes of this chapter is that the changes that have taken place can be seen, and even possibly justified, as meaningful in the context of a new government coming to power; and furthermore, that the changes are not necessarily as dysfunctional as has been portrayed, particularly in accounts written in the 'heat of the moment'; and, finally, that one cannot separate wider political imperatives and styles of government from the communications infrastructures that support them, and that the key may be to try and find some balance between political advocates, on the one hand, and neutral servants of the state, on the other. Before we arrive at that stage, however, we need to locate those points of change that have occurred since New Labour came to power in 1997 and transformed the communications infrastructure.

The Mountfield Report and the Phillis Review

One of the major transformations within the British government communications machinery came with the election of New Labour in 1997 and the publication, and subsequently implementation, of a series of reports and reviews on government communication. The Mountfield Report (1997) can be seen as significant in setting the tone for the operation of government post-1997. The changes that followed, and the widespread use of 'special advisers' under New Labour, was seen by many as bringing about a transformation in the way in which governments tried to control, and drive, the agenda.

Soon after New Labour came to power, an inquiry was set up to look at the Government Information Service (GIS) with the aim, primarily, of reforming it so as to make it fit for the purpose of the new government (Mountfield Report, 1997). The Mountfield Report was clearly prompted by the experience of New Labour when it was in opposition and, according to Seldon, Alastair Campbell's view that the Government Information Service was not up to the task of driving through a government agenda in the dying years of the mediated 20th century (see quote above, p. 126). But the changes, according to Nic Jones (1999), were also prompted by other motives and these included the desire to exert greater centralized control on information so as to ensure that everyone across government would speak with one voice.

In this scenario, the Mountfield Committee was a means of achieving that end and, at the same time, to deal with the series of leaks, media problems and accusations of damaging the Civil Service tradition of political impartiality that the New Labour government encountered in its first few months in office. Nic Jones believes that 'asking a top civil servant (Mountfield) to undertake what could be presented as an arm's-length review was an astute move by the New Labour administration, in view of the accusations of politicisation' (1999: 103). It was, in his view, a set-up and the conclusions of the report – and it should be remembered that Campbell sat on the committee – were not likely to be out of line from what Campbell had wished to create. Jones quotes Jill Rutter, at the time Head of Communications at the Treasury, as saying: '... [Mountfield] was a cop-out for the benefit of Alastair Campbell. It's fine if the Labour Party want to spend their money on publicity but it's an entirely different matter for the state to provide a huge government machine for Labour' (1999: 217).

But it can also be argued that Alastair Campbell's view of the GIS was perhaps less heretical than might be supposed. Sir Christopher Meyer, John Major's Press Secretary (1992–4), revealed the parlous state of Downing Street's media operation in his book *DC Confidential*:

When I arrived at No. 10, I assumed that there was a well-oiled machine that would deliver newspapers to my doorstep. No such machine existed. When I asked about arrangements for getting the papers to me before I left for work, the reaction was, 'You must be joking – make your own arrangements like everyone else.'

As for getting the first editions the night before, it was as if I was asking for caviar and lobster in a fish and chip shop. It was horrible.

Half my brain would be tuned to the BBC *Today* programme on the car radio, while by the time we got to Downing Street I was ready to throw up from car sickness.

This was typical of Downing Street. Tradition is one thing, amateurish improvisation another. It took an election victory like Blair's and a force of nature like Alastair Campbell to sweep away the barnacles and cobwebs from the No. 10 press operation. (2006: 13–14)

The Select Committee on Public Administration made some equally critical comments in its *Sixth Report*. It observed that 'The Mountfield Report noted its authors' agreement with the view that within many departments "insufficient emphasis is placed by civil servants involved in policy development on the communication strategy that every important initiative or decision will require. Some observers have noted something approaching disdain for media and communications matters." We consider the lack of interest in communications matters (where it is relevant) by some civil servants to be a serious issue which needs to be addressed ...' (Public Administration Select Committee, 1998a: para. 12).

For many, the case for reform was immensely strong. The Mountfield Report, more of which below, not only endorsed the case for reform but also set out a framework for it. Not surprisingly, perhaps, its recommendations placed New Labour's advisers in key positions. Alastair Campbell was given the role of Chief Press Secretary in 1997 and there was a view that his appointment as a special adviser meant that he was 'not formally bound by Civil Service rules regarding objectivity and impartiality' (Blick, 2004: 286). He was, in his own words, 'freer than my predecessors' to rebut political attacks on the Prime Minister (quoted in Blick, 2004: 287).

Other appointed special advisers in the New Labour government also took on the role of giving political advice to ministers and to frequently dealing with the media. Whether this represented a very significant departure from the past, a politicization of the Civil Service and a radically different way of treating the Civil Service, ministers and the public is a matter for discussion and debate. Andrew Blick's study of special advisers post-1945 is perhaps more balanced than any of the extreme opposing views put forward. As he points out, 'ever since 1964 special advisers had taken an interest in public relations, which could entail, as well as functions such as planning presentational strategy and speech-writing, the maintenance of contact with journalists' (2004: 265). In the same chapter, he quotes Mike

Grannatt, Head of the Profession of the Government Information and Communication Service (GICS) as estimating that in the late 1990s 'about 40' (of approximately 80) special advisers dealt with the media (2004: 265–6). Although not a large figure, it is regarded as significant given their location and clustering in the governmental machinery, for example Downing Street, key departments and so on. At one point in 1998, four ex-*Daily Mirror* journalists – Campbell being one of the four – were working on government publicity (Jones, 1997: 215). The location and clustering may also be significant because of the fact that they have dealings with a tight media world comprising a dozen newspapers, a handful of television services and a 'Westminster Village culture' where dissent, rumours and gossip circulate freely, easily and speedily. So, whilst the numbers themselves may not be significant, the concentration and absence of media diversity – and habits of 'pack journalism' – may exaggerate their importance (see Tunstall, 1996).

The recommendations made in the Mountfield Report led to concerns about the machinery of government becoming politicized and of 'spin' dictating government communication strategies (see Franklin, 1998; Jones, 1999; and below). Whilst some of these concerns were undoubtedly grave and genuine, it is not possible to reconcile them easily with the needs of a proactive government, on the one hand, and the real routine news-gathering practices of journalists, on the other. If a government wishes to drive forward its agenda, it needs an efficient, coordinated and committed piece of machinery; similarly, if it makes spin the order of the day and/or is able to control the media agenda, it is because it has learned to control the media and exposed the overreliance of journalists on sources and handouts. The fact that Labour's fortunes soon took a tumble amidst reports of sleaze and spin-as-sleaze suggests that despite the concerns and protestations, governments are less cohesive and coordinated than communication professionals would wish them to be. As I shall argue below, we need to see the criticisms of Mountfield and New Labour's communications machinery as emerging from a realization that although the media can often easily be led, it can also quickly turn against those that feed it, if only to protect its self-image as oppositional and 'holding truth to power'.

The Mountfield Report

The terms of reference of the review were 'To consider proposals to respond to concerns about how far the GIS is equipped in all areas to meet the demands of a fast-changing media world; to build on the skills and resources of the career GIS; and to maintain the established, and recently reconfirmed, propriety guidelines.' Its position on the way forward emerges early in its report:

> The effectiveness of Government communications depends not only on the technologically competent performance of media relations within a Press Office, but on two key elements of co-ordination: co-ordination *across Government*, not only day-to-day media handling but of strategic coherence, especially through central machinery; and integration *within a Department* of the development of policy and its communication.

> … For any large complex organisation pursuing a strategy, leaving presentation to chance is not an option …

> The overall political strategy, direction and style of the Government is set by the Prime Minister. He looks to the Chief Press Secretary and the No. 10 Press Office to ensure that the essential messages and key themes which underpin the Government's strategy are sustained and not lost in the clamour of events. (1997: 6. Original emphasis)

The need for better coordination by more skilled professional communicators underpinned much of the report, and the recommendations were intended to bring the GIS up to a level of performance that could stand proudly against the record of New Labour in opposition. Or, to put it differently, New Labour intended to re-create the machinery of communication it ran whilst in opposition in government. With Alastair Campbell at the helm of the party communications machinery in opposition and then in government, it is easy to see the continuities in structure and thinking.

Its advice to the Prime Minister, which he accepted, was summed up as follows:

- to retain a politically impartial service and to sustain the trusted values of the service embodied in its rules of guidance;
- to improve co-ordination with and from the Centre, so as to get across consistently the Government's key policy themes and messages:
  - through a new strategic communications unit serving the whole Government
  - through a reformed Cab-E-Net system (AGENDA) and
  - through clearer rules on attribution;

- to improve co-ordination within each Government Department so that Ministers, their special advisers, their Press Offices and their policy civil servants all play their part in the coherent formulation and communication of policy;
- to bring the practice and procedures of all Government Press Offices up to the standards of the best, geared to quick response round the clock with help from a new central monitoring unit;
- on the basis that communication is an integral part of policy formulation, to develop closer and better working relations between policy civil servants and Press Offices. (Mountfield Report, 1997: 1)

Much has been written about these recommendations and consequent changes to the communications machinery of government and much of that has been quite critical of the centralization and politicization of the government machinery (see, for example, Franklin, 1998; Scammell, 2001). Certainly, the consequences of the change and the demonizing of 'spin' (McNair, 2004) did give rise to concerns about the extent to which cynicism was beginning to infect public views of politics and government. The controversies that ensued from the creation of a proactive government communications machine and of special advisers managing news and allegedly spinning all the time forced the government to concede to yet another enquiry into the nature of communication in the modern age. These controversies, alongside related concerns about the so-called politicization of the Civil Service and the lack of clarity over divisions of responsibility between Civil Servants and special advisers, led to the setting up of the 2004 Government Communications Review Group, chaired by Bob Phillis (henceforth the Phillis Review).

The Phillis Review

The Review Group spent much time reflecting on the unease about the employment of special advisers and the use of spin inasmuch as it impacted on trust in government and engagement in politics. This concern and unease underpinned much of the critical analysis of New Labour's communications strategy. As the Committee observed:

> The response of the media to a rigorous and proactive government news management strategy has been to match claim with counterclaim in a challenging and adversarial way, making it difficult for any accurate communication of real achievement to pass unchal-

lenged. Our research suggests that this adversarial relationship between Government and the media has resulted in all information being mistrusted when it is believed to have come from 'political' sources. (2004)

Its final report, published in June 2004, sought to clarify and streamline much of what the Review Group saw as weaknesses in the communications machinery. For example, it drew attention to the need for clarifying the rules governing the relationship between civil servants and special advisers; it also urged government and media to reconsider the terms of engagement in lobby and other briefings, and it pleaded for a greater and better dialogue between government and public if only in order to overcome what it recognized as a breakdown of trust between 'governments, media and public'.

However, there was no way it could disguise its surprise at the lack of professionalism in GICS and the absence of coordination and strategy across the whole sector of government communications. For instance, it wrote that:

we found a culture in which communication is not seen as a core function of the mainstream Civil Service. In theory, communications staff are a part of the Civil Service like any other. But we too often found a 'them and us' attitude between policy civil servants and communications staff. We found a culture where the way in which policies will be perceived by the public, and how these policies are to be communicated, are issues that still tend to be tagged on to the end of policy formulation, not treated as an integral part of it. (2004: 9)

In a section headed 'Service Not Fit For Purpose', it pointed out that the Review Group's work 'was made harder by the lack of readily available statistics on the scale of the government's communications effort – an illustration, perhaps, of its current status. ... Some 2,600 people work directly in communications directorates at an annual cost of £90 million. Of these, however, according to the numbers supplied to us, only 850 are members of the GICS, which is a body that we regard as no longer fit for purpose because of a number of structural and systems weaknesses', inasmuch as there is an absence of coordination and unity of purpose across the whole communications sector (2004: 9).

And as one turns to the conclusion, one can see how the Phillis Review implicitly lends support to the changes that had taken place from 1997 onwards and makes a case for a stronger centre of communication rather than a weaker one. In other words, the essence of the Phillis Report is a call for a greater professionalization and, to an extent, for a greater centralization of the communications function of government so as to create and deliver a service fit for the modern age – to remedy, in effect, the 'failure of government to develop and implement professional, modern and integrated communication' (2004: 29).

Although one of the immediate outcomes of the Review was that the GICS was restructured and renamed the Government Communication Network, other injunctions for change will take longer to assess as they call for a wholesale reassessment of the relationship between government, the media and the public. At the same time, it draws attention to the tension – perhaps more apparent under New Labour – between a traditional and long-standing Civil Service 'mentality' of impartiality and service and a government in a hurry to bring about major changes in society. While the former can continue to work as it has done in the past, a government driven by a determined Prime Minister and a reforming party would see it as an essential prerequisite to reform the whole infrastructure of communication to the public – because presentation is now part of the policy process – in order to begin to bring about change. For those interested in political communication, the fascinating question – and this may be the test of the success of New Labour's strategies – is whether incoming governments would undo what has been done and so seek to return to a different way of doing things.

A transformation in government communication?

The concerns, reports and controversies surrounding the special advisers and government communication inevitably highlight the question of change and of transformation. Did New Labour radically change the infrastructure of communication and transform the process? Rather than provide an immediate answer to these questions, it may be useful to locate the changes identified above within a longer historical overview of how governments communicate. In this respect, there are three questions that perhaps are central to this review of the changes that have taken place:

● First, there is the question of whether or not the recommendations to recreate the GIS into GICS and into a more professional organization of communication are a departure from anything that had gone before. Was the new communications infrastructure so very different from what preceded it?

- Second, and following on from the above, is the question of whether Alastair Campbell's role differed significantly from the role of previous Prime Ministerial press officers.
- Thirdly, there is the question of the extent to which the changes that were made reflected a particular style of government – more presidential than before, less cabinet government and so on – and could thus be undone or modified by subsequent Prime Ministers with different styles of governing?

There are no easy answers to any of these questions and attempting to give any more than elements of an answer would be beyond the aims of this chapter. Nevertheless, some attempt must be made to answer them since they place the development of government communications strategies in context.

The communications infrastructure: continuity or radical change?

It is now generally accepted that under New Labour, the communications machine worked efficiently and to the advantage of the government: it enabled the government to dictate the agenda and to actively manage the media, particularly in the early years of the new government (see Price, 2006). There were some obvious instances of things going wrong – that is, when advisers were overzealous in their dealings with the media – but on the whole the government and its advisers were able to dictate the agenda to a remarkable extent. And to the extent that Alastair Campbell was in charge of that machinery of communications, he must take some responsibility – and pride – for making sure that the government got its message across.

Whether this represented a significant departure from what had gone on before is more difficult to say. For a start, New Labour came to power in the 24/7 media environment. Responses to media enquiries had to be fast and accurate and unless the government took on board the need to be proactive, there was a danger that it would end up being no more than a reactive operation at the mercy of the media. Sir Christopher Meyer's comments – reproduced above – implicitly suggest the need for radical change in the early 1990s, but they also acknowledge, perhaps again implicitly, the need to be proactive. One could therefore argue that New Labour's communications operation was built on prior experiences and is no more than an extension of these in a changing new media landscape. (The proliferation of the internet at the turn of the 20th century posed its own set of problems and created its own momentum for change.)

The changed media environment created its own pressure for change, so it could be argued that New Labour was only seeking to meet the challenge of change. Even if this argument is discounted, there is some evidence to show that Campbell was operating in a way that one of his predecessors, Bernard Ingham, was also prone to do. Ken Newton makes the point that in 1989 Ingham was made head of the GIS and that 'in effect, he became the country's Minister of Information' (2001: 153). Other similarities between these two suggest that there are some continuities but, at the same time, the level of coordination required in the 1990s and beyond brought about a step-change in the level of organization.

Campbell and Ingham: similar or different?

As to whether or not Alastair Campbell's role differed significantly from some of his predecessors, the likely answer is that it depends on how one views the evidence. Reference has already been made to the fact that both these individuals were placed in charge of the government machinery but other similarities can be found. Campbell was forthright and forceful, and sought to drive the agenda and this was not dissimilar to the Ingham style of operation. More generally, the practice of news management may be an intrinsic part of the relationship between press spokespeople and journalists and is certainly at the heart of the lobby system where journalists and PM spokespeople meet. James Margach, reflecting on his many years of experience as a lobby correspondent from the 1930s onwards, expressed the situation in this way: 'the modern centralized system of controlling Press contacts (represented by such things as Lobby briefings) is the master key in the machine which keeps news, and access to news, under rigid control at the centre' (1979: 139).

Such practices did not suddenly reappear in the 1990s and even a glance at comments about Bernard Ingham, Margaret Thatcher's Press Secretary from 1979 through to 1990, would testify to the continuing efforts by prime ministers, amongst others, to manage the machinery of government. Although Ingham has sought to distance his role and his actions from that of his most famous successor, Alastair Campbell, there are strong similarities. When asked by members of the Select Committee on Public Administration about his job under Thatcher, he gave a considered answer that could be interpreted as describing a role that was similar, rather than different from, that occupied by his successor:

> 3. (*Sir Bernard Ingham*) ... I think that a professional Government Information Service is important and I think it was important in Margaret

Thatcher's day and I think it was very important that you had some-
body there to manage her relations with the media as she did not
exactly regard journalists as her natural habitat. That was really the
role I played; my job was to manage relations with the media and to
keep them on as even a keel as it is possible ever to keep the media ...
(Public Administration Select Committee, 1998b: para. 3)

When asked about a direct comparison between himself and Campbell, Ingham focused on the status of Campbell within the Civil Service
and the government rather than on the substance of the work itself.
Tellingly, he added a comment that points to similarities rather than
differences:

You asked first what is the job of an information officer and I wrote
in 1967 when I was invited to write my job specification in the
Department of Employment, that it *is to promote an informed press and
public about the Government's policies and measures and to advise Ministers and officials on the presentation of those policies and measures and I
think that that stands the test of time.* ... (Public Administration Select
Committee, 1998b: para. 8. Emphasis added)

Whilst Ingham's comments are carefully worded, others have been
more explicit about his role and his work and his ability to direct the
Prime Minister's media agenda. Jeremy Tunstall has described his
behaviour as 'unprecedentedly belligerent and uncouth' (1996: 274)
and he acknowledges that Ingham was 'encouraged to establish a
dominance of government media relations which had not been previously been attempted in peacetime' (1996: 274).

As for the accusations of spin and news management that have been
levelled at New Labour and its communication advisers, these can be
dealt with by pointing out that these practices are not new – as we have
seen above concerning news management – nor are they new with
respect to spin. In a review of his own 1997 report, Sir Robin Mountfield made the point that commentators such as Nicholas Jones (in his
book *The Control Freaks*, 2001):

exaggerate[s] how much of a change there has been in 'trailing'
announcements, in by-passing Parliament, and in selective release of
news or comment to temporarily favoured recipients. I also think he,
and others, fail to recognize that 'spinning' has so far over-reached
itself that it has become almost counter-productive, and that a self-
correcting mechanism is therefore at work. (Mountfield, 2002)

Does a 'new-style Prime Minister' need a new style of communications strategy?

The impetus for reforming the government information machinery may be only a part of what made New Labour distinctive post-1997, since one of the things that underpinned its reforms was the style of government that Tony Blair brought to government with a greater centralization of power and control of the machinery of government and communication. Such 'new-style prime ministers' (Rose, 2001: 3; see also Seymour-Ure, 2003; Tunstall, 1996) have increased their powers enormously. They run their government in a very centralized and almost personalized way and the greater the 'presidentialization' of the role of the PM, the lesser the powers and roles of others, be it the party, ministers, or Cabinet.

But there is another feature of such 'new-style prime ministers' that cannot be overlooked and that is the tendency to approach the problem and the prospects of government in a highly instrumental way. Hence, the often used phrases to describe Tony Blair's style: a command style, command-and-control, Napoleonic, a proactive approach, 'a what Tony wants' phenomenon (see, for example, Hennessy, 2005). It is a description of a prime minister in charge of the ship of state and intent on using his powers to steer it at will and in whatever direction he wants. The PM dispenses power and patronage, and makes every effort to ensure that the electorate is aware of his singular position in the political firmament.

The problem for the 'new-style prime minister' – as for others – is that governments are made up of people who often disagree, who are competitive and opinionated, and who have to deal with issues and events that may be unexpected or have no single or natural resolution. In a competitive media environment, there will always be an outlet for dissenting views, for leaks and for public dissent (see Tunstall, 1996). With a growing interest in the personal as political, the media are happy to reproduce politics as a struggle between people, rather than ideas: the history of New Labour has been dominated by the Blair–Brown conflict, for example. In such circumstances – competitive media, leaky Cabinets, personal public and private posturing – attempts to control events and people even become counter-productive. Hence the dilemma at the heart of modern-day centralized governments: on the one hand, there is a growing awareness of the need to listen and to be transparent, to explain and to communicate ideas, strategies and policies; on the other, there is the overwhelming urge to steer and control, particularly on the part of powerful 'new-style prime ministers'. It is, after all, their government and their fortunes rest on how successfully they have delivered on their promises. How to tread that fine line – without the danger of appearing 'hyperactive and divisive' – must be a constant concern.

It is a concern made worse, perhaps, because the 'new-style prime minister' is a prime minister in an age of electronic communication. If the 'age of television' made prime ministers aware of the need to be on guard and prepared, of being part-politician, part-celebrity, and always in focus, the age of 'electronic glut' (Seymour-Ure, 1996) forces prime ministers and their governments to be on constant lookout for fear of things slipping out and escaping beyond their control. Colin Seymour-Ure has gone so far as to suggest that 'the growth of media and the growth of the premiership come together in a puzzle about the nature and extent of prime ministerial power' (2003: 2). Furthermore, 'awareness of public communication, both as a task … and as a resource' has grown immeasurably since the 1970s. But, as always, there is a tension – something 'inherently unstable' – in this: 'A prime minister ideally wants *focused* power – in other words, control. His news operations pit him in a continuous struggle to be understood as he would wish' (Seymour-Ure, 2003: 3–4) but the media – and sometimes his or her colleagues – will not, cannot and should not, grant him that wish.

In order to understand the transformation of government communication in the past 30 or so years, one needs therefore to have a good grasp of a range of factors that contribute to that transformation. Some, like technological change, are external to governments, but they force governments and the machinery of government to ponder on how they impact on their operations. To return to an earlier point, in an era of 24/7 media and 'electronic glut' it is not possible to deal with the media as if it worked with a regular and known news cycle. Prime ministers, politicians and press spokespeople are consequently forced to change, as are those who claim to control the government's communications machinery.

Other changes are of a more internal character inasmuch as they reflect particular approaches to government. As I have argued, Tony Blair adopted an instrumental and personalized style of government, as do many modern chief executive officers. They are in post to bring about change, they have been appointed to do so and it is their role and duty to ensure that change takes place. They have to make it happen. They have to deliver. To make it happen and to deliver may involve changes in government machinery – in communications, departments, individual approaches – in order to make it more professional and responsive to the political imperatives of the prime minister. The machine of government must, in other words, be fit for the purpose of government and be responsive to gentle, as well as radical, changes in direction.

One clear instance where the machinery has expanded and been made more responsive is the case of No. 10 Downing Street, the Prime Minister's residence and office. In the mid-1990s, the Downing Street office was comparatively small. Jeremy Tunstall suggests that in the mid-1990s, the PM's press secretary was in charge of a small office of 'only about 100 people (including secretaries, cleaners, and messengers)' (1996: 275). This was not much different from the late 1960s and led Tunstall to conclude that the 'Prime Ministerial apparatus was archaic and inadequate in the 1960s and has changed little since' (1996: 279–80) despite changes in the politics, media and journalism.

That there has been an expansion of the office in the wake of Tony Blair's election is clear. Colin Seymour-Ure gives the following figures, albeit 'approximate' ones: Edward Heath in the 1970s had a staff of 18, Thatcher of 30 (2003: 131). By 1998, the 'Number Ten staff' is put at 148, although what this includes or excludes in unclear. The reason for the growth, according to Seymour-Ure, was 'the expansion of a *press office staff*' (2003: 131. Original emphasis). Whilst Tunstall was clear in his conclusion that the Number Ten office in the early to mid-1990s did not represent a British version of the Washington White House, the French Presidential Palace or the Canadian or Australian equivalent's (1996: 275), Seymour-Ure concludes his review in the following way: 'more than under any previous prime minister ... the organization of the Blair communications machine now resembled that of the White House' (2003: 136). It had expanded to deal with a range of activities – 'all permeated with public communication roles' (2003: 136) – that were now part and parcel of modern prime ministerial work. In October 2006, the PM's office comprised 24 senior staff with a range of functions (Ministerial Statement, 2006).

Post-Blair, what?

If New Labour under Blair created a particular template that enabled certain agendas to be pursued, what is likely to happen post-Blair? Is there another template that could be used or have the centralization of power and the coordination of activities become so embedded that they cannot be undone?

As other chapters in this book have indicated, much political activity is now centred on the work of the leader and the small entourage that surrounds them. Contemporary electioneering, for example, is now almost entirely focused on the leader (David Cameron, Gordon Brown) and policy-making emerges from the nexus surrounding the Prime Minister and Number Ten. In these circumstances, it is unlikely that there will be a reversal of this trend and that true democracy will suddenly break loose and multiple centres of power will be allowed free reign. With the media, including the internet, continually chasing stories, the danger for prime ministers and their governments lies in not making efforts to deal with the media in an efficient, proactive and professional way.

If the argument that prime ministers must use their powers of communication and their communication skills as an appendage of power is valid, then not doing so is likely to lead to a situation where the centre is weak and dissent is rife. This certainly happened during John Major's premiership (1990–7) as Chris Meyer, Major's Press Secretary explains:

> Their [the Euro-sceptic rebels] ferocious polemic and guerrilla warfare carried into the Cabinet itself, where discipline was lamentable. I preferred the dentist's chair to briefing the Lobby on a Monday morning. It would be a bloodbath after a weekend of speeches and pronouncements by senior cabinet ministers … Together they managed to contradict each other as well as official government policy on Europe. (2006: 17)

The 'sleaze' factor post-1992 made matters worse for Major's government as it nose-dived to an eventual defeat at the 1997 election.

But controlling the media in an efficient and professional way can also end in tears. Lance Price admits that within a few years of coming to office, New Labour 'was more spinned against than spinning' (2006: xxvi) and that it had lost its grip on the levers of communications. For New Labour, 'spin' became the new 'sleaze' and it too left the government open to accusations of misusing its powers and distorting facts and outcomes. Subsequent events – the Hutton inquiry, the invasion of Iraq, resignations of Ministers (Peter Mandelson, David Blunkett) – left the government unpopular and vulnerable to attack, in spite of its third term of office. The goodwill that greeted victory in 1997 was soon to turn to suspicion and doubt and by 2003–4 into unpopularity; a pattern not dissimilar to John Major's own situation in the 1990s when a period of seeming success (1990–2 which included an election victory in 1992), soon gave way to unpopularity following 'Black Wednesday', 'sleaze' and dissent.

What may lie behind this pattern is a cycle that both Tunstall (1996) and Kavanagh and Seldon (2000) have remarked upon: that the early years of each new Prime Minister are a 'honeymoon' period of sorts – the media are gentle and docile, and political calm pervades the air – but that events soon make themselves felt and how they are dealt with then impacts on the fortunes of the government and the Prime Minister. Tunstall forcefully argues that the 'Downing Street press operation is only fully capable of smoothly functioning in politically quiet times; immediately there is some kind of political excitement, or crisis, the press operation itself is in crisis' (1996: 276).

At the time when that was written, in 1996, Tunstall went on to argue that 'this was at least partly due to its small size, its lack of expertise, and the lack of continuity in personnel' (1996: 276). Changes made by Tony Blair may have dealt with some of these reasons – staff were increased, there was considerably more expertise brought in, and there was some continuity – yet the underlying pattern remained the same. Years of popularity for the Prime Minister and the government were followed by years of unpopularity as events took their toll on ministers, members and the Prime Minister himself.

Even Gordon Brown's brief tenure in office (from June 2007–) has seen this pattern repeated. The honeymoon period was soon followed by events that had enormous negative impact on his popularity, aided and abetted no doubt by a hungry and combative media. Furthermore, the promise of 'no spin' has been modified rather than completely broken. According to journalist Fraser Nelson, not one but two members of Brown's staff are now briefing the media: '[Michael] Ellam and [Damian] McBride, effectively, are of equal seniority. But Ellam is the face of official civil service briefing which Brown wants us to think is the post-Blair, anti-spin fresh start; McBride is the hidden face of spinning as usual' (Nelson, 2007; see also Oborne, 2007).

In other respects, the broad contours of the Brown administration are not substantially different from that which had preceded him. Like Blair, he has been criticized for relying on a small group of insiders and of seeking to exert control over the machinery of government. And, as during Blair's tenure of office, the media are courted and cajoled, so reflecting the continuing tension between those in government and those who report on the personalities and the tensions between those who are in government.

The Transformation of a Political Communication: the Global Context

7

Introduction

The aim of this chapter is to explore some common accounts of transitions and transformations in political communication and to look at these in the context of a number of country-specific studies of transformations in political communication. The first substantive part of this chapter will explore accounts of how changes in both societies and technologies of communication may have led to transformations in political communication, whilst the second part will look at the transformation of political communication in three quite different countries: Germany, Italy and Greece. The final part will review the evidence of transformations in political communication.

At the heart of this chapter is a concern with how we come to understand and explain change and, more specifically, how we comprehend the complex relationship between technologies of communication and societal change. In theory, these issues are quite simple and straightforward: over time, industrial (capitalist, democratic) societies change, and the evidence of that change can be readily observed. We now live in societies that are radically different from those inhabited by our parents and they, in turn, lived in societies that differed from those of their parents and so on. But acknowledging the evidence of change is not the same as providing adequate theories or words to describe the significance of those changes or their underlying causes. Is it adequate merely to observe that societies are now more 'modern', or more 'differentiated', or more 'complex' than before? Or that they are just 'different' from what they were? And what sort of changes do these words signify? Furthermore, what triggers those changes: is it conflict (for example wars), industrialization, globalization, technological change, changes in communication technologies, a combination of these, or something else altogether?

143

At times, as we noted in Chapter 2, technologies of communication are foregrounded as a means of designating changes between time periods. For example, Farrell et al. (2001) use the terms 'the television age' and 'the digital age' as a way of describing transitions (transformations?) in communication and political party structures from one era to the next. Pippa Norris (2002) uses such terms as the 'modern' and 'post-modern' form of campaign communications to designate transformations in political communication and party political structures, whilst Gibson and Römmele (2001) use terms such as the 'modern' and 'professional' campaign to distinguish between campaign styles and party structures.

Some of these ways of exploring change over time appear to apportion transformative powers to technologies of communications – for example from the 'television age' to the 'digital age' and so on – and it cannot be denied that technologies of communication are important contributory factors for understanding change. The medium of television, for instance, undoubtedly contributed to change in the many societies in which it developed *but it also fed off changes that were also taking place in those societies*. What is often missing, however, from analyses of changes in political communication is a conceptualization of change that does not ignore the power of technology to bring about change but supplements this with an analysis of societal change more generally.

One reason for seeking such an account of change is that it would draw attention to the broader changes in social structures within which technologies of communication themselves develop. Rather than privileging technologies of communication as drivers of change, such an account would necessarily offer a more balanced and more nuanced account of how things develop within societies. A second reason for seeking such an account is that it could offer a better understanding of transformations in political communication in a global context. It could, in other words, provide a way of exploring and understanding changes that have taken place across boundaries and political systems. Instead of seeing changes in particular political systems as being specific to them, it could thus offer a more generalized way of exploring and understanding transformations. More generally, it could offer a way of looking at change – in societies, technologies of communication, political communication – that blends together elements of historical, political, sociological and technological analyses.

One attempt to do so can be found in David Swanson and Paolo Mancini's work and their discussion of 'the modern model of campaigning' (1996). Many of the attributes of 'the modern model of campaigning' relate to the changes that have taken place in media and politics over the past half-century. As they put it, its 'key attributes' include the 'personalization of politics, expanding reliance on technical experts and professional advisers, growing detachment of political parties from citizens, development of autonomous structures of communication, and casting citizens in the role of spectator ...' (1996: 249).

But what gave rise to 'the modern model of campaigning'? To answer this question they turn to the idea of 'modernization'. For Swanson and Mancini, 'modernization' is a hypothesis of a 'general and fundamental process of change that ... leads to the adoption' of American-style electioneering techniques in different national contexts (1996: 6). In the relationship between Americanization and modernization 'lie the keys to understanding the causes, significance, and implications of changing campaign methods and practices' (1996: 6).

Whilst the idea of Americanization is fairly easy to grasp, the idea of modernization is more complex. Its 'most basic and far-reaching attribute' is 'steadily increasing social complexity' (1996: 7). They go on: 'In general terms ... modernization fragments social organizations, interests and identity, creating a complicated landscape of competing structures and conflicting symbolic realities which citizens must navigate' (1996: 9). There is, hence, a 'functional differentiation' in society which leads to the emergence of many 'differentiated groups and sub-systems' that seek to advance their own needs and demands (1996: 253).

Such 'increasing social complexity' inevitably impacts on social and political relations and on those organizations and institutions that inhabit the social and political spheres. In the case of the mass media, they 'emerge as an autonomous power centre in reciprocal competition with other power centres' (1996: 11). Of other media-related changes they describe, one stands out: 'the development of commercial television has radically changed the character of election campaigns. It has even changed the nature and role of election coverage provided by the public broadcasting services, introducing new opportunities and new formats' (1996: 13).

In their concluding chapter they summarize their ideas:

Modernization leads to a weakening of political parties and emergence of a powerful role for mass media. These conditions seem to be the immediate causes of changes in electoral practices, and thus mediate between modernization on the one hand and the modern model of campaigning on the other. To this view of underlying causes (modernization), intermediate facilitating conditions (weakened parties and powerful autonomous media), and results (modern campaign practices) should be added three variations. (1996: 255)

These include, for example, instances where political consultants are employed 'before the conditions that favour them are in place' (1996: 255).

One can present this argument in a diagrammatic form as follows:

Causes   *facilitating conditions* *results*

Modernization ⟶ weakened parties ⟶ modern campaign

        powerful autonomous practices

        media

The account offered by Swanson and Mancini (1996) helps us to get a better sense of what modern political campaign communication practices comprise, and the variations they identify demonstrate the numerous ways through which different political systems arrive at the 'modern model of campaigning'. However, there are a number of grounds on which one can query the overall validity of the idea of 'modernization' as it is applied in this context:

- The first is the problem of cause and effect: does modernization *lead to* weakened parties and powerful and autonomous media or do weakened parties and powerful autonomous media *contribute* to a process of modernization?
- The second problem is the relationship between the idea of modernization and those accounts of change in campaign communications that, on the whole, privilege technologies, for example the 'digital' age, or even 'a *continuous* transition from a premodern to a modern and postmodern stage of electioneering' (Plasser and Plasser, 2002: 241. Emphasis added).
- The third problem is that when we begin to explore specific countries, the validity of the hypothesis is open to question in so far as the details throw up significant variations. This, I would argue, is particularly so when we examine the British example.

So, while the idea of modernization remains useful in that it draws attention to change and how changes in societies can be explored and understood, it does have some limitations as we shall see. Nevertheless, it offers a coherent way of supplementing an analysis of technological change with a broader understanding of how societies themselves change over time. For this reason, and the other reasons indicated above, it deserves closer scrutiny.

Understanding change: modernization

While this chapter does not seek to unpack fully the concepts of 'modernization' – or indeed others that touch on similar processes such as 'Americanization' and 'professionalization' – it needs to tackle some of the implications of these concepts and their use as a means of understanding transformations in social structures and processes, including political communication. And, as has already been indicated, one of the issues that requires some further exploration is the relationship between changes taking place in society ('modernization') and the attributes of modern campaigning, such as the use of professional consultants, the rise of autonomous powerful media and so on, to which changes in society are linked. To return briefly to Swanson and Mancini's view of 'modernization', does it *lead*, as they argue, 'to a weakening of political parties and to the emergence of a powerful role for mass media' (1996: 255) or does the 'weakening of political parties and the emergence of a powerful role for mass media' *contribute* to 'modernization'? In other words, are the changing roles of the mass media and/or political parties *constitutive of* changes in social structures and processes rather than driven by them?

As I have argued in Chapter 2, it is possible to see many of the changes taking place in the conduct and content of political communication as coming out of the *interaction* between emerging/maturing media and emerging/maturing political parties. Widespread social change, in this view, is little more than a backdrop to the changes taking place. A brief digression will illustrate the significance of the point. In Britain, television developed in the early 1950s but it was not until the late 1950s and early 1960s that television began to exert itself on the conduct and content of political communication. Prior to this period, roughly between 1951 and 1957, politics on television was still very much a product of a broadcast medium that had still not quite developed an independent and well-defined role and a party political system that was still powerful enough to dictate the way television should operate in matters of political communication. This period corresponds to what Blumler and Kavanagh have called 'Age 1' of political communication: 'the political system was regarded as the prime source of initiatives and debate for social reform ... and much political communication was subordinate to relatively strong and stable political institutions and beliefs' (1999: 211–2).

Sometime after 1960 and with television developing its own styles and practices, political parties were forced to confront television head-on and develop ways and means to get their messages across. Political parties, in 'Age 2', 'had to work harder and learn new tricks. They accordingly adopted an array of tactics to get into the news, shape the media agenda, and project a pre-planned "line" in press conferences, briefings, interviews, and broadcast' (Blumler and Kavanagh, 1999: 211–13). At this time, political parties still dominated the political landscape and garnered substantial numbers of votes: in 1955, total voter turnout in England was nearly 77%; in 1966 it stood at 76%, as it did in 1979 (see http://www.psr.keele.ac.uk/election.htm#U). On the one hand, we see the media growing their power and, on the other, political parties continuing to be important and strong, at least in relation to the media if not in terms of the size of their membership base. Contrary to the hypothesis of modernization, in the Britain of the 1950s and 1960s, we can find the growth of powerful and independent media and a strong party political system. Unless, that is, one puts forward the unlikely proposal that Britain had not undergone a process of modernization by then.

Yet, there is much evidence to show that sometime around 1960, the nature of the relationship between media and politics began to change and the 'first age' of political communication gave way to the 'second age' (Blumler and Kavanagh, 1999). A more subtle account of the transitions that took place around this period is offered by Colin Seymour-Ure (1996). In contrast to the proposition that there were 'three ages of political communication', Seymour-Ure plots five stages in the evolving relationship between broadcast media and politics: two stages prior to 'the watershed year' of 1959 and three after:

- 'inauguration: TV at the heels of radio'
- 'adjustment, exploration, initiative' – 'the balance started to tip [in favour of broadcasters]: politics began to adapt to broadcasting, as politicians became keener to use it ...' (1996: 186)
- 'political broadcasting comes of age: 1960–1974'. A stage in which television would lose the occasional battle against the politicians, but 'the TV medium was now too entrenched to lose the war' (1996: 190)
- TV ascendant: 1975–1990. 'The fourth stage in the intrusion of TV involves changes of degree rather than of kind' (1996: 192)
- 'Electronic glut? Political television disintegrates, 1990–?' (Seymour-Ure, 1996: 194).

What accounts for the significance of 1959–60, and how does this help us understand the idea of modernization and the development of political communication in the global context?

'Modernization', as we have seen, suggests long-term social change which creates a more complex society which in turn impacts on processes and practices. Yet, although Britain was undergoing change in the 1950s – just as before and after – there is nothing specific in the period of the late 1950s that would immediately stand out as a more significant cause of 'modernization' than any other. Political parties were generally adapting to broader political and social change although there was a lessening of the ideological divide that had featured so prominently a decade earlier. As Sandbrook has written, 'for many contemporary observers, what characterized the fifties was not fierce political disagreement but an underlying mood of consensus and contentment' (2005: 59). There were some key political crises, such as the Suez crisis of 1956, that impacted on the then existing arrangements for political broadcasting but, on the whole, this was a period of prosperity and the emergence of the consumer society.

Although in this period political parties still retained the allegiance of a substantial part of the electorate, there are indications that they had much less of a grip on the loyalties of voters than before (see Curtice, 2002) and that they were much less clearly positioned on the political spectrum. The Labour Party faced this problem more than the Conservatives since 'the fulfillment of its programme between 1945 and 1951 had left it with something of a vacuum of ideas' (Butler, 1955: 14; see also Beer, 1997). In one sense, it could do no more than subscribe to the agenda for the pursuit of prosperity that the Conservatives had succeeded in developing. Little wonder, then, that by 1959, one poll found 38% 'of people thinking that it mattered little or not at all which party was in power (compared with 20% eight years earlier)' (Butler and Rose, 1960: 19).

Yet from the late 1950s, a new, more questioning, relationship between the broadcast media and political parties was beginning to be established: on the one hand, the rules that constrained political television, for example the 14-Day Rule, (Negrine, 1999) were swept aside in 1957; and, on the other, new forms of political interviewing and election coverage developed (Day, 1989). Was this a consequence of 'modernization' and of broad social change (meaning what precisely?)? Or was it a response to the emergence of a more competitive media system, and a growing awareness of the manners and properties of television? Finally, did the broadcast media – and their new style of coverage – help undermine the dominance of the political parties?

The significance of these questions cannot be overestimated since they touch on bigger questions of how change in societies, in media and in politics come about and how, for example, we might wish to explore the impact of new means of communication such as the internet. These questions also throw up interesting issues in respect of how we look at developments in electoral campaigning in a global context. Since each political system exhibits particular properties, does 'modernization' adequately deal with conditions in each one of these? Swanson and Mancini, for instance, hypothesized that 'the more advanced the process of modernization in a country, the more likely we are to find innovations in campaigning being adopted and adapted' (1996: 6). However, recent evidence drawn from Fritz Plasser's work (Plasser and Plasser, 2002) shows how countries where the process of modernization is not particularly well advanced – in the Far East or Latin America – can still be adopters and adapters of modern campaigning techniques. It may be that the common links between these disparate political systems and examples is not so much the process of modernization per se but the one thing that they have in common, namely, *the medium of television*. To put the point differently, while societies are in constant flux ('modernizing' or just changing), it is the development of the medium of television – its grammar, institutionalization, regulation, use and so on – that helps us to understand why campaign communications develop in fairly similar ways in different political contexts. Swanson and Mancini sort of acknowledge this point but do not develop it, preferring instead to work with the idea of 'modernization', although they write of 'the *epochal change associated with television*' but qualify this with the statement that we need 'to appreciate, but not exaggerate, television's influence' (1996: 13. Emphasis added).

Other writers, as we shall see, have been less reluctant to give television pride of place in explanations of change. Plasser and Plasser, for example, write of five 'macro-trends observable in advanced industrial societies' of which the first 'and *presumably most momentous* trend is the increasing TV-centeredness' of campaign communication (2002: 241. Emphasis added). They draw further attention to the importance of television a few pages later on in their book:

> Overall, there is one outstanding element of modernization that can be considered revolutionary in most parts of the world: the *growing importance of mass media*, especially the *use of television* during campaigns. Secondly, there has been a noticeable *increase in professional campaign management*, and thirdly, a strong *increase in required budgets* in order to finance television-driven and survey-based campaigns. (2002: 244. Original emphasis)

By acknowledging the importance of the development of the medium of television for understanding changes in political communication over the past half-century, including in campaign communications, one inevitably minimizes the importance of the 'modernization' thesis as an explanation for changes in political communication. To return briefly to the case of Britain in the 1950s: one can point to evidence of the growing appreciation of the importance of television as a medium of communication in the 1953–5 period, even though its ability to significantly alter forms of communication was limited by the formal and informal controls that kept it in check. This was particularly so whilst the BBC was a monopoly broadcaster. Once competition was introduced into the television landscape in 1955, the nature and content of political television changed dramatically. This suggests that it is not the development of new technologies per se that brings about change but the development of new technologies within particular structures and frameworks that may have consequences. As Michael Tracey has forcefully argued:

technology did not … provide the central drive [for change in broadcasting in the 1950s]. This came from the pursuit of an audience in a competitive market – it was the initial formulation of new formats followed by their success in terms of audience size which provided the shift in form that characterized the movement from one historical context, an essentially pre-war one, to the present historical one, a commercial environment which emphasizes the maximization of audience size … (1977: 59)

Later on, he uses the phrase 'epistemological rupture' to describe the 'transition from monopoly broadcasting … to a competitive situation …' (1977: 59).

If the argument that it is a particular – competitive – arrangement of television that brings about a transformation in political communication, then we should be able to find similar elements in other political systems. Rather than take for granted that all political systems have experienced a process of modernization in a more or less similar fashion – as Swanson and Mancini's (1996) thesis would generally hold – we should be looking at changes in the landscape of broadcasting for the causes of transformations of political communication. As Part 4 below suggests, there is some evidence for this in the case of Germany, Italy and Greece.

But the 'modernization' idea is not the only way in which the transformation of political communication in the global context can be examined. In Chapter 1, references were made to the idea of studying historical change as 'histoire croisée', (Werner and Zimmerman, 2006: 32) as comprising intersections and transfers of practices, people and cultures. The Americanization thesis, for instance, explores changes in communication practices as an outcome of a transfer of influences from one continent to another and from one media system to another (see Blumler and Gurevitch, 2001; Negrine and Papathanassopoulos, 1996). By contrast, the professionalization thesis – if that is what it is – suggests that there are common pools of knowledge about political communication from which all practitioners can draw. In both cases, though, specific cultural, social and political arrangements might limit the extent to which unbridled transfers can take place. So, for example, the prohibitions on selling airtime to political parties that exist across most of Europe, limit the full Americanization of political communication.

Unlike the modernization hypothesis, these other ways of exploring the transformation of political communication in the past half century make less of broad societal change and more of transfers and developments specific to particular media, especially television. And, as we shall see in the next section, they make some important contributions to how we should examine the transformation of political communication in the global context.

The transformation of political communication: Americanization and professionalization

At its simplest, the idea of Americanization draws attention to the existence of practices that were first developed in the US and that were then adopted into other political systems and absorbed into political communication practices. The list of such practices is indeed a long one and many those practices have had an impact – usually perceived to be negative – in other political systems (see, amongst others, Blumler and Gurevitch, 2001; Negrine and Papathanassopoulos, 1996; Plasser and Plasser, 2002). In his account of the French presidency under Giscard D'Estaing, Michel makes the point that the changing face of French politics in the 1960s and 1970s was seen as having come about 'under the influence of new methods of communication imported from the United States and based on political advertising and marketing' (2005: 293). This influence was of concern because it had the potential to bring about the 'deterioration of the quality of public debate and the substance of politics itself as an inevitable consequence of the oversimplification of political issues and the excessive reliance upon vague and consensual vote-seeking arguments' (Michel, 2005: 293).

Similar examples from elsewhere would not be hard to find and it is generally acknowledged that practices developed in the US quickly make their way overseas, often helped along by eager media professionals and consultants. In her work on German elections, Holtz-Bacha (2002) has pointed out that whilst many would query the nature of the process of transfer from the US to other continents, 'in a survey of European consultants, almost two-thirds said that knowledge of the latest US campaign literature is absolutely necessary in order to be a professional political marketer' (2002: 29). One way or another the US is an important source of ideas and practices in the field of political communication.

The problem with the idea of Americanization as a way of accounting for change lies not so much in the identification of the process of transfer of practices but in assessing the significance of the transfers. To use a common example, just because political consultants are now commonly used across the globe, it does not mean that all political systems have become Americanized. What it does mean, though, is that others have found those practices useful, effective and an additional tool in their election box of tricks. What it also means is that the practices that are widely used in the US are practices that work in that context and increasingly elsewhere. What has made that possible is that European political systems have either been transformed in such ways that the practices common in the US could then be employed elsewhere or that such practices can work elsewhere because certain elements – the rise of mediated (television) politics in a competitive political system – are now common elsewhere. The latter offers a fertile ground in which practices can develop. So, whilst Americanization as an idea is a pointer to practices that have been transferred across borders, something else points to the circumstances or conditions that make it possible for those practices to become established elsewhere.

This can be explored in a number of different ways and each of these goes back to features of the US political system that create a suitable environment for particular political communication practices to develop. A good example of this would be the 30-second television political spot. This developed in the US in the post-1945 period and it made use of quite advanced American knowledge of how the moving image could be used to persuade and mobilize voters (see http://www.pbs.org/30secondcandidate/). Its restriction to 30 seconds was probably based on two major considerations: cost and impact.

The cost of buying prime-time television would limit how many such time slots could be bought across a campaign that might stretch over many months; whilst the length of the political slot would also ensure maximum impact given that longer commercials – for that is what they are – are more difficult to construct and have more difficulty engaging the interest of the viewers.

In a commercial and unregulated media context, political slots can thrive. More so if political parties do not really exist as organic and functioning ideological units, and individual candidates are the focus of most political activity in a majoritarian political system. In contrast, where parties remain reasonably strong ideologically and work to contest seats – as in Europe in the 1950s and 1960s – it becomes more difficult to pursue the logic of American electioneering. Furthermore, in countries where the regulatory system does not permit airtime to be sold to political parties, there is an added obstacle (although the one major advantage of these regulations is that it keeps down the cost of electioneering).

However, changing conditions in the European political and media landscape have made it easier for American-influenced practices to develop. The commercialization of the German broadcasting system in the late 1980s, for example, made it possible for political parties to buy airtime and, because of the expense, the 30-, or so, second commercial was commonly used. The same is true for Greece. In Britain, where the prohibition on the sale of airtime to political parties remains in place, it is not possible to create the 30-second commercial as the political parties are given blocks of time – now 2 minutes and 45 seconds per broadcast as a minimum – which they must use. They cannot produce the 30-second political spot typical in the US but, if they are adventurous, they can create a series of 30-second scenarios. So, in Britain, as political election slots (PEBs   Party Election Broadcasts) have shrunk from 15 minutes or so in the 1950s to the 3-minute slot or thereabouts in the 1990s, the nature of the political discourse has necessarily changed to resemble less an argued case for why someone should vote for a particular party and more of a series of short statements about why one should not vote for the opposition parties.

While there is no direct and obvious connection between the construction and use of political spots in the US and their construction and use in, say, Britain or Germany, it may be possible to argue that those who produce political spots in Europe (or elsewhere) are probably familiar with practices in the US (or elsewhere). This does not signify that practices have been copied or even adapted, only that familiarity with practices can act as a backdrop to developments elsewhere. To an extent, the same would be true of the use of the 'war room' model for campaign strategizing with Britain and its Millbank operation (Scammell, 1998; Wring, 2005) and the Kampa (Social Democrats' campaign headquarters) in Germany. The use of consultants would be yet another example of the way in which practices and practitioners move across the globe.

In an increasingly globalized world where different political systems can no longer remain as hermetically sealed as they may have once been and where migration, travel, finance and so on cross geographic and imaginary borders easily, the patterns of change may even accelerate in particular contexts. As Plasser and Plasser (2002) show, the use of professional consultants is now common in a range of countries that display quite different socioeconomic and political features: European countries, South Africa, India, East Asia and so on. Processes of transformation may, therefore, not only be dependent on internal factors (for example development of television, internet, parties becoming weaker and so on) but also external factors as practices are imported and or adapted from elsewhere. Hence, Plasser and Plasser's preference for the use of the word 'hybridization' (2002: 250) to describe the transfers and adaptations that have taken place in the world of political communication. 'Hybridization', for Plasser and Plasser suggests a 'shopping model' where there is much borrowing and choosing of practices from amidst culture-specific factors which give rise to hybrid forms of political communication.

But running through all these accounts and explanations of change, one can also find references to a range of actors – from politicians to journalists, political parties to pollsters – who are becoming/have become more professional in the way they deal with aspects of their political communication work (see Negrine, 2005). 'Western European parties', according to Plasser and Plasser, 'have responded to dealignment tendencies within the electorate with a strategy of professionalization of party management and reliance on modern campaign techniques' (2002: 307). Schulz et al. have made similar observations in the context of developments in Germany:

As in many other European countries, the political parties in Germany have adjusted to these changes [in broadcast media] by professionalizing their campaign management, starting gradually in the 1970s and implementing more radical measures in the 1990s. … Ever since television viewing occupied most of the voters' media attention, campaign managers of all the major parties have focused heavily on television … (2005: 58)

Professionalization, in these cases, refers to the ways in which a range of political actors have in some way improved their practices or brought them up to a level that is commonly recognized as the most suitable for the modern period. We now have, as previous chapters have shown, politicians who are more professional than they used to be, political consultants and party managers who are now professional and so on.

The problem is not so much that this trend is an easily identifiable one, but that it is difficult to work out precisely how the idea of professionalization – as used, for example, by either Plasser and Plasser or Schulz (above) – sits alongside other ways of thinking about change highlighted in this chapter. Is the process of professionalization independent of 'Americanization' or is it one of its constitutive features? The same applies to the idea of modernization discussed earlier in this chapter: is professionalization part of the process or independent of it? And, finally, is the transformation of political communication in, say, Britain or Germany, a process that can be represented as a consequence of professionalization, Americanization, modernization, hybridization or a combination of these centred around the changing nature of the medium of television?

The answers to these difficult questions are likely to be quite complex and to vary from case to case, context to context. To end this section with an example: politicians may have become more professional in their handling of the media (see Chapter 5) because:

1. they have come to appreciate the different properties and manners of the various media and drawn on specific domestic experiences, that is, professionalization (see Chapter 2);
2. they have become aware of experiences in other contexts, for example the US, that is, Americanization;
3. they have adapted lessons from elsewhere and the outcome is a 'hybrid' practice, that is, 'hybridization';
4. of the growth of different skill sets around different people and media;
5. they have drawn on elements of all the above.

In short, in seeking to explore the transformation of political communication in the global context, we inevitably confront a complex set of issues that makes it difficult to identify transformations as processes that are both simple and unproblematic. While the idea of 'the modern model of campaigning' may be a useful description of what broadly happens in most democratic political systems – for there is not a 'uniform standardization of campaign practices' (Plasser and Plasser, 2002: 351) – it does not help us to find out how we have arrived at that stage. Moreover, by seeking to offer a more theoretically informed account of change, it underplays what is perhaps the one and key motor of change, that is, a competitive television environment. This is more fully explored in the next section.

Understanding transformations in a global context

To understand 'transformations' in a global context, therefore, we must be able to combine a number of different aspects of change in contemporary societies. In the background, and in a general indeterminate way, must be some consideration of societal change whether seen as 'modernization', 'modernity' (Giddens, 1990) or some variant. Alongside this must be some consideration of the theses of 'Americanization' and 'professionalization' as forces that point to a borderless global world in which things are transported, copied, adapted, and emulated. This is part of the thesis of 'hybridization'. But at the heart of many of these processes of change, lies the medium of television; a medium that became a central focus of political communication almost as soon as it developed and began to take up so much of the public's spare time. Obviously, the pattern of change is not identical in all countries and there are culture-specific and political system characteristics that mediate the processes of change. Nonetheless, the grammar of television has forced all, as Schulz et al. note above, to adapt to it, to respond to it and to seek to control it.

Before we turn to country-specific discussions, it is useful to summarize those areas in which change has taken place and in which that change can be taken to contribute towards a transformation of political communication. The descriptions of areas of change are indicative of general trends and these will certainly differ in different political systems. Nevertheless, they encapsulate the main areas of change and describe change at the level of *media*, at the level of *media practice*, at the *media–politics juncture*, at the level of the *political party*, and at the *organizational–operational* level of political parties.

Change at the level of media refers to changes *in* media (for example from newspapers to television) but also to changes in the ways in which media work. Thus, one must include here the processes of commercialization that privilege 'media logic' over 'political logic' (Mazzoleni, 1987) with the effect of forcing those in politics to become aware of the needs of the media. Thomas Meyer (2002 58) has described the process as the 'colonization' of politics by media logic, and this gives a proper sense of the ways in which politics has altered, and those who practise it have come to deal with the media. More generally, it is important to acknowledge the impact that commercialization of media – through deregulation or privatization, for example – has had on political communication. Winfried Schulz et al. (2005) implicitly acknowledge the importance of the increase in the supply of media – new media, different media – on German political communication. Jens Tenscher has also observed that important changes in the sociocultural make-up of Germany took place in the 1970s and impacted on the nature and content of political communication, but he goes on to note that 'it might be just a coincidence, but the second most important factor [explaining change] is the introduction of a semi-commercial (dual) broadcasting system back in 1984' (2007. Private communication).

In reviewing the Swedish scene, Lars Nord expressed similar ideas:

> recent years have seen dramatic changes on the national media scene where deregulations and technological advances have introduced more market-oriented broadcast media companies. At the same time there have been enormous changes in the newspaper market, which has seen a market-driven development ... Thus, a party-related media system has to a large extent been replaced by an independent and market-oriented media system. All the main actors in the Swedish political communication system now have to adjust to new conditions where marketing logic and highly volatile public opinion are distinctive features. (2007: 83)

The force of 'media logic' must therefore be taken into account when considering the transformation of political communication. Indeed, as Tracey has argued (1977) it may be the single most important reason why change came about.

Change at the level of media can result in *change at the level of media practice* whereby individual political actors – and individuals who are strategically placed in organizations – not only learn to respond to the prerequisites of 'media logic' but also learn to use the media to their advantage. The change can be characterized as denoting a shift from being responsive or reactive to becoming proactive in dealing with the media. Such a change in practice was the hallmark of New Labour's early years in office and suggests that the relationship between political actors and the media is more complex and more fluid than the picture drawn by, say, Blumler and Kavanagh (1999): although political actors may lose direct control over the media as journalism also becomes more critical, they can often find other and different ways to exert their control over the media. To paraphrase Leon Mayhew, we are currently experiencing a 'rationalization of persuasion' where the intent on the part of political actors as a broad category is to find and utilize 'effective means of persuasion based on research on audiences and the organization of systematic campaigns' (1997: 190). Political actors, in other words, become more professional too.

Although the rise of more proactive strategies can imply that the balance of power has shifted towards those in the world of politics, there is a range of factors that have conspired against the exercise of *total* control. *At the media–politics juncture* – where the 'negotiation of newsworthiness' takes place (Cook, 1998) – it is no longer the case that politicians and the media are the only participants in the negotiation process. A range of other intermediaries – consultants, spin doctors, advisers – has been placed at the political end of the spectrum to deal with, that is, manage and control, political communication on the part of political actors, and the media has pulled in other participants from a spectrum of non-governmental but interested bodies. This – and the fact that events conspire to create conflict, divisions and dissent – means that the objective of total media control is nearly always problematic. Whether it is the issue of the war in Iraq or clashes of personalities, the outcome can often be similar, with spats played out in public by an eager media. Raymond Kuhn's (2005) account of politics and the media in France gives a good flavour of this and has much wider relevance:

> Executive diarchy, experiences of cohabitation, ministerial turf wars, coalition government and the career rivalry engendered by presidential ambitions – the structures and functioning of the political system of the Fifth Republic contribute to a picture of division and disunity which makes coordination of executive communication both highly desirable and at the same time extremely difficult to achieve. The significant degree of pluralism and competition among official executive sources often gives rise to confused and conflicting messages and severely undermines any top-down 'command and control' news management strategy. Instead, coordination in French executive communication tends to remain loose at best, despite attempts to impose coherence by the Prime Minister's office. (2005: 314)

At the level of the political party, there have been enormous changes as well. The transformation of parties into electoral professional political parties is an example of this. The consequences are a different approach to the practice of political communication, political advocacy and political engagement. Much of this is common across Europe where political parties have witnessed a decline in their membership (see also Mair and Biezen, 2001) and a changed relationship between voter and public. The most often referred-to trend is one of de-alignment, whereby voters are no longer making political decisions on the basis of traditional allegiances (for example class, religion) and are more prepared to switch votes, and hence are more open to persuasion. This has major implications for the political process. Political parties must therefore turn their attention to how they can communicate with the public/voters, how they can get their messages across, how they can persuade and mobilize voters. Furthermore, in a situation where citizens have become less supportive of political parties, less trusting of the political system and more likely to abstain, there is likely to be a greater incentive to employ those skilled in the arts of communication and marketing – the 'professional' consultants, communicators and organizers – to help the political parties to position themselves in the minds of the citizen/voter.

This has led to considerable organizational change, ranging from a greater centralization of operations to a reassessment of the role of members, and the relationship of the centre to the periphery (for example constituencies, local campaigns). The decline of the political party's traditional position of pre-eminence within the political process (and in the media) is leading to a greater questioning of how they must operate in competitive elections not only in the present but also in the future. The 'settlement' that may have characterized the place of the parties in 'Age 2' (Blumler and Kavanagh, 1999) – dominant, central to political processes, part of the core source of news for the media (part of the *raison d'être* of media?) – no longer holds. Indeed, in the relatively short history of political parties – roughly 1850 to 2000 – that settlement may be no more than a short period when certain features dominated rather than a template.

At an organizational–operational level of political parties, there have been large changes as well. Some, such as the view that organizations should operate with a single vision and should communicate that throughout, have infected political parties and the ways in which they interact with their members, the media and others; others, such as the need to act in a 'professional' way, have also entered the vocabulary and the practice of organizations, as well as individuals. Another indication of these changes is the process of centralization, both within political parties but also in government, that has created a

tight framework for the control and conduct of communication functions. In probably all cases, more care has been taken to deal with
communication, and to reflect and alter the processes and content
of communication to meet the challenges that have arisen from the
changing nature of media, changing nature of government and the
changing nature of the parties themselves.

All these feature in one way or another in the transformation of
political communication in the different political settings that we
shall explore in three countries: Germany, Italy and Greece. And
quite central to all, is the development of television and especially
its transformation from a highly regulated medium into one that
operates in a competitive environment and privileges 'media logic'
over 'party logic'.

Transformation in the global context: Germany

The common theme linking the Western European countries discussed
here – Greece, Germany, Italy – is the changing nature of their societies and of their political arrangements. In the case of Italy, three key
characteristics emerge from the account provided above: the weakening of the political parties, the growth of commercial broadcast (TV)
services and the role of Berlusconi. Whilst the third of these is clearly
specific to Italy, and the demise of the political parties has been more
rapid and extreme than elsewhere, the common theme of weakening
of parties and rise of commercial television features in any examination of change in the German political system. According to Holtz-
Bacha, certain changes in the early 1980s created a novel situation
in Germany:

> While political communication during the 1970s gradually took
> into account that television had taken the lead among the mass
> media and started to adapt to its logic, the late 1980s saw another
> turning point. Although commercial television went on air in 1984,
> it only started to play a role for election campaigning in the 1990s.
> (2007: 69)

The onset of private television and the subsequent commercialization forced those in politics to adapt to a new situation. Commercial
television, unlike the public broadcasters, operated with a different logic in Germany, as elsewhere. The changes brought about
included, according to Barbara Pfetsch, 'a reorientation away from
normative towards commercial goals; from political system towards

market principle' (1996: 432) and there were consequences for the outputs of political communication. In particular, as the public and commercial broadcasters converged in their presentation of politics, it was the public broadcasters who effectively changed their practices most: 'private channels caught up with public channels regarding the contents of political information, while public channels caught up with commercial stations in their presentation formats' (Pfetsch,1996: 446).

One response to these sorts of changes, according to Holtz-Bacha (2002), was a 'professionalization of politics' that aimed to deal with changes in the media: political parties sought to influence and control the presentation of politics, at the same time as they sought to devise ways to persuade an electorate that was less politically committed or aligned than it once was. A similar account can be found in Jens Tenscher's work on changes in political communication in Germany although he also tries to connect the loosening of political ties and commercialization of the broadcast media to changes in political communication practices:

> The image-building function has become more important during recent years because of loosening ties between political organizations and the citizens. Simultaneously, we have witnessed an acceleration of the commercialization of the broadcasting system, which has developed new formats for political (self)-presentation ... Hence, although the German parliamentary system still favours strong political parties and inherently limits the process of personalization, individual political actors have been gaining relevance as principal means to reduce political complexity within the processes of political communication, political coverage and political understanding. Therefore, image-building and news management may be labelled the two major and indispensable tools of modern political communication to achieve their primary political objectives. (2004: 529–30)

More specific changes have been identified in the context of election campaigning. Although each successive federal election campaign has tended to include ever newer methods of campaigning and electioneering, the 1998 election is often seen as the quintessentially 'Americanized campaign' (Holtz-Bacha, 2002). That is, a campaign that does not focus on traditional considerations of issues and policies but rather on candidates and personalities and which is conducted around the medium of television and run by experts (professionals) using techniques adapted from the US experience. As elsewhere, it was not that some of these elements had not intruded into electoral practices in the past – campaign consultants had been cooperating with US consultants since the 1970s (Plasser and Plasser, 2002: 27) – but that the 1998 campaign had the appearance of something different: 'nothing was really new but everything was a little more sophisticated than before' (Holtz-Bacha, 2007: 70).

Features of the campaign that made it seem different included a new degree of 'centralization and specialization, personalization, and entertainization'. The processes of centralization and specialization were in evidence when the SPD set up its campaign headquarters, the Kampa. This was set up in 1997 – a year before the election – 'as a central unit along the lines of Clinton's War Room in the 1992 U.S. presidential campaign, as well as of Blair's campaign headquarters during the 1997 British general election' (Holtz-Bacha, 2002: 30). Holtz-Bacha later comments that the 'image of a centralized campaign management pulling the strings demonstrated professionalism to the party members and the public' (Holtz-Bacha, 2002: 31).

Plasser and Plasser are quite critical of the Kampa and the idea behind it. They argue that it was 'designated foremost to attract journalists and to symbolize the modernity of the Social Democrats' rather than a tactical and strategic move that was of great success in the election. More than this, they argue that these actions were no more than 'imitations' and 'reactions to changed news values of TV journalists exerting pressure' on party managers to deliver newsworthy and visually interesting material (2002: 76). In other words, it was a response to changes in the media rather than a deeper modernization of electioneering per se; a point also made by Holtz-Bacha when she points out that 'in the sense that professionalization means the shift of campaign management to experts outside the parties, the SPD's 1998 campaign can be regarded as professionalized to a high degree. However, if one takes the criteria that Scammell (1997) developed … it soon becomes obvious that this was not the case in Germany' (2002: 35). That is, many of the experts used came from within the political party, there was no specific or special training for consultants, and there was more of a sense of continuity rather than massive discontinuity with the past. It was not so much the product of 'Americanization' as of 'hybridization' of forms (see Schulz et al. 2005: 79).

Changes that have taken place in the German political and media systems have given rise to election coverage that is more personalized, dramatized and more negative than in the past. At the same time, one can quite easily identify a higher level of professionalization across a range of political actors and their helpers (see Schulz and Zeh, 2007). And the factor that has brought about these changes appears to be, as elsewhere, the medium of television. As Schulz et al. observe: 'The media changes in the 1980s altered the presentation formats of politics on television in Germany, as in other countries. ... These developments appear to be the inevitable consequence of increased media competition and the commercialization of broadcasting' (2005: 5).

Italy

Accounts of changes in political communication in Italy (Mancini, 2007; Mazzoleni, 1987, 1995, 1996) usually begin with a brief review of the massive changes in the political system that took place post-1980s. The period leading up to this point is seen as one in which there were strong ties between the political parties and the citizenry and those strong links ensured that parties were directly connected to their membership and supporters. This period was also, therefore, a period when the parties were strongly connected to the mass media. According to Mazzoleni, the:

> main consequences of this media–parties interrelationship have been: 1) a strong politicization of the newsmaking profession, especially in broadcasting, so that it has been fairly easy to label a television channel ... as 'Catholic', 'Communist', 'Socialist', and so on; 2) a tendency for the newspapers to serve as partisan vehicles ...; 3) overwhelming coverage of the inter-party debate in news reporting. (1987: 82)

From the 1980s onwards, a number of changes in the Italian political and broadcasting landscape took place and these created a new environment for political communication, weakening the strong relationship that had hitherto existed. These changes included 'a de-ideologizing of Italian party politics' along with greater electoral volatility, and a 'crisis of the "mass party"' (Mazzoleni, 1987: 82–3). As elsewhere in Western Europe, the political parties lost the grip on society they once had and ceased to be the recruiting, ideological trope that they once were. Whilst these longer term changes could be traced back to the 1970s, it was in the 1980s that they began to have an impact on the nature of political communication. At this point in time, though, the changes that were taking place were far from clear or dramatic. Things were still in flux, although there were signs that the political parties were beginning to take on board the need to deal with a more powerful and less dependent media system. It was a period of transition: 'a phase of transition between old and new patterns, between dependence and autonomy, between the traditional domination of party logic and the growing strength of media logic' (Mazzoleni, 1987: 102).

The ongoing changes were to accelerate when corruption scandals (*tangentopoli*) hit the political party system and undermined its legitimacy. By the 1990s, Mazzoleni could write of the '*fall* of the old party establishment' (1995: 295, emphasis added) and of the vacuum that this collapse created; a vacuum that would subsequently be filled by Silvio Berlusconi and his *Forza Italia* party. One indicator of the decline of the parties was the decline in membership; as Mancini has pointed out, in '1955, the PCI (the Communist Party) had 2,090,006 paid up members, in 1995 the figure was 682,290; in 1955, the DC (Christian Democrats) had 1,186,785 members but in 1995 only 160,000' (Mancini, 2007: 112). The 'crumbling of the establishment and of the party system' (Mazzoleni, 1995: 294) and the increasing volatility of the electorate created a space for a new political force, led by Berlusconi, to make a mark in the 1990s.

Two other factors helped complete the transformation that had begun a decade or more earlier. One was the emergence of a commercial system of broadcasting – controlled by Berlusconi – that rivalled the public broadcaster, RAI; the other was what Mazzoleni describes as changes in the '"rules" of the democratic game': the de-legitimizing of the old political system, changes to the electoral system, and demands for new broadcasting rules (1995: 298–9).

As a result of these changes, elections were to be conducted differently – the proportional representation system was replaced by the majoritarian one – and candidates developed strategies and tactics to deal with or court the media, which had itself changed in the process. This led to 'the commercialization of politics and eventually of political communication' (Mazzoleni, 1995: 307).

The role of Berlusconi in this transformation of Italian political communication cannot be overestimated. He brought 'a new attitude and approach to the media' which grew out of his own background as an entrepreneur keen to satisfy the needs of the public – the voters – and to offer them something new. Under Berlusconi, the trend towards the professionalization of political communication became particularly noticeable. He introduced new forms of political communication based on the marketization, trivialization and the ownership of the mass media. A common element in these attitudes has been a process of professionalization. Many have spoken of *Forza Italia*, Berlusconi's party, as *partito azienda* (a company party) pointing out how it was established thanks to the transfer of Berlusconi's staff from his companies (essentially his advertising firm) into the new party structure: these people brought with them their business-oriented and professional skills (Mancini, 2007: 116).

For Plasser and Plasser, the moment of transformation in Italian political communication is quite specific: only since the parliamentary elections of 1994 and the end or transformation of the old parties, was a trend towards professionalization started in Italy, ushered in primarily by Berlusconi's party (2002: 309).

The contemporary situation in Italy suggests that Italian politics is now quite similar to politics in other Western democracies: there is a greater personalization of politics and focus on political leaders; there is a greater use of political professionals and consultants; and a greater use of the techniques of modern campaigning. Whilst this pattern may be more obvious at the national than the local level, it does indicate that elements of 'modern campaigning' are now commonly found in Italian politics.

The above brief account of the background to the transformation of political communication in Italy suggests that a range of factors need to be taken into consideration when looking at explanations for change. As elsewhere, traditional political parties were separated from their traditional base but this process was compounded by the *tangentopoli* scandals. The growing importance of 'media logic' – and the emergence of a less dependent media – undoubtedly forced political parties to adopt a more professional approach to electioneering. As with the German example, the transformation of political communication in Italy is the outcome of many forces, of which the development of a more autonomous, more audience-directed broadcast media is a key one.

Greece

Greece differs significantly from the other countries explored here for two main reasons. The first is that it was, until the early 1970s, ruled by a dictatorship; the second, that it is commonly seen as a country where 'clientelistic' relations still exist and still constrain the development of more modernized systems of communication (Hallin and Mancini, 2004: 58–9). Nevertheless, there are aspects of the Greek case that point to similarities between trends there and elsewhere. For example, political consultants have been regularly used during election campaigns, political advertising is now possible on the broadcast media, and the television services have been commercialized and deregulated with consequences for both the conduct and the practice of political communication. But differences between Greece and other countries still persist.

At a general and overarching level, Greece shares common features with the other countries dealt with here. As Papathanassopoulos points out, 'Greece has been undergoing a series of social transformations, ... the deregulation and privatization of the television sector, [and] television has become a significant, if not indispensable, medium for political parties and politicians in their efforts to communicate with the public' (2007: 127). Other changes have a familiar ring to them; the differences between the political parties are now much less obvious than they once were and the public is less enchanted with traditional politics than it once was, although identification with political parties is still quite significant (see Plasser and Plasser, 2002: 306) and the political parties still play a significant part in political life. Thus, 'despite using and adapting to new media techniques, communication and marketing practices – particularly during the election campaigning period – [political parties] have remained strong' (Papathanassopoulos, 2007: 129).

The changes that have taken place in respect of the use of television during campaigns has been quite dramatic. 'Overall, spending on political television advertising has increased from 29 per cent of parties' total campaign expenditure in 1990 to 83 per cent in the 1996 election campaign ... unlimited access to paid *poli spots* changed the style of Greek campaigns substantially' (Plasser and Plasser, 2002: 227). Indeed, from the 1993 general election and the rise of 'telepolitics', there has been a greater degree of professionalization in the use of the media in order to get the message across to the voters.

As in Germany and Italy – and to an extent in Britain – the use of professionals/experts in political communication is widespread. In the Greek context, they have been in use since the 1980s but they are subordinate to the political party and its leadership. Moreover, such professionals/experts are 'usually party members and do not come from outside the party or the political system. The difference is that their political marketing techniques are adapted to the new communications environment and media landscape' (Papathanassopoulos, 2007: 132). This is reminiscent of the situation in Germany (see above) where the level of professionalization is seen to fall short of the 'hired gun' model of political consultancy normally associated with the Americanized model of election campaigning. As Papathanassopoulos puts it:

it is uncertain to what extent these professional communication practices have come to dominate the development of political parties or whether they only make sense in the context of the development of the political parties themselves. First of all, the evolution from a party-centred system to a candidate-centred system has not yet materialised in Greece, although the campaigning is indeed focused on the parties' leaders' images. This is because the parties have maintained the dominance over individual MPs, while the party leader personalises the party. (2007: 135)

Summary and conclusion

The three country-specific examples, although brief, draw our attention not only to changes in society and in political parties but also – and importantly – to significant changes in the make-up of their broadcast media. In all three cases, the changes in the broadcast media involve some degree of commercialization and in all cases they took place in the 1980s or later. Unlike as in Britain, where a strong commercial presence was established in the 1950s, the driving force of change which brought about an emerging 'media logic' is identified much later in Germany, Italy and Greece.

If we were to add the case of France to our list we would probably find similar patterns. As in other West European democracies, politicians in France have had to learn how to use the media to great effect although Philippe Maarek (2007) has pointed out that the greater appreciation of the need to use the media has a long history. He cites several examples: Michel Bongrand, 'a promising marketing consultant ... who had spent several months in Joe Napolitan's staff in the United States learning the new rules of the game' came to prominence in France in the 1965 election (2007: 146); and in 1981, Jacques Séguéla came to prominence for his work with François Mitterand. Both Bongard and Séguéla are described by Plasser and Plasser as 'internationally renowned specialists in *marketing electorale*' alongside a small number of other '*conseils politiques*' and '*conseils en communication*' (2002: 34).

In more recent times, restrictions on election expenditure and on the ways in which political actors can make use of available free time on television – airtime cannot be bought – have increased pressure on media and journalists by politicians and their press agents to manage the news agenda. Such activities inevitably call for an increased professionalization in the candidates' public relations. However, Maarek suggests that in the French case, professionalization may have reached some sort of 'limit' precisely because 'campaigning and campaigning techniques by themselves have become news items' (2007: 152). By being exposed, the public can not only see through efforts to manipulate it but also approaches politics with a more cynical perspective.

Yet it is hard to deny the continuing relevance of marketing and professionalization in the French context and particularly as a result of the 'media logic' of media in a competitive environment – French broadcast media were also deregulated in the 1980s – although this does not mean that the 'modern model of campaigning' (Swanson and Mancini, 1996) is not refracted by domestic considerations. As Raymond Kuhn has pointed out, there is now:

> pressure on politicians to professionalize their public communication [which] has been generated by the increased demands of the news media and the changing expectations of the electorate. In no political system, however, do these demands and expectations simply determine the communicative strategies and behaviour of elite political actors in the mediated public sphere. Instead, common transnational pressures for change are filtered, shaped and reconfigured by national (and sub-national) practices, institutional arrangements and elite cultures. (2000: 310)

Whilst this is an argument in support of the 'hybrid' thesis, the roots of change are, according to Maarek, decidedly American and the French political communication has followed 'more or less willingly the American role model of the use of modern media' (2007: 157). Here, as elsewhere, we have the competing accounts of transformations: commercialization of broadcast media bringing about a more audience-oriented perspective; elements of Americanization, with the US as a source; elements of 'hybridization' as practices are adapted; elements of professionalization as new tricks are learned and older ones updated – all giving rise to a different set of practices than before, all pointing to transformations of sorts.

In all cases, there is a common link and that is the media-centredness of political systems and, more critically, the input of a commercial dimension into the broadcast medium of each of the countries concerned.

The Internet: Transforming Political Communication?

8

Introduction

It is perhaps fitting to devote the penultimate chapter of this book to the newest development in communication to have an impact on contemporary societies, the internet. Whilst the focus of this chapter will be mainly on the internet, it is important that we see the internet as part of a continuing process of technological change whereby the powers and capacity of computers are combined with forms of communication via wire as well as wireless technologies to give shape to new infrastructures of communication (see, for example, Winston, 2004).

One reason for taking a broader view of change is that we often forget that prior to the rise of the internet as a mass phenomenon, other information and communication technologies (ICTs) such as cable and satellite television also began to challenge the hegemony of earlier forms of broadcast communication. By the early 1990s, for example, cable and satellite television had created a television of abundance where there was once scarcity. Equally important, these newer forms of television gave rise to round-the-clock services, for example in news provision, that forced politicians, amongst others, to rethink their communication strategies. This change is captured well in the views expressed by Chris Meyer and Alastair Campbell (see Chapter 6) when they were helping their respective political masters to adjust to the new media environment.

Whilst the newer ICTs brought about what Seymour-Ure (1996) called 'electronic glut' and others have referred to as the 'third age' of political communication (Blumler and Kavanagh, 1999), it could be argued that the emergence of the internet pushed all these developments in a direction that had hitherto only been dreamt of. Henceforth, political communication would no longer need to be *mass* communication: it could be targeted at individuals as well as groups; it could be direct and not mediated by traditional professional journalists; it could be interactive; it could be plentiful since there was no restriction on supply; and so on. This was the era of digital communication in which all forms of communication – visual, audio or text – could be converted into a digital format, processed by computers and pushed (or pulled) around the globe with the greatest of ease.

With such momentous changes taking place in the infrastructure of communication – although we must still acknowledge that the penetration of the internet in the UK is at around 60% of households, and access varies by age and gender (Livingstone et al., 2007) – it was perhaps inevitable that questions would be raised about how politics and political communication would be affected by it. How would political parties adapt to such change? How would individuals adapt? What of politicians themselves and what about institutions? In other words, how would the internet transform – or not – the nature and practice of politics and of political communication? In seeking to deal with these questions, this chapter:

- will review some of the ways in which the internet is currently being used in the realm of politics, with particular emphasis on political parties and parliamentary representatives
- will review those developments in the context of the broader discussion of how different technologies have been used in the past in the realm of politics (see also Chapter 2)
- will offer a tentative conclusion as to whether the internet has, or has not, transformed and professionalized the conduct and practice of political communication.

Before we begin the analysis of the transformative qualities of the internet, it is worth bearing in mind Agre's comments on the internet and its potential and properties:

> If we ask what effect the Internet will have on the political process, for example, then the question is ill-posed: The Internet has its effect only in the ways that it is appropriated, and it is appropriated in so many different ways that nobody has enough information to add them up. Some of the changes will take the form of 'the same, only more so'; others will be qualitative, as the existing accommodations become untenable. Institutions may implode, or they may fragment and reconfigure, or their functions may be absorbed by rivals. ... (Agre, 2002: 316)

The political impact of new media

In his 1974 study *The Political Impact of Mass Media*, Colin Seymour-Ure (1974) sought to establish a framework that could be used to explore the 'impact' of mass media. According to Seymour-Ure, we needed to move away from looking at 'impact' and its close cousin 'effects' in a simplistic way so that we could become more aware of the many and different ways in which the mass media could change the nature of the political system and of political communication. One of his suggestions was that we should ask the question 'How far and in what ways are the political relationships of groups and individuals affected by the communication between them?' (1974: 16). In this way, analysing the 'impact' of mass media meant looking at how relationships – between individuals and individuals, institutions and institutions and so on – changed as a consequence of the communication that took place between them. At one point he goes so far as to argue that 'at its broadest, "effect" is defined ... as any change within the political system induced directly or indirectly by the mass media' (1974: 21).

This sort of approach makes sense in at least two ways. First, it accepts that the nature of 'effects' can be varied and on a range of actors, in the first instance, and then on institutions. So, 'the effect of mass media on Parliament means some kind of change caused by media in the political relationship of Members of Parliament to each other or to non-members' (1974: 22). In this way, one can begin to explore both individual 'effects' and broader 'effects' on political culture or institutions. Second, in the context of the study of *mass* media this approach makes sense because the political communication that does take place usually occurs between one source and a large (a *mass*) audience. Consequently, how things that are communicated in a news broadcast or a party election programme intended to reach a large number of people, may engender some set of 'effects' or responses, is a legitimate area of study. That the communication is directed at *individuals* who make up the *mass* audience is a point worth emphasizing, although the properties of the media in question – newspapers, television – direct content at everyone in an undifferentiated way.

Whilst some of these elements are applicable today, because we still live in an age of mass media – television and newspapers continue to be important players within the political system – the digital age creates different conditions for political communication. On the one hand, the internet complements and supplements the older forms of communication by creating other sources of information; on the other hand, the internet becomes a means of communication per se enhanced, no doubt, by the interactivity that it offers. In many ways, the internet needs to be seen as separate and different from traditional mainstream mass media, whether print or broadcast. Some recent evidence from the Pew Internet & American Life Project shows how the communication environment for politics has changed:

> Some 25% of all Americans (or 37% of internet users) say they got information online about the 2006 elections and 10% of Americans (15% of internet users) say they exchanged emails about the candidates. Many people used the internet both ways – for news and for communication about politics. Altogether, 31% of all Americans (or 46% of internet users) say they were online during the campaign season gathering information and exchanging views via email. Throughout this report, we call this group *campaign internet users*. They represent more than 60 million people. (Jarvis, 2007a)

Moreover, many of these users not only accessed information but used facilities to communicate with others:

> About 14 million Americans – almost a quarter of those 'campaign internet users' (11% of internet users, 7% of Americans) – *used* the read-write web to 'contribute to political discussion and activity.' They didn't just read. They *did*: 8% of 'campaign internet users' posted their own comment online; 13% forwarded or posted someone else's commentary; 1% created and 8% forwarded audio or video ... (Jarvis, 2007a)

While there are no similar figures about the UK political environment, the figures that are available suggest that the internet is becoming important as a source of news and information and as a means for engaging in political activities. A study conducted for the Hansard Society by the Electoral Commission in 2007, found that 14% of adults (18 years and over) obtained their information and news from the internet. Although this lagged behind television (76% of respondents), the national press (56%), the local press (33%) and radio (34%), it was a large enough figure to suggest that the internet could not be overlooked in matters of political communication (Hansard Society, 2007: 54). Other research has also found that online access provided opportunities for political engagement. Gibson et al. (2005) found that 17% of those online in 2002 reported engaging in some form of online political activity, such as seeking political information or visiting political websites. While this figure is small, one might expect it to grow as more go on line: in 2002, 49% of the UK population was online compared with 57% in 2007 (National Statistics, 2007). The implications of both these bits of data are many: on the one hand they point to the need for political communicators to consider the internet in all media planning; on the other, they suggest that the properties inherent in the use of the internet – ranging from search facilities to networking, blogging to e-petitions – can begin to shift the nature of political communication and the relationships that have long characterized it.

The extent to which this new communication environment brings about a transformation of political communication is something to which we shall return, but there is no doubt that significant changes have come about. In Chapter 2, I argued that as newer media – newspapers, radio, film, television – came on stream *outside* the direct control of political parties and/or the state, the opportunities for direct control lessened considerably and political actors had to adapt to 'media logic' and all its consequences. Political parties could no longer assume that they were central to the business of the media; they would have to consider new ways of gaining a presence there. With the internet in place – although we must not overlook the phenomenal growth in commercial media and the competitive and fragmented media environment that the new information and communication technologies also brought about – political parties have, it seems, an even more limited power to exercise control over the mainstream media. This argument is captured in Brian McNair's analysis of news and journalism in the 21st century. In the introduction to his book *Cultural Chaos* he writes:

> while the desire for control of the news agenda, and for definitional power in the journalistic construction of meaning, are powerful and ever-present ... the capacity of elite groups to wield it effectively is more limited than it has been since the emergence of the first news media in the sixteenth century ... The chaos paradigm does not abolish the desire for control; it focuses on the shrinking media space available for securing it ideologically. (2006: 4)

Whilst it is true that there is a 'shrinking media space ... for securing it ideologically', when applied to the digital era – or to the internet more specifically – this argument is only partially correct. To understand why this should be so, we need to look more closely at how elites (of which political parties are a prime example) work with the media generally.

In the case of the mainstream media – principally television and the press – elites seek to control the agenda through a series of well-established tactics. Often the positions of elites can be challenged because of the ways in which the media work, (Schlesinger and Tumber, 1994) and so in the pursuit of the newsworthy, elite positions and counter-positions usually sit side-by-side on news broadcasts or on the pages of daily newspapers. It follows from this, that attentive viewers and readers will be exposed to a range of sometimes conflicting views. This is admittedly a fairly simplistic account of what happens in day-to-day news production but the underlying processes at play are well known and well established: in the mainstream media coverage of the Middle East, for instance, the Israeli position will be balanced by that of Palestinians and other groups, and if it is not, someone will surely point out that it should be so.

The internet works very differently and has different properties. The most obvious difference is that apart from the online versions of the mainstream media, there is no single or dominant source of information. Elites cannot compete for space as they do on the *BBC* or in the *Guardian*. They can create their own vehicles of communication, their own websites, but the 'impact' of these will depend on whether anyone (or what number of people) accesses them. So, while the 'media space' has undoubtedly shrunk, on the internet elites can create their own vehicles of communication: be it a political leader's weblog (http://www.webcameron.org.uk/) or an internet television channel (http://www.18doughtystreet.com/).

There are, then, contradictory forces at play. With the internet developing rapidly in most modern societies, there are countless ways in which connections between organizations and people can be made. Yet in respect of the communication of politics:

- Mainstream news media are still dominant as sources of news.
- Although elites can create and control their own media space (their websites, blogs and so on) these are of little use unless they are accessed. However, the potential for interactivity exposes elites to interrogation and contradiction.
- Websites compete with, and link with, other websites so creating a network of information.
- With many sites on the internet providing tools for interactivity, individuals can not only feed back comments but create their own networks of information.
- Lastly, the networks of information can open up discussions beyond what is made available through elites or traditional media outlets.

To return to the example of the Middle East, news about the Middle East will most likely be accessed from the online versions of the mainstream media (for example www.bbc.co.uk/news) but it can then be supplemented by news from a whole host of other sources which will, in turn, link up to other sources of information, including http://www.melaniephillips.com/diary, http://www.engageonline.org.uk/blog/article.php?id=1071, http://www.arabmediawatch.com/amw/ and http://www. palestineremembered.com/. At some points in this process, those accessing sites will be able to add their own comments.

However, the fact that the internet is a 'pull' technology – we have to 'pull' the information – contrary to the 'push' of traditional technologies where the content is pushed to us in digestible chunks whether we wish it or not, is both its strength and its weakness. It can give rise to millions of websites (its strength) but if no one accesses them, they are of little use (its weakness). Which is why the digital era has not completely eroded the strength of the mainstream media for day-to-day coverage of events and opinions: political debate is still debate that takes place in traditional media. Another example will illustrate this point. In the summer of 2007, the Conservative Party was having to deal with a minor controversy over its policy towards selective (so-called 'grammar') schools. Much of that controversy was inflamed by the mainstream media – both press and television – with their relish for a story about political dissent and resignations within the party (see, for example, http://news.bbc.co.uk/1/hi/uk_politics/6708511.stm). While this story also featured on other websites, for example Iain Dale and Guido Fawkes (http://iaindale.blogspot.com/ and http://www.order-order.com/ respectively) it would be difficult to argue that those sites were critical for the development of the story or – and this is perhaps more of a key point – are important for the general public. As far as the Conservative Party is concerned, their aim is still to control the agenda of the *mainstream* media.

So, while the argument that 'media space' has shrunk is valid, it is valid up to a point in that it does not explore the details of how different media work and how traditional media remain dominant despite the erosion of their pre-eminence. Equally, it does not explore the extent to which elites will try to control their own media space through the creation of their own websites. Finally, it does not consider the extent to which elites will shift their efforts away from mediated communication via mainstream media to unmediated communication via the internet. All this suggests, therefore, that when we speak of the digital age/internet age in the context of politics and political communication, we need to be aware of the interaction and adaptation of media to other media and of elites adapting their own practices to the newer media. To follow up an argument set out in Chapter 2, elites/political parties will adapt to newer media in order to gain advantage from them and to gain any advantage they can over their rivals. They will continue to use them to the extent that they feel they have to in a competitive electoral environment: we now have, on the Conservative Party side, the party website, the leader's website, individual MPs' websites, blogs and newsletters. This is mirrored on the side of the Labour Party and so on.

Has this transformed and professionalized the nature and content of political communication in Britain? While it has certainly led to the creation of more outlets, and more outlets run by more professional webmasters, that is somewhat different from claims that it has (or has not) transformed political communication. For those claims to have any credibility, we need to explore in greater depth how the internet is used in politics and to return to the question of how we can study the 'impact' of the new media.

Politics on the net

Clearly, there is no shortage of political and governmental (institutional) information on the internet. Much of it is produced by individuals, groups and institutions but established political parties are by no means absent from the web. Simple or raw numbers, however, do not necessarily translate into significance. During the 2005 British General Election, James Stanyer counted 312 political blogs representing a whole range of established and non-established political views (quoted in Wring et al., 2007: 103). Is this a large number, or remarkably few, considering the ease of blogging? In a similar vein, a report on the internet and political communication in the 2004 presidential election noted that 'the [Howard] Dean campaign posted 2,910 entries on its "Blog for America" and received 314,121 comments which were also posted here' (Cornfield, undated, c.2006: 2). Whilst this is a large number, it is small by comparison to the size of the US adult population.

Although numbers do begin to indicate the extent to which use of the internet has begun to reshape patterns of communication and political activity, on their own they are unlikely to resolve the question of how significant the internet has been/or is in major political struggles; or how significant different/novel uses of the internet have been or are. For this, we have to turn to commentaries on national elections.

Reviewing the experience of the 2004 presidential election, Cornfield conceded that:

the internet's distinctive role in politics has arisen because it can be used in multiple ways. Part deliberative town square, part raucous debating society, part research library, part instant news source, and part political comedy club, the internet connects voters to a wealth of content and commentary about politics. At the same time, campaigners learned a great deal about how to use the internet to attract and aggregate viewers, donors, message forwarders, volunteers, and voters during the 2003–4 election cycle. (undated, *c*.2006: 1)

In this respect, the evidence from the US does point to increasing use of the internet in politics but, beyond this, there is still room for debate as to the significance of all this. Will it do anything more than reward the media rich? Will it overturn decades of ingrained behaviour? Will it, dare one ask, 'transform' political communication?

To begin to answer these 'bigger' questions one has to tackle two separate problems, one theoretical, the other experiential. The theoretical one is bound up with the question of how we come to understand the ways in which technologies (television, computers, the internet) develop within societies. The second question is, by comparison, more straightforward: what is our experience of the uses of the internet in politics? Whilst the two are indeed connected, it is useful to look at them separately before we pass any considered judgements on the ways in which the internet and politics interact.

Exploring the interactions of technologies and politics

There are at least two different ways in which the themes of the internet in the political process have been explored. On the one hand, there are positions which privilege the potential of the internet to bring about major changes in the political process. On the other hand, there are positions that see the internet being appropriated by existing bodies rather than bringing about change; in this latter case, it is very much a matter of 'things as before'. Both these sets of positions are discussed briefly below but, in the context of this book, it is fairly obvious that it is the latter set of positions that is favoured. This is not only because they are neither optimistic nor pessimistic – perhaps more 'realist' (Agre, 2002: 316) – but also because they tend to lend support, if only implicitly, to the view expressed throughout this book that political organizations will use newer technologies to the extent that they can benefit from them. Over time, the interactions that take place between political parties and (those who organize) the new means of communication can begin to transform the nature and content of political communication. We can see this process in the case of the development of television: while television as a new medium did force political actors and parties to rethink how they should communicate to a mass audience via that particular medium, once those in charge of television (executives, journalists and so on) began to exert their power and skills as mediators of content, we were able to see the transformation of political communication. The power to communicate, in other words, shifted away from the political parties or, and perhaps more often, was the outcome of negotiations. Transformations are therefore more likely to be the result of gradual, incremental and phased change rather than of a one-time, big-bang sort.

Such a gradualist/incrementalist position has one other advantage and that is its take on how change comes about. Adopting the view that new technologies bring about change – views that can too often be found in the literature – simplifies the interactions that take place within a social, economic and political context. Thus, the gradualist/incrementalist position does not deny the possibility of change, including transformative change, but sees that as being part of a longer and more gradual process. It favours a more sophisticated approach to the study of technologies within society.

By contrast, positions that privilege the potential of the internet to bring about change not only simplify how social forces work but also, more critically, appear to hanker for a vision of the future that magically cures all the ills of today's societies. So, if levels of participation in the political process are low, if people are not knowledgeable, if individuals find it difficult to make contact with their elected representatives, if people find it difficult to walk to the local school to vote and so on, technology can come to the rescue. The 'fix' in all these cases is a technological one. In these scenarios, the internet can reconnect people, reinvigorate democracy and so on. As Philip Agre put it, 'the political process is being intensively reimagined in the context of new information and communications technologies' (2002: 311).

The irony is that we have been here before in other times and with other technologies. In the 1960s, cable television and cable systems acquired similar 'healing' properties. For example:

- It promised an abundance of communication (thus ending scarcity).
- It gave rise to the possibility of creating new structures of communication (local TV systems, local TV, everyone becoming a communicator).

- It predicted better communities by enhancing communication within them through its ability to connect everyone and allowing access for all to the means of communication.
- It would heighten participation and challenge the status quo and create the potential for participatory democracy and town-hall democracy.

Hailed as 'the television of abundance' by the American Sloan Commission inquiry into cable communication, it became a solution to contemporary problems. As the Commission remarked, as the 'urgent problems' confronting society were in some ways 'problems in communication' (Sloan Commission, 1971: 4), improving the means and content of communication would help solve society's ills. Brenda Maddox was moved to declare that the new revolution in communication made it possible 'to think of ending isolation, illiteracy and the tyranny of the mass medium' (1972: 15). Or it could be 'used to solve the problems of the cities, to reduce traffic on the roads, to give the poor more contact with a larger world' (1972: 23). The underlying assumption appears to be that the solution to many, or all, of the ills of society lies in the greater, and more effective, use of communication, and any technology that enhances that process of communication becomes either the solution or at the very least a critical part of the solution. As Carey and Quirk pointed out, the potential for the predicted improvement is derived not from the ability of the technology to fulfil its primary aim, but from 'the supposed capacity to transform the commonplace into the extraordinary; to create novel forms of human community; new standards of efficiency and progress, newer and more democratic forms of politics, and finally to usher a "new man" into history' (1973: 498). This is the process of 'reimagining' that Agre (2002) described.

With hindsight, we can see how limited such analyses of futuristic technological change were and how these visions of the future were based on a very simplistic understanding of larger processes. But if we can say that of other writings on 'new technologies', maybe we should adopt the same critical edge when we explore the statements surrounding the development of the internet. This is not to deny the possibility of change, nor to deny that some change will inevitably take place. Rather, it is to accept that the change that will take place is likely to be less radical than one thinks and circumscribed by existing social forces. We now accept, or should do, that technology cannot build a future in which 'the human condition is somehow transcended, politics evaporated and a blessed stage of peace and democratic order achieved' (Carey and Quirk, 1973: 489). That what happens, in reality, is that technologies become sidelined or appropriated, become superseded by others, are adapted in many different ways, and are shaped by a set of competing forces – economic and business interests, governmental and regulatory ones, consumer and practical preferences and desires. Furthermore, that the promise does not become obliterated but is reduced to a small part of a much more complex mosaic of activities and processes.

What one rarely finds within futuristic perspectives is a close examination of how technologies – of communications or otherwise – develop within existing societal structures; the expectation tends to be that the introduction of a new technology brings about change in an almost deterministic fashion. This expectation of change runs counter to positions that take as their starting point the expectation that change will be more gradual and within existing structures. Thus, the 'normalization hypothesis' developed by Margolis et al. 'runs counter to the popular notion that the internet provides the means for minor political parties and marginal political interest groups to compete with major political parties and interests on a more or less equal basis in cyberspace', although they admit that it is hardly 'conclusive' and more ongoing research is required (1999: 26). A study of the British general election of 2005 arrived at conclusions that tend to lend support to Margolis et al.: 'Both political parties and mainstream news providers have tended to "normalize" [that is, made into a quasi-traditional medium] the internet. It is very much politics or news as normal repackaged for well-to-do internet users' (Downey and Davidson, 2007: 106). This is not to say that new things were not tried on the internet, but that in terms of how they were used and their potential for overturning or revolutionizing existing modes of politics and of political communication, the prospect of change was small.

A similar conclusion, albeit based on a much more sophisticated understanding of how new technologies develop within societies, is the approach used by Philip Agre and his notion of 'amplification'. Agre suggests that:

> the political process comprises a complicated institutional circuitry of routinized information flows … and information technology accelerates many of this circuitry's constituent activities. A question that naturally arises is this: In what sense can the internet change anything? The amplification model gives a clear answer to this question: The internet changes nothing on its own, but it can amplify existing forces, and those amplified forces might change something. (2002: 317)

Instead of saying that technologies are 'reinforcing the system rather than repairing it' – a view he attributes to 'the reinforcement model' – his amplification model works with the idea that if change does come about, it will come about as a 'consequence of "forces," which are the aggregate effects of the actions that institutions organize people to perform. Modern institutions evolve through the interaction of numerous forces, and the amplification model asks how the interaction among forces might be changing' (2002: 318).

The reference to institutions is critical because it highlights the way that much of politics and political communication *even in the context of the internet* takes place through established institutions such as governments or political parties, social movements and so on. (See, for example, de Jong et al., 2005). Institutions are important precisely because they have not only taken on the role of representing aggregated views and positions but also because they 'provide a terrain upon which individuals and groups can pursue their goals' (Agre, 2002: 315). It follows, Agre continues, 'that the internet creates little that is qualitatively new: instead, for the most part, it amplifies existing forces' (Agre, 2002: 315).

Whether we accept Agre's statement to the effect that 'little that is qualitatively new' is likely to be created or his views on 'normalization', depends on how we *interpret* the evidence relating to the use of the internet in politics. As with the raw data (above), the construction of an interpretative framework is critical and no examples of internet use, on their own, can be conclusive evidence of anything in particular. It may also be far too early to be able to make any proper assessment of how the internet will alter our lives, let alone political communication. All we can do at this stage is simply turn to examples of its uses and then begin to see the extent to which the world of politics and political communication may, or may not, be transformed.

The internet in national political contests

In addition to highlighting some common uses of the internet such as fund raising and blogging in the 2004 US presidential election campaign, Michael Cornfield drew attention to other features:

> after decades of mass-media domination, interpersonal campaigning has undergone a renaissance in the early years of the millennium. The resurgence of the so-called 'ground war' entails canvassing citizens to discern their preferences, engaging them to persuade and mobilize supporters, and finally, getting out the vote (GOTV),

both on election day and before through programs aimed at taking advantage of the burgeoning early and absentee voter programs in many states. (undated, *c.*2006: 5)

He concludes:

As broadband connections proliferate and hum, the old mass audience for campaigns is being transformed into a collection of interconnected and overlapping audiences (global, national, partisan, group, issue-based, candidate-centered). Each online audience has a larger potential for activism than its offline counterparts simply because it has more communications and persuasion tools to exploit. This transformation makes life in the public arena more complex.

The more citizens use the internet, the more they might expect from campaigners and political journalists: rapid responses to information searches; a multiplicity of perspectives available on controversies; short and visually arresting promotional messages; drill-down capacities into referenced databases; more transparency from, and access to, institutions and players. Meanwhile, on the supply side of the political equation, candidates, groups, and parties now have models for how to use the internet to raise money, mobilize voters, and create public buzz. The new benchmarks established in 2004 could well be matched and surpassed in 2008. (undated, *c.*2006: 7)

The picture painted by Cornfield is one of change, yet it is change that has taken place within existing definitions of politics and a somewhat expanded adaptation of political communication as commonly understood. As Davis has pointed out 'the Bush and Kerry campaigns were command-and-control operations' (2005: 243) led by the parties seeking election. So, whilst the newer means of contacting individuals via the internet was undoubtedly important, the campaigns took the lead and directed activities. Without organization, the whole thing comes apart. In these ways, one could argue, the broad outlines of the political system have been readjusted rather than erased and redesigned and the internet has been appropriated by existing social forces.

Political elites/forces/actors thus used the internet in many different ways *to further their own specific aims to get elected*. What did not happen, although this is an abiding hope of those who tend to prophesy dramatic change, was for politics as it is commonly understood or as it is usually organized to be completely redefined. And so, and in spite of action groups, activities on Facebook, YouTube and so on, political action is still channelled through political parties, political leaders are still chosen from the political parties and politics is mostly organized as it was before. The core features of representative democracy remain in place, not only because they have been so completely normalized in Western capitalist societies but also because those who have invested most in such structures are themselves able to adapt and co-opt forces of change: which is why political parties will make use of the internet and why they will modernize themselves.

What about politics and the internet in the most recent (2005) British general election? In almost direct contrast to the US, the British case shows less change. Admittedly, it was a somewhat lacklustre campaign and the outcome was pretty well a foregone conclusion, giving the Labour Party its third victory in a row. And so despite the numerous weblogs and activities online, the campaign did not even generate the sorts of features that appeared in the US in 2004: there were certainly no 'meet-ups' and little or no citizen activism. Some funds were raised by the parties through the internet and parties were able to target content to different geographical constituencies, but overall the impact was small (Campbell, 2006). Part of the explanation for this could be that the nature of the parliamentary political system with its fairly strong political parties contesting local constituencies does not permit the more individualistic, expensive and lengthy campaigns common in the US. The official British election campaign averages about four weeks and although party leaders dominate, votes are cast for individuals standing in constituencies. This means that campaigning activity has to take place at both national levels and local levels and that parties as well as candidates must make themselves known. As a global medium, the internet can be used to advantage by the national parties, but it is less useful when it comes to local candidates wishing to communicate to all local constituents. While targeting of communication by the internet is possible, it is not possible unless all contacts are individually accessible. So the roles of the local candidate or representative are differently affected by the emergence of the internet, as we shall see in the next section.

Obviously, as in the US presidential election of 2004, more people went online than before and more access to more websites was the order of the day. Similarly, there were some interesting developments, such as websites where statements made by politicians would be put to the test, although even these were often run by traditional media outlets such as Channel Four. Despite the very obvious increased activity around the internet by parties, candidates and voters, Downey and Davidson conclude their study of the 2005 general election by stressing that 'the internet played an insignificant role in the 2005 General Election. Political parties, realistically, clearly do not see their websites as large-scale direct vote-winners and tend to focus their on-line activities on providing information ... to a small information elite' (2007: 106). This may be too pessimistic a conclusion given the variety of ways in which the internet was used and may reflect no more than the fact that the internet is still in its infancy. The view of many is that politics will change – must change – once the internet becomes part of the media mix.

Politics as usual ... or new possibilities?

Restricting the discussion of the internet to its place in electoral political communication significantly minimizes the importance of the roles it has developed or can potentially develop in the realm of politics. As we have seen, the internet can create new networks of communication, of information and of news. With the internet, communication takes place without mediation: governments, political parties, social movements, political leaders and actors can bypass traditional media outlets and this gives them the power to communicate directly with individuals or each other. Perhaps more significantly, political parties can also interact continually with their supporters, as well as with other citizens. In this way, they can consult and so be better placed to create or modify policies in line with what citizens want.

The architecture of the internet thus creates numerous possibilities for citizens and voters to play a part in politics, policy-making and the decision-making process itself. Political communication need no longer be from government or party to the citizen or voter; it can include elements of feedback, response, discussion and so on. Equally important is the possibility of interaction taking place amongst citizens or voters themselves with scant reference to those who are in government or politics. Social movements, for example, have found the internet useful as a means of building support and encouraging direct action.

What all these different ways of connecting peoples and organizations means is that the 'political impact' of the internet can take many forms and be looked at from a number of different perspectives. The discussion thus far has been about how parties communicate at elections and how the internet has been used in recent elections, but the other ways in which the internet can play a part in politics are by no means unimportant.

We need to consider here how the make-up of politics will be reshaped by the internet. Radio and television, in their different ways, forced political parties to reconsider how they communicated with the electorate: radio emphasized a particular and more informal style and form of communication, television brought about a more visual form of political communication. With journalists, for whatever reason, becoming more confrontational, political parties also developed new strategies to deal with these media. The arrangements that have dominated political communication in the recent past are thus the product of a particular conjunction of forces – parties in decline, television in the ascendant, a certain form of political journalism (Swanson, 1997) – and the question that we must confront is whether those fundamentals will change with the internet. We do know that the internet has a potential to create new networks of communication, we also know that it has had quite a severe impact on the existence of other technologies of communication. We know, furthermore, that it offers facilities for easier and cheaper communication across distances and time and that it can be used to create enormous repositories of information. All in all, it may have the potential to alter the relationships that existed in the very recent past between political institutions and citizens, between political representatives and the institutions within which they work, between political representatives and constituents, and between citizens themselves often as they organize themselves for political action. As the discussion and examples below will illustrate, there are countless ways in which the 'new' media can have a 'political impact'. Most of these can be subsumed under the heading of e-democracy.

e-democracy

Discussions of 'electronic democracy' or e-democracy usually focus on the power of the new technology of the internet to enhance the democratic process. By creating systems and structures whereby citizens can participate more easily, more frequently and more efficiently in decision-making processes at all levels (local, regional and national), where citizens can be in more direct contact with their representatives, leaders and governments (for example email contact, petitions and direct democracy), and where representatives and political institutions are themselves more readily and easily scrutinized by the citizenry and better able to meet their needs and desires, the internet is accorded powers to alter, for the better, the democratic process. ICTs can thus be used to 'improve communications', 'enhance scrutiny and performance' and 'strengthen democratic transactions' (Ferguson and Miller, 2007 1). One very obvious criticism of such scenarios is that it suggests that the 'new' media can 'fix' the problems of democracy such as low turnout, disengagement, disconnection and apathy.

But if we look closely at the ways in which the internet is being used, we can see how it can be employed to aid – rather than necessarily enhance or improve – aspects of the democratic process.

Consultations

Traditionally, political parties have written manifestos and then presented them to the electorate. But it is now possible for parties – as well as governments – to engage the public in a dialogue and in consultations and therefore in the process of policy-making itself. If politics is to be treated as a consumer good – in line with the idea of political marketing – then making the public part of the process of generating policies is indeed sensible. Parties can then decide which policies to pursue having taken the feedback into account. How widely used this sort of consultative activity will be is difficult to judge, since there are problems attached to it. When political parties try to gauge the views of supporters, as the Labour Party sought to do in 2002/3 with its *Big Conversation*, the exercise was criticized for being window dressing and/or a stunt. Similarly, when politicians seek the opinion of the public – in the 2007 French presidential elections, Ségolène Royal was reported to have said that her position would depend on what the French people wanted – they can be readily accused of having no political compass.

Assuming that an appropriate way of bringing the public into the political communication process can be found, then it is possible to see how the internet can facilitate the discussion between those who seek to govern and the governed. In this respect, the governed are no longer outside the process but a party to it, so fundamentally changing the relationship between political parties and the public.

Similar comments could be made about the place of the internet in communication from government and in governmental policy-making. Rather than keeping the governed at bay, it is perfectly possible to solicit their views through, for example, e-consultations and e-petitions and to build on this as part of the process of public inclusion into policy-making and governing. A report by Mayo and Steinberg, *The Power of Information*, took this a step further: the UK government, it concluded, should 'engage with grassroots web activism. This means communicating with the public through user-generated communities rather than official websites and greatly freeing up access to, and controls on the use of data held by the public sector' (Mayo and Sternberg, 2007: 3–4). Cabinet Office Minister Hilary Armstrong was quoted:

> Government cannot afford to overlook this phenomenon of citizens changing their lives through their use of information, especially what they find on the internet. We need to support ordinary people to take advantage of these opportunities to build community networks and make informed decisions on issues relating to their day to day lives. (Armstrong, 2007)

The aim here is to make use of the knowledge and information that individuals may have about their own circumstances, and by individuals coming together and generating their own content about issues and problems, grass-roots knowledge can be fed into the policy-making process. As with other examples, the internet facilitates the process of communication from the individuals into other arenas and facilitates the e-participation of citizens.

The role of representatives

If the way government is conducted could change because of the possibilities inherent in how the internet works, another relationship that could change is that between the political representative and his/her party, constituents and media.

Political representatives such as MPs relate to a number of different sets of constituents. They have a constituency role and spend a considerable part of their time dealing with constituency matters. They are also members of political parties and so connect to leaders as well as colleagues. Lastly, they are involved in policy-making – lobbying, recommending, supporting, opposing and so on. Some of these roles are likely to change with the onset of the internet. For example, MPs can create their own webpages, send out their own newsletters online, email constituents and create their own blogs. In these ways, MPs can raise their profile as well as solicit information, advice and help. Rather than being a relationship based on more traditional connections – letters, visits, leaflets – the internet creates the possibility for faster, continuous communication that can, at the same time, include the prospect of response through interactive features. A more 'genuine two-way process of debate and engagement' (Campbell, 2006) may develop as a consequence. In a similar fashion, the relationship between the MP and the media can change: by accessing websites, the media can also find out what MPs are doing.

There is some evidence already that MPs – and representatives elsewhere – have taken on board the need to go online. According to Ward and Lusoli the number of MPs online in 2003 was substantially higher than in 2002 (2005: 66) and the younger the MP the more likely he/she was to have a web presence (2005: 68). However, not all have advanced features on their websites so the extent to which they can create more than a platform for themselves is open to debate. Interestingly, when David Cameron, leader of the Conservative Party, revamped his webcameron website in 2007, he was criticized for removing interactive facilities from it. Nonetheless, if the Ward and Lusoli research is right in detecting age/cohort factors in the setting up of websites, it is probable that in the near future a substantial number of, if not all, MPs will have a fully functioning website with a considerable range of features.

For some MPs, then, making use of the internet is part of the process of professionalization and a process of enhancing and improving their skills and using them to their best advantage. This is akin to what Ward and Lusoli refer to as '*modernization* where new media technologies are used simply to increase the administrative efficiency of existing services and to improve the image of MPs and parliaments generally' (Ward and Lusoli, 2005: 61. Original emphasis). Although others might see it as creating the circumstances for a 'reinvigoration' of representative politics – providing 'additional opportunities for public participation which in turn might help to re-engage public interest and trust and reconnect MPs with the electorate' (Ward and Lusoli, 2005 61).

In such circumstances, the idea of 'reinvigoration' may be overstated since what is most likely to be happening is that more people are engaging in communication with, say, their representatives because it is now much easier and simpler to do so. Whether the behaviour of those who have little interest in politics and little engagement with it changes when they go online, that is an 'e-effect', (Gibson et al., 2005) remains an interesting question.

An 'e-effect'?

Whilst a large body of opinion appears to favour the 'normalization' of technologies idea, that is, that there is no real change and that those who have social and other capital benefit most from new technologies, some have sought to argue that the internet can have a positive impact on political behaviour. This may be part of the 'reinvigoration' process but it also points to the ways in which a dialogue with the disconnected may emerge. Gibson et al. (2005) 'stop short of inferring any immediate or even medium-term radical changes in patterns of participation in the UK given the relatively small numbers of individuals involved', but they suggest that 'the findings are significant in the challenge they present to the ideas of normalization and reinforcement that currently dominate the field' (2005: 562). In effect what they point to is a possibility that 'the online world is offering a space for political engagement among those who might not have been otherwise active' and that the reason for that:

> may lie in the technology itself. Even with a pre-existing interest in politics, receiving e-stimuli and developing experience of the Internet increase the likelihood that one will engage in organizational contacting and online participation. Such findings support the idea that there is a new set of resources coming to the fore in the sphere of online politics that are Internet-specific and unrelated to those linked to offline participation. (2005: 578)

Only further research will confirm or refute such findings, but the consequences are potentially significant in that this might be a way for technology to bring about a re-engagement in politics amongst those who are traditionally disengaged. At present, though, and given data on levels of participation in politics via the web (Livingstone et al., 2007) the evidence for a momentous re-engagement in politics because of the web is not yet there.

Citizens, the internet and new social movements

The above discussion has been predominantly focused on how individuals can become more involved and enter into more fruitful dialogues with those who govern them. But the internet can also be potentially helpful in creating the infrastructure for individuals to come together, locally and transnationally, and to build on the strength of that unity. As Lance Bennett (2003) has argued, the properties of the internet create the potential for movements of different types to come into being. The new technology creates new possibilities and new circumstances which were not possible when other modes of communication were dominant. Movements can be loosely organized, leaderless, flexible and continually regenerating; they can be local or global, they can change their nature and adapt rapidly to changing circumstances. The global reach and speed of the new information and communication technologies make them useful for rapid, global and easy communication and organization.

Internet websites created by such movements become, in effect, sources and resources of information and action. They become those elements that link individuals to one another and to larger groupings, so as to advance, protect or challenge authority or centres of power. For many contemporary movements, the new technologies are the means of linking up. Often, there is no single centre of activity but a range of different centres; no leadership but a range of independently run groupings. Pickerill and Webster employ the phrase 'an "electronic spine" that connects key activists' to describe the process of connecting (2006: 418). In the same vein, words such as 'polycentric (distributed) communication networks' and 'hubs' give further indications of how the internet connects diverse and 'ideologically thin' organizational links (Bennett, 2003: 150).

The creation of connections across space and time enables not only movements to come into being but also enables dispersed peoples to unite in their endeavour to come together and redefine their own identities. In the process, they can begin to exert a political power that can challenge existing arrangements and the definitions of problems and solutions. A good example of this is the way in which the Palestinian community has created what is, in effect, a virtual community or a set of communities that calls attention to its existence and consequently seeks to be heard, for example www.palestineremembered. com/. In the process, it is able to amplify its voice and ensure that it too can be heard when discussions about the Middle East are taking place. Needless to say, such voices are, in turn, countered.

These particular examples work with a somewhat different understanding of how the new information and communications technologies can provide opportunities for individuals to come together and, in the process, create larger bodies for action. As with much of the previous discussion, it is not that these opportunities did not exist in the past: we could always contact our MPs, we could always get access to parliamentary reports, we could always organize. With the ICTs, we can do all of these things much more easily and much more rapidly than before.

The factors of ease and speed cannot be overestimated but even here their mention often ignores such basic considerations as the skills required to establish even a simple website (and the language, design skills and so on to go along with that) and the availability, or otherwise, of broadband connections. Although the 'digital divide' highlights the major differences between those who have and those who do not have internet connections, these probably map onto other factors such as educational background and income/occupational status. Put differently, there may be differences in not only physical access to the technology but the cultural, social and linguistic skills that tend to accompany the use of ICTs. Interestingly, the use of mobile phones for the purposes of organizing dissent, as happened during the 'fuel protests' in the UK in 2001 (Doherty et al., 2003) illustrates that other technologies of communication may be more flexible than fixed connections and, because they depend on verbal communication, are more 'user friendly'. They are also more easily available and have more widespread use.

Summary and conclusion

The above examples of internet use amongst different groups and in different circumstances are illustrative of the numerous ways in which its insertion in the media mix alters well-established relationships. In each case, the use of the internet subtly – and sometimes not so subtly – changes the way relationships develop. Yet in all cases, we should see these examples as a part of ongoing change: parties and representatives, movements and governments will all employ the newest and/or the most appropriate techniques to connect with their constituents.

In recent national elections – the US in 2004, Britain in 2005 and France in 2007 – we have seen a mix of communication tools used by politicians, with web presence and the mainstream media coverage building on each other. Paradoxically, the use of a mix of tools only goes to affirm the supremacy of the established political parties and representative system. What has not been in evidence, and this takes us back to an earlier point, is a direct challenge to the political parties during election campaigns. The few websites that challenge the idea of voting or question the usefulness of the process are dwarfed by the power of others who seek to underpin the system that is in place.

But if we deal with the internet as only an extension of traditional forms of political communication by other means, we are in danger of minimizing the ways in which its properties differ from those of mainstream media. We are in danger, in other words, of not appreciating the ways in which communicating via the internet differs from communicating via, say, television and how it might, just might, begin the process of transforming political communication. Just as Stanley

Baldwin needed advice on how to speak on radio (see p. 103 above), political communicators of today also need to be versed in how to communicate via the internet.

In a recent *Personal Democracy Forum* reported on Jeff Jarvis's website (Jarvis, 2007b) on the 2008 presidential campaign (www.prezvid. com), a selection of webmasters pointed out that communicating via the internet differed from communicating by other means. The 'advice' to candidates included:

- Not engaging in 'stunts', looking 'real', looking 'authentic'. For example, Barack Obama's 'Walk for Change' video on how to canvass was criticized as coming across 'like a bunch of snotty carpetbagging kids from out of town'.
- Candidates should not treat internet videos as formal television appearances. When those videos appeared on YouTube (www. youtube.com) – as they mostly did – they had to have the quality of being 'amateurish', namely, handheld, genuine and 'real' and 'not directed by a commercial director'.
- Videos on the internet had to have the quality of being 'real' and not 'formal'. But if they were 'real' and 'amateurish' – points made about the Conservative Party leader's website, www.webcam-eron.org.uk – they were in danger of also being accused of being 'not authentic' (whatever that means) and inadequate means of persuasion. There is, then, a very fine line to tread between coming across on the internet – in blogs or videos – as somehow manufactured and not very successful at getting messages, visual and verbal, across to internet users.
- Representatives and candidates also had to beware of being caught in an 'embarrassing' moment since there was always the risk that someone would capture that moment, for example on a mobile phone, and make it available on the internet.

If one adds to this list that communication on the internet tends to favour the short and the dramatic – internet videos, even on YouTube, are comparatively short – then the space for communicating to a large audience is restricted. (Internet channels of communication such as 18DoughtyStreet – 'Politics for Adults' – are unlikely ever to have a large audience.)

The point behind this – sometimes contradictory – advice is that as people become used to the internet and develop an understanding of how it works best, those in politics who want to gain advantage from it will also have to become familiar with its grammar. In 2008, it is far too early to say how the internet will transform politics or political communication. The evidence to date points to a range of different uses and a range of different activities taking place around it and of individuals, groups and political elites adapting to it and dealing with it at the same time as dealing with other media.

There are interesting parallels with the development of television in Britain: a decade elapsed between the emergence of television in Britain as a mass medium (around 1953) and its incursion into politics in a significant and extensive way (around the early 1960s). At that point in time, there were very few media academics pondering the big question of television's impact on politics. In time, academics and politicians began to appreciate the way television had transformed the political landscape by emphasizing the importance of image and presentation and the best means to achieve a good televisual presence. The internet, in many ways, builds on what we have learned via television: the importance of visual communication, of presentation, of presence, of sincerity. In that way, it may be less of a transformative technology than television. Or maybe it is just too early to say. As the internet becomes more established and a more established way of conducting political communication, political parties and social movements, amongst many other organizations, will turn more often and more regularly to those who know how best to use it. It is in this manner that 'Internet teams edged closer to being "at the table," where the decisions are made' (Max Fose, adviser to John McCain in the 2000 presidential campaign, quoted in Davis, 2005: 241).

For those outside traditional political processes – the social movements, the bloggers, the outcasts – the internet offers a means of sending out information to large numbers. But is anyone receiving these messages or acting upon them? These are the sorts of connections that need to be established for the communicators to begin to engage and enhance not only the processes of communication but communication among citizens.

Conclusion: The Transformation and Professionalization of Communication and its Impact on Politics

9

The central argument of this book has been that the nature and content of political communication has inevitably changed with every new technology of communication and with every new method of managing public perceptions of events and causes. But rather than seeing clear and clean breaks between periods and eras, the changes have reflected an ongoing professionalization of skills surrounding the practice of political communication. To return to one example featured in an earlier chapter: as radio developed as a mass medium, political actors had to learn how to use it and would often turn to those who claimed to know how best to use the medium. The same logic applied when television replaced the medium of radio and when the internet's importance as a method of political communication was recognized.

It is important, however, to recognize that new technologies of communication are not the only factor that can usher in change. In Chapters 2 and 3, it was argued that the use of skills gained in advertising and public relations were also of importance to those who sought to gain political office. To understand how the public think and feel about issues and events and to be able to manage that process to advantage is of great help to those who seek election (or to those who seek to sell something to the public). This explains, in part, why political parties employ professional advisers.

The previous eight chapters have offered a range of examples where a process of professionalization has been identified, where the skills that are currently in use are different – qualitatively – from what they were in the past. The examples have included such things as better and more professional use of the media; better use of opinion polling and persuasive techniques; political parties becoming much more strategic in the ways in which they pursue election victories; individual politicians becoming more skilled and tuned into the needs of (more professional) media; and those in government also becoming more aware of the need to communicate better, that is, more professionally, as part and parcel of governing. In all these examples, one can identify the process of change and the ways in which those involved are made aware of the need for a more professional – knowing, skilful, strategic – approach to a range of circumstances.

This process of professionalization is not unique to the world of politics and the media. Other institutions and occupations have similarly refined their ways of working in such a way that they too can point to moves towards degrees of professionalization. This may not be professionalization in the more traditional sense of the word as it applies to the world of medicine or law where there are codified rules and codes of behaviour (Negrine, 2005; Scammell, 1997; Webb and Fisher, 2003) but it is professionalization in the sense that the skills are delivered in a way that is more thought out than before and is based on some analysis and understanding of how things work. The contemporary politician and the contemporary television producer both know – in the sense of having learned from experience or from others – what works best, say, on television. That is the sort of professionalism that is discussed in this book.

To look at professionalization in this way suggests that things are continually changing in the light of increasing knowledge and experience. There are continuities and transitions from one set of practices to another, or from one form of activity to another, sometimes with an underlying purpose. Political parties and their leaders seek office and they will use whatever means they can to gain advantage: whether it is in respect of media (radio, television, the internet) or those individuals who can assist them to attain their goals.

What, then, of transformations? If transformation implies 'a marked change in nature, form or appearance', then the greater degree of professionalization that is now brought to bear on the conduct of political communication is one such transformation. Elections 'are no places for amateurs' as they might have been in the past. There are other transformations and these identify much bigger changes than can be contained in the word 'professionalization': political communication has been totally transformed by television. Whether the internet will have a transformative effect on the same scale it is too early to say. Our political leaders, too, have been transformed in the sense that they are more aware and more knowing of the expectations of office and of the public. More generally, political communication in the 21st century is a different endeavour from what it was in the early 20th century: there are more and different media and these have had an impact on who, what and how things are communicated.

Transformations point to large, encompassing changes, whilst professionalization points to changes of degrees and to continuities. Professionalization also illustrates the processes through which change has come about.

Have these transformations altered the role of the public in considerations of political communication?

In charting the changing relationship between those in politics and the developing technologies of communication, this book has by-passed a discussion of the place of the public in the transformation and professionalization of political communication. One obvious reason for not dealing with the public at length is that the focus of this book has been on the ways in which the nature and content of political communication has changed over the past 150 or so years. Another, and perhaps more significant reason, is that a discussion of 'the public' deserves its own lengthy exegesis and that this is not the place for it.

That said, one should also add that references to 'the public' do appear in the course of this book – sometimes explicitly, often implicitly – although in a more loosely defined way than might be desirable. This is so for two important reasons. The first is that how 'the public' is constituted is itself a contentious point. The second is that 'the public' is more often than not an invisible yet ever present concern and target for those in both politics and the media. It is not so much that the public never makes an appearance but more a matter of those in politics and in the media acting in ways that have an impact on the public as the targets of communication.

This brief section offers a fuller discussion of these two points.

The starting point for this discussion is Sonia Livingstone's helpful analysis of the distinction between 'audience' and 'public'. As she observes, while the same people make up each of these designations, one is defined in opposition to the other. 'In both popular and elite discourses, audiences are denigrated as trivial, passive, individualised, while publics are valued as active, critically engaged and politically significant' (Livingstone, 2005: 18). There is, one should add, a parallel in the ways in which popular culture is placed in opposition to political communication with the former being seen as less important or serious ('newzak', tabloid) than the latter (see, for example, van Zoonen, 1998).

Livingstone also goes on to point out that in political communication research, one tends 'to ascribe a clear meaning to the public in terms of political citizenship and then ask how the media support or … undermine public understanding and participation. … all too often [research suggests] that the effect of media on their audience is seen to reposition what was or might be or should be, a public (knowing, thinking, influential) as a mere crowd (watching, sharing and emoting) or mass of consumers (driven by tastes, preferences and motivations)' (Livingstone, 2005: 18).

In fact, Livingstone could have gone further in developing her point regarding how those who study political communication conceive of 'the public' since other ways of looking at it are also commonplace and are often used in this book, including such terms as 'the electorate', 'voters', 'citizens' and 'the people'. Whether any of these are synonymous with 'the public' and how we conceive of the public is a moot point, although they do illustrate the ways in which those in politics and probably in the media also think of the role of *individual members* of the public in the political process. So, for example, in discussions of efforts to use the newer technologies of communication (film, radio, television) to reach the public (Chapter 3), it is principally the voters amongst the wider public that are the intended targets. More generally, whilst politicians may wish to be viewed favourably by the public as a whole, they are probably prepared to court some displeasure with the public so long as they are favoured by a sufficient number of voters – their intended public.

In many ways, the 'old' media created the environment in which these sorts of considerations were paramount: *mass* media were intended for *mass* communication and so could potentially reach everyone, voters as well as non-voters. With the 'new' media, other considerations apply since segments of the public and of voters can be reached in new and different ways. The sense of there being a public out there does not disappear; rather it is supplemented by the knowledge that there are publics that cannot be subsumed under a singular public. Consequently, the conduct of politics and of political communication has to adapt to these newer conditions and different ways of looking at those intended to be persuaded and mobilized.

However, irrespective of the differences in the terminology used, Livingstone is correct in identifying a critical feature of the public (or of publics) in discussions of political communication, namely, that the public (or publics) is increasingly seen to be made up of individuals – although in the past these individuals may have had strong ties to social groups or classes – who are supposed to act rationally in their sifting of political information before passing a judgement on people who are seeking their votes. This view of the public and how it behaves, that is, this view of what citizenship entails, reduced, as it often is, to a particular form of limited political participation, runs through a considerable part of the discussion of the professionalization of political communication and of politics, more generally. Politicians, to give just one example, are seen to seek the approval of voters by setting out their plans and outlining their performances whilst in office. Having considered the arguments and presentations, voters are then expected to respond to these appeals by exercising their right to vote.

Yet it could be argued that not only has this ideal typical 'model' of voting behaviour been exaggerated[1] but that recent experiences with newer media have undermined this model altogether. As Michael Schudson has argued in respect of the 1960 Kennedy–Nixon television debates, they 'ushered in a new model of how citizenship has gone wrong. Now, it seemed, citizens judged not character, as in colonial days, and not party, as in the nineteenth century, but *performance*. They judged television presence. … The surprisingly intimate link people feel to candidates they know – but know only through television – is discounted as dangerously false pseudo-knowledge' (1999: 234. Emphasis added).

One need not go as far as Schudson in pointing to the allegedly negative effects of television in politics but his comments are a reminder of how new, more professionalized, ways of conducting politics – through television, with 'negative' campaigning, with 'spin', employing professionals to dress, tutor and guide candidates, and the like – change the ways in which those in politics seek to persuade and mobilize the public. Politicians and their professional advisers are now often accused of using words and images to manipulate voters rather than seeking to persuade them with solid and well-founded arguments. The voter becomes a target that needs to be reached, persuaded and mobilized and, perhaps inevitably, politicians will now turn to those who have the skills and knowledge of how the targets can be reached and mobilized. The point that needs to be emphasized here is that the relationship between the politician and the voter becomes less of a conversation or dialogue and more of a one-way process of communication with the individual as the target of communication, and more an audience of politics than a thinking and active citizen.

The nature of this relationship is perhaps further underpinned by the nature of the 'old' *mass* media and by considerations of 'media logic'. The mass media, and particularly commercial mass media, tread a fine line between serving the public as citizens and serving the public as an audience. At times, media professionals take on the role of representatives of the public (for example 'I am asking the questions the public may ask of you ...') and/or as the professionals who create or guide the vehicles of political communication that are intended to place politicians 'on the spot'. But when acting as representatives of the public or when creating appropriate vehicles for political communication, those in the media also need to ensure that these vehicles of communication have an audience. This is the essence of 'media logic' with its emphasis on reaching a larger audience (or should this be a larger public?) with the contents of political communication. When broadcasters consider what sorts of programmes should be created for covering an election, do they consider primarily the needs of the public as rational, thinking and active citizens and/or, at the same time, as members of a passive audience that needs to be entertained? In practice, as research by Justin Lewis and his colleagues shows, the public rarely makes an appearance as a 'knowing, thinking, influential' collectivity (or subsets of that) in the news media. More often than not, the public is essentially media fodder. As Lewis at al. observe, the 'news media mainly represent the image of a passive public, whose main form of participation in the public sphere is, at best, following the agenda set by political leaders' (2005: 116).

If the relationship between the politician and the public as citizens is problematic, it becomes even more so in an age in which the dominant media fragment and the newer media offer opportunities for more targeted communication. The fragmentation of the media creates problems for those in politics who wish to reach all citizens. As Tony Blair pointed out in his last major speech as Prime Minister, the main British news bulletins 'used to have audiences of 8, even 10 million. Today the average is half that. ... In 1995, 225 TV shows had audiences of over 15 million. Today it is almost none' (Blair, 2007).

Consequently, not only can the public, the voters or the citizens not be reached as easily as they had been in the past, but the media can no longer be as easily controlled as in the past to do the bidding of politicians. If in the 'first and second age' of political communication (Blumler and Kavanagh, 1999), political parties dominated the political agenda and guided much political communication, the 'third age' is one which exhibits fragmentation and 'cultural chaos' (McNair, 2006). Equally, the political leaders' powers of control have greatly diminished as the number of media has greatly increased. In the

1930s, for example, political leaders persuaded the national British press not to report stories relating to the relationship between Edward VIII and Mrs Simpson, a relationship that led to the abdication crisis of 1936. In Richard Cockett's study, *Twilight of Truth* (1989) we can find other examples of how the press was controlled, this time by Neville Chamberlain. This was achieved through contacts with press owners or through a stranglehold over political journalists. Whilst anti-appeasement news was not totally absent from those sections of the press not being pressured by Chamberlain, a large section of the press did follow his lead. The public, in this instance, was being 'manipulated' by those in power and the press participated in that process. In one sense, then as perhaps now, the public is only sought as a source of legitimacy through the vote and not as an active participant in the political process.

With a fragmented media landscape and with the internet in place, many elements of the relationships between politicians, the media and the public necessarily change. Politicians still need to reach, persuade and mobilize the public – and do so in increasingly professional ways – but they do so by using both the 'old' and the 'new' media. In turn, the 'old' and the 'new' media develop new ways of reaching the audience as public with the added factor that (a section of) the public ceases to act as an audience and becomes both citizens and communicators. Finally, the public as a whole need no longer behave as an audience and can take on the role of active, thinking, knowing citizens in pursuit of information. To return to a point made in Chapter 8, we have yet to work out just how much the new media will alter the parameters of political communication.

The outcome of all these changes is not so much that the public ceases to be of interest to politicians or the media (and academics) but that the complexity of the terms and the changing political and media landscape give rise to multiple sets of relationships. What has not changed, though, is the theme outlined in Chapter 2 of this book, that is, the continuing need for politicians to find ways to communicate in an effective and persuasive way with voters as citizens. In essence, that is still the core interest of political communication; the transformation and professionalization of political communication merely points to the ways in which the fragmentation of the media landscape, the growth of knowledge about how best to communicate, better understanding of what motivates voters, better ways of identifying the needs and wishes of voters, and a more cynical outlook amongst voters add layers of complexity to the essentially simple matter of winning votes.

Finally, have either transformations or processes of professionalization been, on the whole, benign and beneficial?

Those who have felt the need to comment on this subject – in the course of other discussions, by and large – have expressed both doubts and concerns. On the one hand they have highlighted concerns about how the use of professionals has changed the nature of political parties; on the other hand, they have argued that the practices that professionals engage in – from polling right through to political marketing – privilege one side of the equation (those in power) and disempower the rest.

For example, Plasser and Plasser (2002) argue that when consultants are used, the role of the party organization comes under attack and under greater scrutiny. Indeed, they argue further that the use of consultants has a negative effect on parties and voters. 'Apparently, there is a *vicious circle* in modern politics today: the more political parties try to compensate for their lack of support and identification within the electorate with professional strategies, the more they contribute to a further weakening of their shrinking core vote base' (2002: 305). Where parties have no purchase on voters, the effects can be severe as both parties and the polity lose the allegiance of voters. Under the heading 'a democratic dilemma' Lars Nord (2007) put the issue clearly: 'The risk associated with the ongoing process of professionalization is … a further weakening of the position of political parties. … If parties in the future are reduced to become only voting mobilization organizations, then the party-based democracy is surely at stake' (2007: 92).

Another commentator, Cees Hamelink (2007), added the following 'tentative conclusions' to his concluding chapter in 'The Professionalisation of Political Communication':

- the current professionalisation of political communication further widens the inequality between politicians and citizens in terms of the capacity to manipulate political messages, perceptions and opinions;
- professional political communicators contribute to the development of 'democracy without citizens';
- more professional political communication is likely to enlarge the current democratic deficit;
- professionalisation reinforces the role of people not as active participants but as passive supporters of those who represent them. (Hamelink, 2007: 182–5)

If the professionals and the process of professionalization come in for such damning criticisms, what of the practices they engage in? Dominic Wring (2005) provides one set of criticisms of the political marketing approach to politics. It is a critique of a way of dealing with the wishes and desires of the public that ultimately devalues them. For example, he writes that:

> despite its emancipatory pretensions, the reality of opinion research was that it encouraged a secretive, hierarchical culture within the [Labour] party and an ideological conservatism anti-pathetic to spontaneity and transparency.

And:

> Rather the influence [of the real effect of political market research and analysis] can be felt in the focus group evidence amassed and accumulated *over decades* and which has conditioned the Labour elite's thinking about voters' perceived prejudices and convinced them to jettison social democracy.

And that:

> Disquiet has rightly been expressed over the way the packaging of politics has led to debate being manipulated by spin doctoring and image making. But marketing's colonization of campaigning raises other, more fundamental concerns about the ends as well as the means of the democratic process and, more specifically, the way stratified electioneering devalues the importance and influence of the predominantly stable sections of the voting population. The logic of Dick Morris and Philip Gould's position is that it is actually counter-productive to have a fixed principled stance. This is 'political' marketing. ... (Wring, 2005: 174–9)

With these criticisms of the professionalization of political communication still ringing in one's ears, it is difficult to put forward a truly convincing defence of the professionals or their practices. The 'most realistic scenario' offered by Nord offers some measure of comfort:

> It is more likely that professionalization will neither kill existing parties nor give them unlimited success. Instead, it is reasonable to think that the professionalization process poses considerable conflicts for the parties regarding their objectives. They can either

become more professionalized and accept the new conditions for campaigning and opinion formation, or they can remain as a consolidating party organization and balance internal interests within the party. In the first case, they risk party unity and coherence in politics. In the second case, voter support and political influence are in jeopardy. (Nord, 2007: 93)

What of the voters/citizens and of the polity? Cees Hamelink's comments offer a fitting conclusion to this book:

Professional political communication fulfils clear functions within 'thin' democracies. If, however, societies decide for a strong model of democracy, they will need all the professionalism they can muster to engage in the grand scale teaching of democratic minds. (2007: 187)

Notes

Chapter 1

1. At the time of writing (Autumn 2007), both the Conservative and Labour parties were embroiled in a controversy about funding given to them as 'loans' by individuals, only some of whom had been identified. Such loans may contravene electoral legislation and may be in breach of the law but this has yet to be determined. The sums involved are £13.5 million for the Labour Party and £17 million for the Conservative Party.

Chapter 2

1. The typology in Norris, (2002), qualifies these headings by suggesting that these dates refer to 'the predominant era' (Norris, 2002: 135). The qualification is not present in *A Virtuous Circle* (Norris, 2000).
2. Later on, Gibson and Römmele present a figure that sets out 'a comprehensive model of postmodern campaigning' (2001: 38) which has all the characteristics of their professional campaign. Are these terms interchangeable?
3. Interestingly, parties have never successfully launched their own newspaper, and media regulations usually prohibit gaining access to broadcast services. However, the web offers alternatives and direct access to the public, for example www.18DoughtyStreet.com.
4. The one exception to this comment is the continued existence of Party Political Broadcasts which are made by the parties and simply retransmitted by the broadcasters, although even here, their status has declined since their origins in the 1920s.
5. The BBC Trust's latest report on 'impartiality' makes the distinction between the traditional way of looking at the issue, that is, as a 'see-saw', and the need to consider it in the current media and political landscape more like a 'wagon wheel' (BBC, 2007).
6. The exercise of indirect control over the content of coverage of the issue of appeasement by Neville Chamberlain through contacts with proprietors, editors and the lobby system is well documented in Richard Cockett's *The Twilight of Truth* (1989).
7. 'From 1923 to 1977 the [Conservative] party maintained its own national Centre to which trainee agents and local activists would come for short residential courses' (Ball, 1994: 277). The Labour Party also had its own training programme.

8. David Butler had spent some time in the US, along with Tony Benn, in the early 1950s, although this should not be read as supporting the 'Americanization' thesis per se (Winstone, 1995: 166).
9. Gower's comments to Baldwin are similar. See p. 102 above.

Chapter 3

1. Cadre parties are dominated by elites and were the common form of party in the 19th century.
2. The use of the terms 'propaganda' and 'public relations' during the inter-war period are linked and could often be interchangeable. In his 1922 book *Public Opinion*, Walter Lippmann observed: 'But what is propaganda, if not the effort to alter the picture to which men respond, to substitute one social pattern for another?' (1992: 16).
3. Phonograph records of political speeches had been used in the 1908 US presidential election (McGerr, 1986: 160).
4. Harold Wilson was to become leader of the Party and later Prime Minister from 1964–70 and 1974–6.
5. Labour Party headquarters.
6. At various points in the report there were acknowledgments that the Conservatives spent more on activities, for example advertising, because they had more funds to spend.
7. Clause 4 read: 'To secure for all the workers by hand or by brain the full fruits of their industry and the most equitable distribution thereof that may be possible upon the basis of the common ownership of the means of production, distribution and exchange, and the best obtainable system of popular administration and control of each industry of service.' It was finally abandoned in the late 1990s under Tony Blair's leadership.
8. Best and Cotta also argue that 'the emergence of specialized political roles, such as the professional politician ... can be taken as [one of the] indicators of political modernization'. (2000: 496)

Chapter 4

1. Peter Mandelson, who worked for New Labour, earned the title of 'the prince of darkness'. Andrew Blick's (2004) book on special advisers in government is called *People who Live in the Dark*.
2. According to Richard Cockett, Margaret Thatcher received her first training sessions at such an event on 22 February 1956 (1994: 566).
3. Airtime, for example, could not be bought in Britain.
4. The chapter on the Labour Party in the study of the 1964 general election (Butler and King, 1965) is suitably titled 'The modernization of Labour'.
5. After the 1959 defeat, a number of senior Labour politicians had arrived at similar conclusions. They noted that 'the Labour Party had failed to adapt its traditional doctrines to the needs and aspirations of an increasingly prosperous group of would-be middle-class voters who had decided the result of the election' (Windlesham, 1966: 85).

6. The relationship between advisers in the world of professional politics is complex: Hilton's partner is Rachel Whetstone. Whetstone worked in Conservative Central Office for Michael Howard (Leader of the Party in 2004–5) and she is godparent to one of Cameron's children. Whetstone is also a founder of the PR firm Portland which is headed by Tim Allan who was a former deputy to Alastair Campbell, Blair's press spokesman (see Wray, 2006).
7. He was reported as expressing a desire to continue to work for the Party on a consultancy basis.

Chapter 5

1. MP from 1959 to 1964 and from 1970 to 1997.
2. For recent examples see http://www.youtube.com/labourvision.
3. *MPs and the Media: A Study of the Professionalization in Political Communication*, ESRC, 2001–3, R000223540. Unless otherwise stated, all quotes used in this chapter come from interviews conducted during research for the study listed here.
4. Joe McGinnis records this conversation, 'While waiting to go on, Richard Nixon fell into conversation with Roger Ailes. "It's a shame a man has to use gimmicks like this to get elected", Nixon said. "Television is not a gimmick", Ailes said. Richard Nixon liked that kind of thinking. He told Len Garment to hire the man' (McGinniss, 1970: 57).

Chapter 9

1. There is now growing interest in the role of emotions in politics. See, for example, Goodwin et al. (2002) Passionate Politics in *American Communication Journal*.

Bibliography

Abrams, M. (1963) Public opinion polls and political parties. *Public Opinion Quarterly*, **xxvii:** 9–18.

Agre, P. E. (2002) Real-time politics: The internet and the political process. *The Information Society*, **18:** 311–31.

Altheide, D. L. and Snow, R. P. (1979) *Media Logic*. Beverly Hills, CA: Sage.

Armstrong, H. (2007) Press release, 7 June. http://www.cabinetoffice. gov.uk/newsroom/news_releases/2007/stories/070607_power_information.asp accessed 14 June 2007.

Ashcroft, M. (2005) *Smell the Coffee: A Wake-up Call for the Conservative Party*. London: Michael A. Ashcroft.

Ball, S. (1994) Local Conservatism and the evolution of the Party organization. In Seldon, A. and Ball, S. (eds) *The Conservative Century: The Conservative Party Since 1900*. Oxford: Oxford University Press.

Barnett, A. (2006) Q. What price a Tory kingmaker? A. A snip at £276,000 a year. *Observer*. http://www.guardian.co.uk/politics/2006/mar/19/uk.conservatives.

BBC Trust (2007) *From Seesaw to Wagon Wheel: Safeguarding Impartiality in the 21st Century*. London: BBC. http://www.bbc.co.uk/bbctrust/assets/files/pdf/review_report_research/impartiality_21century/report.pdf as at 19 June 2007.

Beer, S. H. (1997) Britain after Blair. *The Political Quarterly*, **4:** 317–24.

Benn, A. W. (1953) *The Labour Party and Broadcasting*. Labour Party archives: BS/BCST/217.

Bennett, L. W. (2003) Communicating global activism: Strengths and vulnerabilities of networked politics. *Information, Communication & Society*, **6:** 143–68.

Best, H. and Cotta, M. (eds) (2000) *Parliamentary Representatives in Europe 1848–2000: Legislative Recruitment and Careers in Eleven European Countries*. Oxford: Oxford University Press.

Black, J. and Macraild, D. M. (2000) *Studying History*. Basingstoke: Palgrave – now Palgrave Macmillan.

Blair, T. (2001) quoted in http://www.publications.parliament.uk/pa/cm200102/cmselect/cmliaisn/1065/106501.htm.

Blair, T. (2007) Tony Blair's speech on the media, delivered at the Reuters Institute, 12 June http://news.bbc.co.uk/1/hi/uk_politics/6744581.stm as at 1 October 2007.

Blears, H. (2006a) Party-time for Democracy. Letter in *The Times*, 14 June.

Blears, H. (2006b) *PM* programme, BBC Radio 4 on 14 June.

Blick, A. (2004) *People Who Live in the Dark*. London: Politico's.

Blumler, J. (1990) Elections, the media and the modern publicity process. In Ferguson, M. (ed.) *Public Communication: The New Imperatives*. London: Sage.

Blumler, J. and Gurevitch, M. (2001) 'Americanization' reconsidered: UK–US campaign communications across time. In Bennett, L. W. and Entman, R. M. (eds) *Mediated Politics: Communications in the Future of Democracy*. Cambridge: Cambridge University Press.

Blumler, J. G. and Kavanagh, D. (1999) The Third Age of political communication: influences and features. *Political Communication*, **16**: 209–30.

Branigan, T. (2006) Primary colours. *Guardian*, 19 April. http://politics. guardian.co.uk/media/story/0,,1756395,00.html.

Briggs, A. (1979) *The History of Broadcasting in the United Kingdom: Sound and Vision. Volume IV*. Oxford: Oxford University Press.

Butler, D. (1952) *The British General Election of 1951*. London: Macmillan – now Palgrave Macmillan.

Butler, D. (1955) *The British General Election of 1955*. London: Macmillan – now Palgrave Macmillan/New York: St. Martin's Press.

Butler, D. and Kavanagh, D. (eds) (1992) *The British General Election of 1992*. London: Macmillan – now Palgrave Macmillan/New York: St. Martin's Press.

Butler, D. and King, A. (eds) (1965) *The British General Election of 1964*. London: Macmillan – now Palgrave Macmillan.

Butler, D. and Rose, R. (1960) *The British General Election of 1959*. London: Macmillan – now Palgrave Macmillan.

Cairney, P. (2007) The professionalisation of MPs: Refining the 'politics-facilitating' explanation. *Parliamentary Affairs*, **60**: 212–33.

Campbell, A. (2006) A technophobe no more. *Guardian*, 20 February. www.guardian.co.uk/print/0,,329416766-103677,00.html.

Caramani, D. (2003) The end of silent elections: The birth of electoral competition, 1832–1915. *Party Politics*, **9**: 411–43.

Carey, J. and Quirk, J. (1973) The history of the future. In Gerbner, G., Gross, L. and Melody, W. (eds) *Communications Technology and Social Policy*. New York: John Wiley and Sons, pp. 485–503.

Clark, T. (2006) The renewal agenda must be brought to the public sector, *Guardian*, 14 September.

Clarke, C. (2007) *New Labour and the Media: Ten Years On*. London: Royal Television Society, 28 March.

Cockerell, M. (1989) *Live from Number 10: The Inside Story of Prime Ministers and Television*. London: Faber & Faber.

Cockett, R. (1989) *Twilight of Truth: Chamberlain, Appeasement and the Manipulation of the Press*. London: Weidenfield and Nicolson.

Cockett, R. (1994) The party, publicity and the media. In Seldon, A. and Ball, S. (eds) *Conservative Century: The Conservative Party since 1900*. Oxford: Oxford University Press.

Conservative Party Archives (1952) Lord Woolton, letter to Conservative MPs. Conservative Central Office archives: 1952/CCO4/4/250.

Conservative Party Archives (1956) Crum-Ewing, note. Conservative Central Office archives: CCO4/7/361.

Conservative Party Report (1951) *Talking on Television*. Conservative Central Office archives: CCO/4/4/260.

Cook, G. (2002) The Labour campaign. In Bartle, J., Atkinson, S. and Mortimore, R. (eds) *Political Communications: The General Election Campaign of 2001*. London: Frank Cass, pp. 87–97.

Cook, T. E. (1998) *Governing with the News: The News Media as a Political Institution*. Chicago: University of Chicago Press.

Cooper, A. (2002) The Conservative campaign. In Bartle, J., Atkinson, S. and Mortimore, R. (eds) *Political Communications: The General Election Campaign of 2001*. London: Frank Cass, pp. 98–108.

Cornfield, Michael (n.d. *c.*2006) *The Internet and Campaign 2004: A Look Back at the Campaigners*. Pew Internet and American Life project http://www.pewinternet.org/pdfs/Cornfield_commentary.pdf as at 5 June 2007.

Craig, D. B. (2000) *Fireside Politics. Radio and Political Culture in the United States, 1920–1940*. Baltimore: Johns Hopkins University Press.

Critchley, J. (1995) *A Bag of Boiled Sweets*. London: Faber & Faber.

Curtice, J. (2002) *Survey Research and Electoral Change in Britain*. Working Paper Number 96. Oxford: CREST (The Centre for Research into Elections and Social Trends).

Davis, A. (2002) *Public Relations Democracy: Public Relations, Politics and the Mass Media in Britain*. Manchester: Manchester University Press.

Davis, S. (2005) Presidential campaigns fine-tune online strategies. *Journalism Studies*, **6**(2): 241–4.

Day, R. (1975) *Day by Day: A Dose of my Own Hemlock*. London: William Kimber.

Day, R. (1989) *Grand Inquisitor*, London: Pan Books.

De Jong, W., Shaw, M. and Stammers, N. (eds) (2005) *Global Activism, Global Media*. London: Pluto.

Delaney, T. (1982) Labour's advertising campaign. In Worcester, R. and Harrop, M. (eds) *Political Communications: The General Election Campaign of 1979*. Hemel Hempstead: George Allen & Unwin.

Doherty, B., Paterson, M., Plows, A. and Wall, D. (2003) Explaining the fuel protests. *British Journal of Politics and International Relations*, **5**(1): 1–23. Oxford: Blackwell.

Donoughie, B. and Jones, G. W. (1973) *Herbert Morrison: Portrait of a Politician*. London: Weidenfield and Nicolson.

Downey, J. and Davidson, S. (2007) The Internet in the UK General Election. In Wring, D., Green, J., Mortimore, R. and Atkinson, S. (eds) *Political Communications: The General Election Campaign of 2005*. Basingstoke: Palgrave Macmillan, pp. 93–107.

Farrell, D. M. and Webb, P. (2002) Political parties as campaign organizations. In Dalton, R. and Wattenberg, M. (eds) *Parties without Partisans: Political Change in Advanced Industrial Societies.* Oxford: Oxford University Press, pp. 102–29.

Farrell, D. M., Kolodny, R. and Medvic, S. (2001) Parties and campaign professionals in a digital age: Political consultants in the United States and their counterparts overseas. *Press/Politics,* **6**: 11–31.

Ferguson, R. and Miller, L. (2007) *Parliament for the Future. Forecasting the Form of a Digitally-enabled Parliament.* Hansard Society Report, August. http://www.democracyseries.org.uk/sites/democracyseries.org.uk/files/PARLIAMENT%20FOR%20THE%20FUTURE%20REPORT.pdf.

Feuchtwanger, E. J. (1968) *Disraeli, Democracy and the Tory Party: Conservative Leadership and Organization After the 2nd Reform Bill.* Oxford: Clarendon Press.

Franklin, B. (1994) *Packaging Politics: Political Communications in Britain's Media Democracy.* London: Edward Arnold.

Franklin, B. (1998) *Tough on Soundbites, Tough on the Causes of Soundbites: New Labour and News Management.* London: Catalyst. Paper 3.

Gandy, O. (1982) *Beyond Agenda Setting: Information Subsidies and Public Policy.* Norwood, NJ: Ablex Publishing Company.

Gibson, R. and Römmele, A. (2001) Changing campaign communications: A party-centered theory of professionalized campaigning. *Press/Politics,* **6**: 31–44.

Gibson, R., Lusoli, W. and Ward, S. (2005) Online participation in the UK: Testing a 'contextualised' model of Internet effects. *British Journal of Politics and International Relations,* **7**: 561–83.

Giddens, A. (1990) *The Consequences of Modernity.* Oxford: Polity.

Goldie, G. W. (1977) *Facing the Nation: Television and Politics 1936–1976.* London: Bodley Head.

Goodwin, J., Jasper, M. and Polletta, F. (2002) (eds) Passionate politics. *American Communication Journal* **5**(3).

Gould, P. (1998a) *The Unfinished Revolution.* London: Little Brown.

Gould, P. (1998b) Why the Conservatives lost. In Crewe, I., Gosschalk, B. and Bartle, J. (eds) *Why Labour Won the General Election of 1997.* London: Frank Cass.

Grant, D. (1986) A comment on Labour's campaign. In Crewe, I. and Harrop, M. (eds) *Political Communications: The General Election Campaign of 1983.* London: Macmillan – now Palgrave Macmillan.

Guardian (2007) Open the gates of information. Technology Guardian, 14 June, p. 1.

Hallin, D. C. and Mancini, P. (2004) *Comparing Media Systems. Three Models of Media and Politics.* Cambridge: Cambridge University Press.

Hamelink, C. (2007) The professionalisation of political communication: Democracy at stake? In Negrine, R. M., Mancini, P., Holtz-Bacha, C.

and Papathanassopoulos, S. (eds) *The Professionalisation of Political Communication*. Bristol: Intellect.

Hansard (2005–6) (http://www.publications.parliament.uk/pa/cm200506/cmhansrd/cm060724/wmstext/60724m0169.htm#0607246000254 as at October 2006).

Hansard Society/Electoral Commission (2007) Audit of Political Engagement 4, http://www.hansardsociety.org.uk/assets/Audit_4_final_2007_without_picsblogs/publications/archive/2007/10/20/Audit-of-Political-Engagenent-4.aspx.pdf at 24 June 2007 as at June 2007.

Harris, L. (1963) Polls and politics in the United States. *Public Opinion Quarterly*, xxvii: 3–8.

Harrison, M. (1965) Television and radio. In Butler, D. and King, A. (eds) *The British General Election of 1964*. London: Macmillan – now Palgrave Macmillan.

Harrop, M. (2001) The rise of campaign professionals. In Bartle, J. and Griffiths, D. (eds) *Political Communications Transformed: From Morrison to Mandelson*. Basingstoke: Palgrave – now Palgrave Macmillan.

Hennessy, P. (2005) Rulers and servants of the State: The Blair style of government 1999–2004. *Parliamentary Affairs*, **58**: 6–16.

Hill, K. A. and Hughes, J. E. (1998) *Cyberpolitics: Citizen Activism in the Age of the Internet*. Lanham, MD: Rowman & Littlefield.

Hitchens, C. (2007) *Cameron*. London: Channel 4 TV.

Hollins, T. (1981) *The representation of politics. The place of party publicity, broadcasting and film in British politics, 1918–1938*. Unpublished Ph.D. University of Leeds.

Holtz-Bacha, C. (2002) Professionalization of political communication: The case of the 1998 SPD campaign. *Journal of Political Marketing*, **1**: 23–37.

Holtz-Bacha, C. (2007) Professionalisation of politics in Germany. In Negrine, R., Mancini, P., Holtz-Bacha, C. and Papathanassopoulos, S. (eds) *The Professionalisation of Political Communication*. Bristol: Intellect.

ICM Polls (2006) http://www.icmresearch.co.uk/reviews/2006/Channel4%20-%20Brown%20v%20Cameron%20-%20April06/Brown-cameron-april06.asp.

Jackson, N. (2007) *Online Political Communication: The Impact of the Internet on MPs 1994–2005*. Bournemouth: University of Bournemouth.

Jarvis, J. (2007a) On http://www.buzzmachine.com/2007/01/19/the-revolution-will-be-youtubed-2/ as on 11 June 2007.

Jarvis, J. (2007b) http://prezvid.com/index.php?tag=show as on 11 June 2007.

Johnson, D. W. (2000) The business of political consulting. In Thurber, J. A. and Nelson, C. J. (eds) *Campaign Warriors*. Washington DC: Brookings Institution.

Jones, N. (1999) *Sultans of Spin*. London: Orion.

Jones, N. (2001) *The Control Freaks: How New Labour Gets its Own Way*. London: Politico's.

Jones, N. (2006) *Trading Information*. London: Politico's.

Katz, R. and Mair, P. (2002) The ascendancy of the party in public office: Party organizational change in twentieth-century democracies. In Gunther, R., Montero, J. R. and Linz, J. J. (eds) *Political Parties*. Oxford: Oxford University Press.

Kavanagh, D. (1970) *Constituency Electioneering in Britain*. London: Longmans.

Kavanagh, D. (1996) Speaking truth to power? Pollsters as campaign advisers. *European Journal of Marketing*, **30**: 104–13.

Kavanagh, D. and Seldon, A. (2000) *The Powers Behind the Prime Minister: The Hidden Influence of Number Ten*. London: HarperCollins.

Kelley, S. Jnr. (1956) *Professional Public Relations and Political Power*. Baltimore: Johns Hopkins University Press.

King, A. (ed.) (1998) *New Labour Triumphs: Britain at the Polls*. London: Chatham House.

Kirchheimer, O. (1966) The transformation of the West European party system. In Palombara, J. and Weinar, M. (eds) *Political Parties and Political Development*. Princeton, NJ: Princeton University Press.

Kolodny, R. and Dulio, D. (2003) Political party adaptations in US congressional campaigns. *PARTY POLITICS*, **9**: 729–46.

Koss, S. (1984) *The Rise and Fall of the Political Press in Britain*. London: Fontana Press.

Krouwel, A. (2003) Otto Kirchheimer and the catch-all party. *West European Politics*, **26**(2): 23–40.

Kuhn, R. (2005) Where's the spin? The executive and news management in France. *Modern and Contemporary France*, **13**: 307–22.

Labour Party Archives (1958) (GS/BCST/266).

Lee, A. J. (1980) *The Origins of the Popular Press, 1855–1914*, London: Croom Helm.

Lees-Marshment, J. (2001) *Political Marketing and British Political Parties: The Party's Just Begun*. Manchester: Manchester University Press.

L'Etang, J. (1998) State propaganda and bureaucratic intelligence: The creation of public relations in 20th century Britain. *Public Relations Review*, **24**: 413–41.

L'Etang, J. (2004) *Public Relations in Britain: A History of Professional Practice in the 20th Century*. Mahwah, NJ: Lawrence Erlbaum Associates.

Lewis, J., Inthorn, S. and Wahl-Jorgensen, K. (2005) *Citizens or Consumers? What the Media Tell Us About Public Participation*. Maidenhead: Open University Press.

Lippmann, W. (1922) *Public Opinion*. New York: Free Press Paperbacks.

Livingstone, S. (2005) On the relation between audiences and publics. In Livingstone, S. (ed.) *Audiences and Publics: When Cultural Engagement Matters for the Public Sphere*. Bristol: Intellect.

Livingstone, S., Bober, M. and Helsper, E. (2007) Active participation or just more information?: Young people's take up of opportunities to act and interact in the internet [online]. London: LSE Research Online. Available at: http://eprints.lse.ac.uk/1014. Available in LSE Research Online: May 2007. Originally published in *Information, Communication & Society*, **8**(3): 287–314 (2005). London: Taylor & Francis Group.

Lloyd, J. (2004) *What the Media are Doing to Our Politics*. London: Constable.

Lynch, P. and Garner, R. (2005) The changing party system. *Parliamentary Affairs*, **58**: 533–54.

Maarek, P. J. (2007) The evolution of French political communication: Reaching the limits of professionalisation? In Negrine, R. M., Mancini, P., Holtz-Bacha, C. and Papathanassopoulos, S. (eds) *The Professionalisation of Political Communication*. Bristol: Intellect.

McGerr, M. E. (1986) *The Decline of Popular Politics. The American North, 1865–1928*. Oxford: Oxford University Press.

McGinniss, J. (1970) *The Selling of the President*. London: Penguin.

McNair, B. (2004) PR must die: Spin, anti-spin and political public relations in the UK, 1997–2004. *Journalism Studies*, **5**: 325–38.

McNair, B. (2006) *Cultural Chaos. Journalism, News and Power in a Globalised World*. London: Routledge.

Maddox, B. (1972) *Beyond Babel. New Directions in Communications*. London: Andre Deutsch.

Magleby, D. B., Patterson, K. D. A. and Thurber, J. A. (2000) Campaign consultants and responsible party government. *APSA* (American Political Science Association). http://polisci.wisc.edu/~party/apsa2000magleby.pdf.

Mair, P. (1998) *Party System Change: Approaches and Interpretations*. Oxford: Clarendon Press.

Mair, P. and Biezen, I. V. (2001) Party membership in twenty European democracies, 1980–2000. *Party Politics*, **7**: 5–21.

Mancini, P. (1999) New frontiers in political professionalism. *Political Communication*, **16**(1): 231–45.

Mancini, P. (2007) Political professionalism in Italy. In Negrine, R. M., Mancini, P., Holtz-Bacha, C. and Papathanassopoulos, S. (eds) *The Professionalisation of Political Communication*. Bristol: Intellect.

Mannheim, J. (1994) *Strategic Public Diplomacy and American Foreign Policy: The Evolution of Influence*. Oxford: Oxford University Press.

Margach, J. (1979) *The Anatomy of Power*. London: W.H. Allen.

Margolis, M., Resnick, D. and Wolfe, J. D. (1999) Party competition on the Internet in the United States and Britain. *Press/Politics*, **4**: 24–47.

Marquis, F. J. E. O. W. (1959) *The Memoirs of the Rt. Hon. the Earl of Woolton*. London: Cassell.

Mayhew, L. (1997) *The New Public*. Cambridge: Cambridge University Press.

Mayo, H. and Steinberg, T. (2007) *The Power of Information* http://www.cabinetoffice.gov.uk/upload/assets/www.cabinetoffice.gov.uk/strategy/power_information.pdf as at February 2008.

Mazzoleni, G. (1987) Media logic and party logic in campaign coverage: The Italian General Election of 1983. *European Journal of Communication*, **2**: 81–104.

Mazzoleni, G. (1995) Towards a 'Videocracy': Italian political communication at a turning point. *European Journal of Communication*, **10**: 291–320.

Mazzoleni, G. (1996) Patterns and effects of recent changes in electoral campaigning in Italy. In Swanson, D. and Mancini, P. (eds) *Politics, Media, and Modern Democracy*. Westport, CT: Praeger.

Mazzoleni, G. and Schulz, W. (1999) 'Mediatization' of politics: A challenge for democracy? *Political Communication*, **16**: 247–61.

Meyer, C. (2006) *DC Confidential*. London: Phoenix.

Meyer, T. with Hinchman, L. (2002) *Media Democracy: How the Media Colonize Politics*. Oxford: Polity.

Michel, F. (2005) Breaking the Gaullian mould: Valery Giscard d'Estaing and the modernisation of French presidential communication. *Modern and Contemporary France*, **13**: 291–306.

Miller, D. and Dinan, W. (2000) The rise of the PR industry in Britain, 1979–1998. *European Journal of Communication*, **15**: 5–35.

Ministerial Statement (2006) http://www.theyworkforyou.com/wms/?id=2006-07-24b.86WS.5 as at May 2007.

Moore, M. (2005) *The Origins of Modern Spin. Democratic Government and the Media in Britain, 1945–51*. Basingstoke: Palgrave Macmillan.

Mountfield Report (1997) *Report of the Working Group on the Government Information Service*. Cabinet Office, November.

Mountfield, R. (2002) *Politicisation and the Civil Service*, http://www.civilservant.org.uk/politicisation.shtml.

National Statistics (2007) http://www.statistics.gov.uk/cci/nugget.asp?id=8.

Negrine, R. (1994) *Politics and the Mass Media in Britain*. London: Routledge.

Negrine, R. M. (1998) *Parliament and the Media: A Study of Britain, Germany and the Media*. London: Pinter.

Negrine, R. M. (1999) *The Press and Broadcasting Since 1945*. Manchester: Manchester University Press.

Negrine, R. M. (2005) Professionalism and the Millbank tendency: A response to Webb and Fisher. *Politics*, **25**: 107–15.

Negrine, R. and Papathanassopoulos, S. (1996) The 'Americanization' of political communications: A critique. *Harvard International Journal of Press/Politics*, **1**: 45–62.

Negrine, R., Mancini, P., Holtz-Bacha, C. and Papathanassopoulos, S. (eds) (2007) *The Professionalisation of Political Communication*. Bristol: Intellect.

Nelson, F. (2007) The PM's curious spin cycle. *Guardian*. 10 December. http://www.guardian.co.uk/media/2007/dec/10/politicsandthemedia. gordonbrown.

Newton, K. (2001) The transformation of governance? In Axford, B. and Huggins, R. (eds) *New Media and Politics*. London: Sage, pp. 151–71.

Nord, L. (2007) The Swedish model becomes less Swedish. In Negrine, R. M., Mancini, P., Holtz-Bacha, C. and Papathanassopoulos, S. (eds) *The Professionalisation of Political Communication*. Bristol: Intellect.

Norris, P. (2000) *A Virtuous Circle: Political Communication in Postindustrial Societies*. Cambridge: Cambridge University Press.

Norris, P. (2002) *Democratic Phoenix: Reinventing Political Activism*. Cambridge: Cambridge University Press.

Norris, P. (2004) The evolution of election campaigns: Eroding political engagement? *Political Communications in the 21st Century*. New Zealand: University of Otago, www.pippanorris.com (as at May 2004).

Oborne, P. (2007) Clean up in Spin-City, *British Journalism Review* **18**(4): 11–18. London: Sage.

Panorama (2002) Tony in Adland. BBC: London.

Papathanassopoulos, S. (2007) Political communication and profession-alisation in Greece. In Negrine, R. M., Mancini, P., Holtz-Bacha, C. and Papathanassopoulos, S. (eds) *The Professionalisation of Political Communi-cation*. Bristol: Intellect.

Pearson, J. and Turner, G. (1965) *The Persuasion Industry*. London: Eyre and Spottiswoode.

Pegg, M. (1983) *Broadcasting and Society, 1918–1939*. London: Croom Helm.

Pew Internet and American Life (2006) *Election 2006 Online* http://www. pewinternet.org/PPF/r/199/report_display.asp) as at 14 June 2007.

Pfetsch, B. (1996) Convergence through privatization? Changing media environments and televised politics in Germany. *European Journal of Communication*, **11**: 427–51.

Phillips, Sir Hayden (2007) *Strengthening Democracy: Fair and Sustainable Funding of Political Parties*. The Review of the Funding of Political Parties, March 2007 http://www.partyfundingreview.gov.uk/files/strengthen-ing_democracy.pdf as at 15 June 2007.

Phillips, Morgan (1958) *TV and the Labour Party*. Interview with Morgan Phillips conducted by Kenneth Mason. Labour Party archives: GS/BCST/266.

Phillis Review (2004) *An Independent Review of Government Communications* http://www.cabinetoffice.gov.uk/publications/reports/communica-tions_review/final_report.pdf and http://archive.cabinetoffice.gov.uk/gcreview/News/index.htm

Pickerill, J. and Webster, F. (2006) The Anti-war/Peace Movement in Britain and the conditions of information war. *International Relations*, **20**: 407–23.

Plasser, F. and Plasser, G. (2002) *Global Political Campaigning: A Worldwide Analysis of Campaign Professionals and their Practices*. London: Praeger.

Price, L. (2006) *The Spin Doctor's Diary: Inside Number 10 with New Labour*. London: Hodder.

Public Administration Select Committee (1998a) *Sixth Report*. The Government Information and Communication Service. http://www.publications.parliament.uk/pa/cm199798/cmselect cmpubadm/770/77006.htm.

Public Administration Select Committee (1998b). *Minutes of Evidence*, 2 June 1998 http://www.publications.parliament.uk/pa/cm199798/cmselect/cmpubadm/770/8060202.htm.

Rathbone, T. (1982) Political communication in the 1979 General Election campaign by one who was in it. In Worcester, R. and Harrop, M. (eds) *Political Communications: The General Election Campaign of 1979*. Hemel Hemsptead: George Allen & Unwin.

Robinson, J. (2007) Andy Coulson. The Tories bring on a new spinner. *Observer*, p. 39.

Rose, R. (1965) Pre-election public relations and advertising. In Butler, D. and King, A. (eds) *The British General Election of 1964*. London: Macmillan – now Palgrave Macmillan.

Rose, R. (2001) *The Prime Minister in a Shrinking World*. Cambridge: Polity.

Rush, M. (2001) *The Role of the Member of Parliament Since 1868: From Gentlemen to Players*. Oxford: Oxford University Press.

Rush, M. and Cromwell, V. (2000) Continuity and change: Legislative recruitment in the United Kingdom, 1968–1999. In Best, H. and Cotta, M. (eds) *Parliamentary Representatives in Europe 1848–2000*. Oxford: Oxford University Press.

Sabato, L. (1981) *The Rise of Political Consultants: New Ways of Winning Elections*. New York Basic Books.

Sandbrook, D. (2005) *Never Had it So Good: A History of Britain from Suez to the Beatles*. London: Little, Brown.

Scammell, M. (1995) *Designer Politics. How Elections are Won*. London: Macmillan – now Palgrave Macmillan.

Scammell, M. (1997) The wisdom of the war room: U.S. campaigning and Americanization. *Joan Shorenstein Center Research Paper R-17*. Cambridge, MA: Harvard University.

Scammell, M. (1998) The wisdom of the war room: US campaigning and Americanization. *Media, Culture and Society*, **20**: 251–75.

Scammell, M. (1999) Political marketing: Issues for political science. *Political Studies*, **XLVII**: 718–39.

Scammell, M. (2001) Media and media management. In Seldon, A. (ed.) *The Blair Effect*. London: Little Brown.

Schlesinger, P. and Tumber, H. (1994) *Reporting Crime. The Media Politics of Criminal Justice*. Oxford: Oxford University Press.

Schudson, M. (1999) *The Good Citizen. A History of American Civic Life.* Cambridge: Harvard University Press.

Schulz, W. and Zeh, R. (2007) *Changing Campaign Coverage of German Television: A Comparison of Five Elections 1990–2005.* Paper presented at the 57th International Communication Association, San Francisco, 24–8 May.

Schulz, W., Zeh, R. and Quiring, O. (2005) Voters in a changing media environment: A data-based retrospective on consequences of media change in Germany. *European Journal of Communication,* **20**: 55–89.

Seldon, A. (2005) *Blair.* London: Free Press.

Self, B. (2000) *The Evolution of the British Party System, 1885–1940.* London: Pearson.

Seymour-Ure, C. (1974) *The Political Impact of Mass Media.* London: Constable.

Seymour-Ure, C. (1977) Parliament and mass communications in the twentieth century. In Walkland, S. A. (ed.) *The House of Commons in the Twentieth Century.* Oxford: Clarendon Press.

Seymour-Ure, C. (1996) *The British Press and Broadcasting Since 1945.* Oxford: Blackwell.

Seymour-Ure, C. K. (1998) Are the broadsheets becoming unhinged? In Seaton, J. (ed.) *Politics and the Media: Harlots and Prerogatives at the Turn of the Millennium.* Oxford: Blackwell.

Seymour-Ure, C. (2003) *Prime Ministers and the Media: Issues of Power and Control.* Oxford: Blackwell.

Shaw, E. (1994) *The Labour Party Since 1979: Crisis and Transformation.* London: Routledge.

Sloan Commission on Cable Communications (1971) *On the Cable: The Television of Abundance.* New York: McGraw-Hill.

Socialist Commentary (1965) Our Penny-Farthing Machine. Labour Archives: Manchester University.

Stannage, T. (1980) *Baldwin Thwarts the Opposition: The British General Election of 1935.* London: Croom Helm.

Stuart, C. (ed.) (1975) *The Reith Diaries.* London: Collins.

Sumpter, R. and Tankard, J. W. J. (1994) The spin doctor: An alternative model of public relations. *Public Relations Review,* **20**(1): 19–27.

Swanson, D. (1997) The political-media complex at 50: Putting the 1996 Presidential Campaign in context. *American Behavioural Scientist,* **40**: 1264–82.

Swanson, D. and Mancini, P. (1996) *Politics, Media and Modern Democracy: An International Study of Innovations in Electoral Campaigning and Their Consequences.* Westport, CT/London: Praeger.

Taylor, P. M. (1999) *British Propaganda in the 20th Century: Selling Democracy.* Edinburgh: Edinburgh University Press.

Tenscher, J. (2004) 'Bridging the Differences': Political communication experts in Germany. *German Politics,* **13**: 516–40.

Thomas, H. and Gill, L. (1989) *Making an Impact.* London: David and Charles.

Tracey, M. (1977) *The Production of Political Television.* London: Routledge & Kegan Paul.

Tunstall, J. (1996) *Newspaper Power: The New National Press in Britain.* Oxford: Oxford University Press.

Van Zoonen, L. (1998) A day at the zoo: political communication, pigs and popular culture. *Media, Culture and Society* **20**(2): 183–200. London: Sage.

Ward, S. and Lusoli, W. (2005) 'From weird to wired': MPs, the Internet and representative politics in the UK. *Journal of Legislative Studies,* **11**: 57–81.

Watt, Nicholas (2004) Fox threatens to deselect poor Tory candidates. *Guardian,* 13 February.

Webb, P. and Fisher, J. (2003) Professionalism and the Millbank tendency: the political sociology of New Labour's employees. *Politics,* **23**: 10–20.

Werner, M. and Zimmerman, B. (2006) Beyond comparison: Histoire croisée and the challenge of reflexivity. *History and Theory,* **45**: 30–50.

Wernick, Λ. (1994) *Promotional Culture.* London: Sage.

Wilson, G. (2006) Labour outspends big stores on ads. *Daily Telegraph,* 24 August.

Wilson, H. H. (1961) *Pressure Group: The Campaign for Commercial Television.* London: Secker & Warburg.

Windlesham, L. (1966) *Communication and Political Power.* London: Jonathan Cape.

Winston, B. (2004) *Media Technology and Society: A History from the Telegraph to the Internet.* London: Routledge.

Winstone, R. (ed.) (1995) *Tony Benn. Years of Hope. Diaries, Papers and Letters, 1940–62.* London: Arrow.

Wintour, P. (2006) Celebs force rewrite of Tory A-list. *Guardian,* 7 August. http://www.guardian.co.uk/uk/2006/aug/07/politics.conservatives as at Feb. 2008

Woodward, W. (2006) Labour warns of possible job cuts as party faces funding shortfall. *Guardian,* 2 August, p. 15.

Woodward, W. (2006a) Contender for Labour deputy post highlights 160,000 lost members. *Guardian,* 27 December.

Woodward, W. (2006b) Cameron hails vote as proof of change in party. *Guardian,* 20 September.

Wray, R. (2006) The search for influence: Google becomes a political player. *Guardian,* 24 October.

Wring, D. (2005) *The Politics of Marketing the Labour Party.* Basingstoke: Palgrave Macmillan.

Wring, D., Green, J., Mortimore, R. and Atkinson, S. (eds) (2007) *Political Communications: The General Election Campaign of 2005.* Basingstoke: Palgrave Macmillan.

Index

A

Abrams, Dr Mark 80, 80–1
actors, political 93–116
advertising 82
  increased government expenditure on
    122–3
advisers, *see* professional advisers
Ailes, Roger 102
Allan, Tim 119
Americanization 14, 145, 152–7, 169
  of media practices 5
American-style electioneering techniques
  145, 162–3
amplification model 181–2
Ashcroft, Michael 87
audience *v.* public 197

B

Baldwin, Stanley
  on changes after the First World War
    18–20
  on the press 30, 32, 42
BBC 30–1, 32–3
  political interference 33–4
  see also broadcasting; radio; television
Benn, Anthony (Tony) Wedgwood 36–7,
  78–9, 102
Berlusconi, Silvio 161, 165
Blair, Tony 57, 58–9, 85
  descriptions of style 138
  and television 96
Blears, Hazel 19–20, 41
blogs 74, 177, 188
Bongrand, Michel 168
Bradley, Clive 80
broadband 183
broadcasting
  14-Day Rule 39
  political, development of 79
  political interference 33
  see also radio; television
Brown, Gordon 142

C

cable broadcasting 27
cable systems 179–80
cable television 170, 179–80
  television of abundance 180

cadre parties 46, 64
Callaghan, Jim, and television 96
Cameron, David 59, 86, 90
  CV after university 103–4
  website revamp 189
campaign communications
  changing nature of 23–8
  evolution 23–5
campaigning
  candidate-centred 69
  command-and-control operations 183
  constituency campaigning 33, 65
  consultants, increasing use of 65
  factors in professionalization of 67
  forms of campaign 23–5
  internet users 173
  long-term 79
  'modern model of' 144–5, 169
  national campaigns 46, 65
  selling v. marketing 65
  stages in development of 66
Campaigning Diploma 95
Campaigns and Communications
  Directorate (Labour Party) 83
Campaign Strategy Committee (Labour
  Party) 83, 85
Campbell, Alastair 12–13, 59, 91, 128,
  135
  as Chief Press Secretary 129
  role compared with that of Bernard
    Ingham 136–7
candidate-centred campaigning 69
candidates
  audit of 95
  changing demands on 94–5
  Conservative Party A-list of 94
  experience categories 104
  job background 105
  media skills 103
  media training for 100–3, 106–8
  need to become more professionalized
    94, 95–105
  seen as party members 94
  timing of selection of 106
  in the US 93
capitalist societies, change in 143
cartel parties 22, 42, 63, 68
  characteristics of 64
Carville, James 91
catch-all parties 39, 61, 68
  characteristics of 64

Central Office of Information (COI)
122–3
Chamberlain, Neville 201
change 143–4
  at an organizational–operation level of
    political parties 160–1
  in communication technologies
    11–12
  exploring 4
  historical change 4–14
  importance of understanding 6–14
  at the level of media 157–8
  at the level of media practice 158–9
  at the level of the political party
    159–60
  at the media–politics juncture 159
  in party structures 7–11
  in political communication 1, 4, 5
  in sociopolitical environment 60,
    61–2, 68
  television and 144, 145, 156, 157
  see also transformation
Churchill, Winston, and television 96, 97
cinema vans 34
Civil Service 125–6
Clarke, Charles 59, 89
class allegiance, and voting behaviour 60
Clause 4: 55
COI (Central Office of Information)
  122–3
Colman, Prentis and Varley 79, 81
command-and-control operations 183
commerce, and politics, communications
  activities interrelationship 119–20
communication
  adaptation or transformation? 21–3,
    42–3
  becoming one-way process 199
  'centrifugal diversification' 27–8
  centripetal 27
  commerce/politics interrelationship
    119–20
  digital 171
  early-20th century developments in
    49
  infrastructure 135–6
  internet role 175
  loss of political parties' control over
    27, 28, 31
  managing 121–4
  potential of 180
  technologies 6, 11–12, 18, 19
  transforming 75–83
  use of professional advisers in 69–92
  verbal 192
  see also campaign communications;
    political communication
Conservative Party
  A-list of candidates 94
  controlling group 82

election 1959 80
election 1979 82
election 2001 89
importance of organization 78–83
organizational developments, reasons
  for 60
professionals in the 1950s 78–83
reorganization in the 1950s 52
constituency campaigning 65
  effect of radio on 33
consultants
  negative effect on parties and voters
    202
  use of, in campaigning 65
  see also professional advisers
consultations 187–8
Coulson, Andy 87, 89
Critchley, Julian 94–5
Crum-Ewing, Mrs 36
'cultural chaos' 200

D

Daily Chronicle 30
Daily Mail 19
Davidson, J. C. C. 76
decision-making process, party members'
  influence on 8
democratic societies, change in 143
digital communication 171
'digital divide' 191–2
documentary movement 51
Downing Street
  growth in staff 123, 140
  media operation 128–9
Duncan Smith, Iain 90

E

e-democracy 186–92
Eden, Anthony, and television 97
e-effect 189–90
effects 172
  e-effect 189–90
electioneering
  American-style 145, 162–3
  contemporary, focused on leader 141
  see also campaign communications;
    campaigning
electoralism 91
electoral success
  based on organization and publicity
    52
  ideology v. broad appeal 61, 62
'electronic glut' 24, 41–2, 139, 148, 170
'electronic spine' 191
elite groups 174–5
elite party 46, 64
Ellam, Michael 142
e-stimuli 190

F

feedback, from consultations 187
films 26–7, 32–5
    commissioned by political parties 34
    impact of 6
First World War, changes after 18–19
flacks, *see* public information specialists
14-Day rule 149
Fox, Dr Liam 95
France 152, 159, 168–9
    election 2007 192
franchise, expansion of 29, 33, 46
fuel protests 192
functional differentiation 3
funding of political parties, changes in
    7–8

G

Gallup Poll 51, 77
Germany 153, 155, 158, 161–4
    commercial television 154, 161–2
    early 1980s 161
    election campaigning 162–3
    image-building 162
    Kampa 163
    professionalization 162, 163–4
GICS, *see* Government Information and
    Communication Service
GIS, *see* Government Information Service
global movements of practices/
    practitioners 155
Globe 30
Gorst, E. J. 10, 66, 68, 76
    party organization changes 47–8
Gould, Philip 57, 59, 73, 84, 89, 91
government communication
    government control over 118, 125–7
    increase in staff 122–3, 124
    transformation in 117–42
Government Communications Network
    134
Government Communications Review
    Group, *see* Phillis Review
Government Information and
    Communication Service (GICS) 133–4
    lack of professionalism in 133
Government Information Service (GIS)
    126, 128
    enquiry into, see Mountfield Report
Gower, Sir Patrick 102
gramophone records, speeches on 26, 50
Grannatt, Mike 129–30
Greece 154, 166–8
    political television spending 167
    professionalization 167–8
    social transformations 167
    telepolitics 167
Greenberg, Stan 91

H

Hague, William 90
Haines, Joe 13
Harris, John 80
Harris, Will 89
Heath, Edward, and television 96
Hewitt, Patricia 84, 89
higher education organizations,
    communications and self-promotion
    124
Hilton, Steve 86–7, 89, 90, 91, 119
'histoire croisée' 5–6, 152
historical change 4–14
Howard, Michael 90
hubs 191
hybridization 155, 157, 163, 169

I

ICTs (information and communication
    technologies) 186–7, 191–2
industrialist societies, change in 143
information and communication
    technologies (ICTs) 186–7, 191–2
information subsidies 121–2
Ingham, Bernard 13, 136
    role compared with that of Alastair
        Campbell 136–7
institutions, communication via 182
internet 170–94
    advice to candidates 193
    blogs 74, 177, 188
    campaign internet users 173
    commercially driven system 27
    effect on communication 6, 11–12,
        27
    effect on political process 171
    election campaigning 114–15
    government information on 177
    impact on political behaviour
        189–90
    in national political contests 182–5
    new challenges 96
    penetration of, in UK 171
    political impact of 185–6
    political information on 177
    potential and properties 171
    a 'pull' technology 176
    realistic expectations of 180–1, 182
    superseding other media 11–12
    in the UK 171, 173–4
    in the US 173, 184
Italy 161, 164–6
    corruption scandals *(tangentopoli)* 165,
        166
    decline in party membership 165
    Forza Italia party 165–6
    'media logic' 166
    professionalization in 166

J

journalists, changing attitude of 98

K

Kinnock, Neil 58–9, 83, 84, 85

L

Labour Party
    Clause 4: 55
    election 1959 80
    election 1983 83
    election 1992 84
    election 1997 86
    election 2001 86
    election 2005 86
    importance of organization 78–83
    organization in the 1950s 53
    professionals in 58, 78–83
    see also New Labour
The Labour Party and Broadcasting (Labour
    Party report) 37–8
Liberal Democrat Party, early placing of
    candidates in constituencies 109
literary bureaus 74
Lloyd George, David 30
local media
    MPs' relationship with 109–13
    role between elections 112–13, 115
    significance to candidates 99
Luntz, Frank 91

M

McBride, Damian 142
MacDonald, Ramsay, and film 96
Major, John 86, 141
Mandelson, Peter 59, 83–4, 84, 89
marginal constituencies, media training
    107
mass media
    individuals as part of mass audience
        172
    for mass communication 198,
        199–200
    political impact of 172
mass-membership parties 45, 59–67
    ceasing to exist 62
    transformation from 39
media
    adapting to politics 20
    adversarial exchange relationship with
        98, 105
    Americanization of media practices 5
    between elections 114
    candidates' skills 103
    changing types of 24–5
    commercialization of 158

'conditioning' power 21, 43
    extent of influence 103–5
    fragmentation of 200, 201
    gaining attention of 48
    mainstream 176
    MPs' skills 103
    New Labour and 59
    political use of 11
    proliferation of outlets 123
    relationship with political parties 22,
        23, 147
    significant events xii–xiv
    see also local media
media experiences 104–5
'media logic' 40, 157–8, 161, 174,
    199–200
    France 169
    Germany 168
    Greece 168
    Italy 166, 168
'media politics' 40
media space 176
'mediatization' 40
media training
    for candidates 100–3, 106–8
    constantly improving 107–8
    in marginal constituencies 107
    for MPs 98
    need for? 107
membership organizations
    recruiting/retaining members 19
    successful 19
membership of political parties 8–11, 60,
    61
Members of Parliament, *see* MPs
ministers, and the media 100
Mitterand, François 168
mobile phones 192
modernization 145–6, 147–52, 156, 189
'modern model of campaigning' 144–5,
    169
Morrison, Herbert 50–1
Mountfield Report 126–7, 127–32
    terms of reference 130–1
MPs
    media skills 103
    personal contact with media 111
    relationship with local media 109–13
    role of 188–9
    websites 99, 115

N

Napolitan, Joe 84, 168
National Executive Council (NEC), Labour
    Party 85
New Labour 57–9, 83–7
    approach to communications 120
    Campaigns and Communications
        Directorate 83

government communication 125–7
post-Blair 140–2
newspapers 28–32
circulation 29
greater independence from political
parties 26, 27, 30
political allegiance 29–30
provincial 47–8
newsreels 6
normalization hypothesis 181
Number 10, *see* Downing Street

O

O'Brien, Toby 78
Observer 30
Operation Turnout 86
Operation Victory 86
organization, electoral success based on 52
Our Penny-Farthing Machine (Labour party
report) 53

P

Pall Mall Gazette 30
parties, *see* political parties
party bureaucracies, growth of 46
party bureaucrats 71
Party Election Broadcasts (PEBs) 154
Phillis Review 122, 127, 132–4
policy-making process, party members'
influence on 8
political actors 93–116
political communication
adaptation or transformation? 21–3
change in 1, 4, 5
global context 143–69
post-modern 12
stages of 147–8
strategic 118
political leaders, less control of media
200–1
political parties
late-19th century 46–8
early-20th century 48–52
post-1945 52–7
adaptation to their environment 18,
32, 42, 66–7, 73–4
attention to organizational matters
76–7, 78
cadre parties 46, 64
cartel parties 22, 42, 63, 64, 68
catch-all parties 39, 61, 64, 68
centralization, danger in 8
changing nature of 22, 44–68
control by leadership 56, 59, 94
decline of 8
evolution 26
loss of control over means of
communication 27, 28, 31

mass-membership parties 39, 45,
59–67, 62
media relationships 22, 23, 147
members 8–11
membership numbers 8, 60, 61
models and characteristics of 64
national campaigns 46
need to engage with members 8–10
organizational change 9–10, 44–68
profile improvements 48
reasons for change 48
relationship with professional advisers
87–91
structure changes 7–11
themes in professional communication
71–2
see also Conservative Party; Labour
Party; Liberal Democrat Party
political representatives, *see* MPs
politics
and commerce, communications
activities interrelationship 119–20
communication of 175
impact of television on 6, 23, 40
marketing of 9
as a profession 63, 68
significant events xii–xiv
technologies' interaction with 178–82
polls
role of 88
see also Gallup Poll
polltakers' role 88
polycentric communication networks 191
Poole, Lord 9–10, 52, 68, 80
Powell, Chris 73, 78, 84
press
'power without responsibility' 30, 32
see also newspapers; *and individual
newspapers*
press bureaus 74
prime ministers
honeymoon period 142
new-style 138–40
spending less time in the House of
Commons 97
see also individual prime ministers
Prime Minister's Office, *see* Downing
Street
professional advisers 69–92, 195
effect on political message and
communication 72–3
employment often short-term 71
firm links with politicians 88–9, 91
increasing use of 62, 63–4
influencing those in politics 2–3
leading or supporting the party? 89
meaning of term 70–1
means of dealing with change 74
payment for services 75–6, 77
relationship with parties 87–91

role in the Labour Party 58, 59
in the US 75–6
professional consultants, across the globe
    155
professionalism
    in communication, meaning of 100
    general increase in 123–4
    intensity and degree of 119
professionalization 169, 196, 197
    in campaigning 67
    meaning of 2–3, 14
    of political communication 1–4, 34–5,
        42, 195, 202–4
    process of 3
professional politicians 63, 68, 103
propaganda 49–50, 51
pseudo-knowledge 199
public
    v. audience 197
    as individuals 172, 198, 198–9
    as media fodder 200
    role of 197–201
    as voters 198, 199, 201
public information specialists (flacks) 122
publicity
    electoral success based on 52
    and politics 123
publicity bureaus 74
public opinion, sampling 51
public relations democracy 119
public relations sector, sudden growth in
    119, 123–4
public relations skills 82

R

radio 27, 32–5
    effect on constituency campaigning 33
    impact of 6
    see also BBC
Reece, Gordon 82
Reeves, Rosser 79
reimagining 180
reinforcement model 182
reinvigoration of representative politics
    189, 190
Reith, John 32
representatives, political, role of 188–9
The Right Spirit (film) 34
Royal, Ségolène 187

S

Saatchi, Maurice 86, 89, 90
Saatchi and Saatchi 82, 121
sampling of public opinion 51, 77
satellite broadcasting 27
satellite television 170
Sawyer, Tom 85
SCA, *see* Shadow Communication Agency

Séguéla, Jacques 168
Shadow Communication Agency (SCA)
    84–5
    initiating or implementing policy? 84
    membership 84
significant events, chronology xii–xiv
sleaze 130, 141
Smith, John 57, 58
social complexity 145
Socialist Commentary 53–5, 81
social movements, involvement of
    internet 190–1
sociopolitical environment, change in 60,
    61–2, 68
special advisers, *see* spin doctors
specialists 71, 88
spin 12–14, 20, 120, 141, 142
    defined 124
spin doctors (special advisers) 12–14, 120,
    129
    emergence of 124
    increase in numbers of 123
Standard 30
strategic political communication 118
strategists 71, 88
Sweden 158

T

'tabloidisation' 31
Talking on Television (Conservative Party
    report) 35–6
technologies
    of communication and 6, 11–12
    contribution to professionalism 116
    harnessing 28–43
    interaction with politics 178–82, 190
    need for professionals 70
    'periods' of 12
    push v. pull 176
television 27, 35–41, 64–5
    cable television 170, 179–80
    as change factor 144, 145, 156, 157
    closed circuit studio 38
    commercial TV 31
    development in UK 194
    as dominant medium of
        communication 21, 39
    dress on 36
    impact of 6, 23, 40
    multi-channel 41
    performance of candidates on 199
    political potential of 21–2
    political spots 79, 153–4, 167
    prime ministers and 96–7
    regional 114
    regulation of 21
    satellite television 170
    television of abundance 180
    'television election' 39–40

training for appearing on 36, 38
transforming political communication 196
web television 41–2
working with 95–7
television channels, increase in number of 123
Thatcher, Margaret, and television 96
Thomas, Harvey 118
transformation 196–7
  effects of 202–4
  in global context 157–68
  in political communication 1
  see also change

U

UK general elections, 2005 181, 184–5, 192
US presidential elections 173, 177–8, 182–3, 184–5, 192–3

V

vendors 71, 88
voluntary workers 51, 76
voters
  class allegiance 60
  political campaigns' orientation to 25
  public as 198, 199, 201
  wooing 46
voting behaviour 199

W

websites, MPs' 99, 115
web television 41–2
Whetstone, Rachel 119
Whitaker and Baxter 76
Wilson, Harold, and television 96
Woolton, Lord 52